"Joe Sweeney is a most persistent and persuasive man. *Networking Is a Contact Sport* exemplifies the value of networking 'outside the box.'"

Bob Costas
Broadcaster

"Joe Sweeney's networking skills helped to significantly increase my off-the-field income."

Brett Favre
Three-Time NFL MVP and Future NFL Hall of Famer

"Joe Sweeney is right. Networking is one of the most crucial aspects of being successful in any workplace. Cultivating personal and business relationships both inside and outside of your workplace will lead to more contacts and greater opportunities."

Bud Selig
Commissioner of Major League Baseball

"Joe has taught me the value of having a 'wingman' in your life. I thank God and my Guardian Angel for protecting me, and having Joe watching out for me during my time in Milwaukee was a blessing, too."

The Most Rev. Timothy Dolan
Archbishop of New York

"I use Joe's networking techniques every day. I've worked with Joe for over fifteen years, and a day doesn't go by that I don't learn something new from him. If you don't learn something from *Networking Is a Contact Sport*, then your mind is not open and you're not listening."

Craig Leipold
Chairman and Owner of the Minnesota Wild

"Joe Sweeney has grasped what it means to network in both the black and the white environment. If you follow the advice in *Networking Is a Contact Sport*, it will help you to transcend racial differences and succeed in any work situation."

Ulice Payne
Businessman, Entrepreneur, and Former President
and CEO of the Milwaukee Brewers Baseball Club

"When you think about it, life is all about relationships, both personal and professional ones. But relationships don't just happen by themselves. Many have to be pursued, and that's where Joe's book, *Networking Is a Contact Sport*, comes into play. A great read that proves that networking is hard work but well worth the while."

Bill Perez
Former CEO of S.C. Johnson & Son, Nike, Inc.,
and Wm. Wrigley Jr. Company

"I teach Joe Sweeney's networking philosophy to all four thousand of our employees. I am reminded every day that they work. The Joe Sweeney way works."

Bob Trunzo
Chief Operating Officer, CUNA Mutual Insurance

"Broadcasting is a people business. Contacts, sources, connections, relationships—that's networking, and that's where Joe's expertise has helped me."

John K. Anderson
ESPN SportsCenter Anchor

"I have known Joe Sweeney for forty years, and if there is one rule he has practiced, it is the Golden Rule. Living by this standard has helped him succeed in all facets of his life. By following the advice found in *Networking Is a Contact Sport*, you will find more meaning to your life and to your work."

Joel Maturi
Director of Athletics at the University of Minnesota

"Joe Sweeney has shown that no matter your background, there are universal keys to successful networking."

Virgis Colbert
Retired Executive Vice President, Miller Brewing Company;
Voted "Top 50 Executives in America" by Ebony *and* Fortune *magazines*

"Joe's networking advice has helped me in recruiting for decades."

Barry Alvarez
Athletic Director and Former Head Football Coach
at the University of Wisconsin–Madison

"The concepts in *Networking Is a Contact Sport* have helped me in my post-Olympic years."

Bonnie Blair
Five-Time Olympic Gold Medal Speed Skater

"Joe explains what's common in all successful people. It's the importance of networking."

Darren Hardy
Publisher of SUCCESS *magazine*

"Joe Sweeney is an authentic leader who knows the real value of mutual support in business and life. In *Networking Is a Contact Sport*, he does a tremendous job explaining the importance of why you need a wingman to watch your back and deal with adversity in these challenging times."

Rob "Waldo" Waldman
Bestselling Author of Never Fly Solo

"*Networking Is a Contact Sport* speaks volumes for the value of connecting with others. Joe Sweeney's principles will enhance your relationships, your business, your career, and your life."

Robin Yount
Two-Time Major League Baseball MVP
and Inductee to the Baseball Hall of Fame

"Practicing the networking skills that Joe Sweeney teaches in this book will give *anyone* from any walk of life the abilities they need to find their own personal success."

Bo Ryan
Head Basketball Coach at the University of Wisconsin–Madison

"Joe has captured the essence of what it takes to be an effective woman networker in today's workplace."

Sheila Stewart
CEO of Empower 180 and Author of
Backwards in High Heels: A Woman's Guide to Succeeding in Business

"Joe Sweeney taught me the networking skills necessary for me to succeed in the business world after my football career. *Networking Is a Contact Sport* details the lessons I learned from Joe as he helped me succeed both on and off the gridiron."

LeRoy Butler
Four-Time Pro Bowl Player with the Green Bay Packers; Entrepreneur

"Everything I know about the world of networking stems from Joe Sweeney's philosophy—networking truly is a place where you go to *give*, not to get. Joe's networking advice has helped us here at OneCoach."

John Assaraf
President and CEO of OneCoach and New York Times
Bestselling Author of The Answer

"Joe Sweeney's networking ability helped put a spotlight on all Wisconsin sports."

Gov. Tommy Thompson
*Former U.S. Secretary of Health and Human Services
and Former Governor of Wisconsin*

"I saw Joe's networking skills on our trip to China. Joe displayed that his networking skills can be applied domestically as well as internationally."

Gov. Jim Doyle
Governor of Wisconsin

"There aren't many people who have the heart and mind of Joe Sweeney, and there are even fewer who have his integrity. The ultimate coach, Joe wants everybody to win."

Lesley Visser
Hall of Fame Sportscaster

"On the field or off the field, networking is a place where you go to give, not to get. If you follow the guidelines in *Networking Is a Contact Sport*, you will find success, regardless if you are a beginning entrepreneur or a CEO."

Dan Jansen
Olympic Gold Medal Speed Skater

"I preach Joe Sweeney's networking advice to all of my employees. I know that if they practice his rules of networking in our work environment, then our company will continue to enjoy success."

John Shiely
Chairman and CEO of the Briggs & Stratton Corporation

"Nobody in the sports business has made networking more fun or funnier than Joe Sweeney...except maybe me."

Bob Uecker
Hall of Fame Baseball Broadcaster

"Joe has nailed it! If I had met Joe when we were selling millions of copies of For Dummies books, I would have signed him to write *Networking for Dummies*. In this book, Joe gives you a gift that keeps on giving. Apply his principles and watch your business grow."

John Kilcullen
Creator and Publisher of the For Dummies Series

"*Networking Is a Contact Sport* has reinforced my research with the two hundred most successful people in the world—networking with passion is the ultimate formula for success."

Mark Thompson
Co-Author of Success Built to Last *and* Forbes Investor
with the Midas Touch

"The concepts in *Networking Is a Contact Sport* have helped the associates at Kohl's Department Stores become a powerhouse in the retailing industry."

Larry Montgomery
Retired Chairman and CEO of Kohl's Department Stores

"Joe's concepts in *Networking Is a Contact Sport* are what I teach in my Ultimate Life workshops."

Jim Bunch
Founder of the Ultimate Life Workshops

"Joe gives new and valuable insight to many of the concepts I offered up in my *New York Times* bestseller *Never Eat Alone*. *Networking Is a Contact Sport* is an outstanding tool for any person who wants to become a master networker."

Keith Ferrazzi
CEO of Ferrazzi Greenlight
and Author of the New York Times *Bestseller* Never Eat Alone

NETWORKING
IS A
CONTACT SPORT

*How Staying Connected and Serving Others
Will Help You Grow Your Business,
Expand Your Influence—
or Even Land Your Next Job*

Joe Sweeney
WITH Mike Yorkey

BENBELLA BOOKS, INC.
DALLAS, TEXAS

BenBella Books, Inc.
103000 N. Central Expressway, Suite 530
Dallas, TX 75231
www.benbellabooks.com
Send feedback to feedback@benbellabooks.com

Printed in the United States of America
10 9 8 7 6 5 4 3 2

Library of Congress Cataloging-in-Publication Data is available for this title.
ISBN 978-1-936661-17-6

Copyediting by Lisa Miller
Proofreading by Erica Lovett and Stacia Seaman
Cover design by Faceout
Cover image by Getty Images
Text design and composition by John Reinhardt Book Design
Printed by Lake Book Manufacturing

Distributed by Perseus Distribution
(www.perseusdistribution.com)

To place orders through Perseus Distribution:
Tel: 800-343-4499
Fax: 800-351-5073
E-mail: orderentry@perseusbooks.com

Significant discounts for bulk sales are available.
Please contact Glenn Yeffeth at glenn@benbellabooks.com or (214) 750-3628.

To Mom, I thank you and Dad for teaching your ten children how to get along and love one another, which is the foundation of networking as a place you go to give, not to get.

Contents

Acknowledgments

WRITING A BOOK about a subject that I'm passionate about—and including stories about my experiences—was like going through intense therapy for a year. *Networking Is a Contact Sport* would never have happened if I hadn't been fortunate enough to grow up in a home with nine siblings, where my parents taught us the value of getting along with others and working together—great foundational networking principles.

To Mike Yorkey, my friend, writing partner, and wingman, your molding of all my crazy clay took the talent of a world-class artist. I could have never produced this book without you. I also want to thank Rick Wood, a photojournalist with the *Milwaukee Journal Sentinel*, who used his expertise to give visual life to my networking stories.

To my friends, relatives, business partners, and advisors. I'm afraid there are way too many of you to name everyone, but thanks for being there and for networking with me and *for* me.

To my dozen wingmen, you've been great listeners and offered wise counsel over the years. I especially want to acknowledge Craig Leipold; my brother, Mark; and my cousins Bobby and Dennis Sweeney for watching my back.

To my four marvelous children, Kyle, Conor, Kelly, and Brendan, you've crystallized what's important in life.

And finally, to my wonderful wife, Tami, I offer my heartfelt thanks for giving me the freedom to be myself and the flexibility to pursue my passions.

Foreword
by Jack Canfield

IT'S AN INSPIRATIONAL tug-at-the-heart story that belongs in one of my *Chicken Soup for the Soul* books, which have sold 144 million copies and been translated into fifty-four languages worldwide.

She asked that her real name not be used, so I'll call her Tina Bennett. She was a mother in the Milwaukee area raising two sons and working part-time so that she could be home when the boys arrived from school. Her life was tipped upside down, however, when she and her husband divorced. The young mother valiantly carried on by increasing her hours at a Milwaukee title company, where she worked as an assistant.

Just as Tina's life was stabilizing, she received another round of distressing news: her ex-husband had lost his job because of fraud he'd committed at work. Before he was sentenced to prison, all child support stopped. Suddenly, Tina was on her own to support two growing boys and keep a mortgage paid.

She was seeking out a new job that would pay her more when she interviewed with a Milwaukee businessman regarding an assistant position at an investment banking firm. During the interviews, she mentioned that her oldest son, Randy, an eighth-grader, dreamed of attending Marquette University High School, an all-boys Catholic secondary school, but that didn't look possible since her ex-husband was headed for a jail term.

The Milwaukee businessman replied that he knew the private school well since his two eldest sons were graduates from that school.

He added that his third son was currently enrolled at Marquette University High School and was excelling in the classroom and on the sports field. He encouraged Tina to be open-minded about Marquette, declaring that the Jesuit-trained teachers would be great male role models in the boy's life.

Tina didn't get the job with the Milwaukee businessman, but she thanked him for his time and his interest in Randy. Meanwhile, her son attended a "Shadow Day" at Marquette University High School that spring, and when Tina picked him up, she asked him how his day went. "Marquette rocks!" said Randy. "I really want to go there next fall."

Tina's heart melted. *Dear God, how will I ever do this?*

"We'll go through this one step at a time and see what happens," she told her son. The cost to attend Marquette for the school year was around $10,000, a daunting sum.

Meanwhile, Tina continued to run into the Milwaukee businessman, who encouraged her to have Randy take the Marquette entrance exam and fill out the scholarship forms. She completed the paperwork and was told that the school could offer Randy a $3,000 scholarship, but that left a $7,000 balance.

All summer, Tina fretted about what to do. A week before the start of school, she still didn't have the money, and she informed Randy that barring a miracle, he would have to attend their local public high school.

Now let me shift gears and introduce the Milwaukee businessman, Joe Sweeney, the author of this book.

This last exchange between Joe and Tina happened in August 2007, just a couple of weeks before the start of the school year. At that time, Joe was facing a different set of challenges. He had taken a leave of absence from Corporate Financial Advisors, an investment banking firm where Joe was a managing director, to pursue a dream job: becoming CEO of the publicly owned Green Bay Packers.

Yes, I'm talking about *the* Green Bay Packers, who play on the "frozen tundra of Lambeau Field," as ESPN's Chris Berman likes to say. Despite being situated in the smallest TV market in the NFL, the Packers have developed one of the largest fan bases in America and have sold out every game since 1960. Eighty thousand people are on the waiting list to buy season tickets, and if you put your name on that list today, the estimated wait time would be more than a hundred years.

When the Packers' CEO position opened up, more than one hundred top-level executives applied for this plum job, including Wisconsin native Joe Sweeney, who was the former president of the Wisconsin Sports Authority and a well-connected business and sports figure in the Badger State. Joe kept making cut after cut. By the summer of 2007, he had made it to the Packers' short list.

Though preparing and interviewing for the Packer CEO position consumed much of his life, Joe hadn't lost the common touch. He felt bad for Tina Bennett, who hoped against hope to send her son to Marquette University High School. When Joe called to see what Marquette offered in the way of scholarship money, he counseled her to keep the faith.

Meanwhile, Joe had a little soul-searching of his own to do. Joe didn't have any salary coming in during his open-field pursuit of the Packers job, which meant bills were being paid from his reserve fund. Two big ones were staring him square in the face: a $20,000 bill for the first semester at St. Louis University, where his daughter, Kelly, was in her junior year; and his own $10,000 tuition invoice from Marquette University High School, where Joe's youngest child, Brendan, would be a senior.

On the morning of August 17, 2007, Joe mailed off a check to St. Louis University and dropped by the Marquette business office to pay off Brendan's tuition. But he couldn't get Tina and Randy Bennett out of his mind. What were they feeling? Were their stomachs in knots?

He inquired what the balance was for Randy Bennett's account.

"Seven thousand dollars," replied the clerk.

Joe thought about that sum for a moment. The amount was like earning $10,000 before taxes. How would he earn that extra income in a year that was already looking extremely lean?

Joe said a prayer that he was doing the right thing. "Here's a check to cover Randy's tuition," he said. Despite the dent this put in his savings account, he felt good about what he'd done. He'd tell Tami, his wife of twenty-six years, about it later. He figured it was better to ask for forgiveness than permission.

Joe stepped out of the Marquette University High School business office and placed a phone call to Tina Bennett, who nearly fainted when she heard the news. Then the tears flowed. He could hear Randy jumping up and down in the background.

But that's not the end of this heart-warming story.

Around 7:15 P.M. that evening, as Joe and Tami were about to head home from a Marquette football game in Burlington, Joe received a phone call from his sister, Mary Beth, who was out of breath with excitement. "Joe, guess what?" she exclaimed. "You're a finalist to win $10,000 in a drawing. You're down to the final twenty."

"What drawing?"

"Didn't Freddy tell you?" Freddy was one of Joe's eight older brothers.

"Tell me what?"

"That he bought a raffle ticket for you. It's a fundraiser for Edgewood High School. They cost $100 each, but he figured you'd be good for it, so he wrote down your name. You now have a one-in-twenty chance of winning $10,000!"

Joe could hear the pandemonium in the background. Mary Beth was standing inside the Edgewood High auditorium, which was packed with hundreds of parents and students at Edgewood's kickoff event for the school year. She said the emcee had pulled out twenty raffle tickets, each with a name written on the back, and dropped them back into the hat. The winner would collect $10,000.

"You know what, Mary Beth? I've never won anything in my life. I'm not getting my hopes up." *But Joe knew that if he won the raffle, the prize would cover Randy's tuition.*

"They're drawing tickets out one by one until we have a winner," Mary Beth explained.

"Fine. If I get down to the final ten, call me."

Fifteen minutes later, as Joe and Tami tooled along Highway 83, Mary Beth phoned his cell. "You're in the final ten," she announced.

Joe and Tami listened on speakerphone as more raffle tickets were drawn and eliminated from winning. None had his name on the back.

Joe still had a chance to win as their car pulled into their driveway back home in Fox Point, a Milwaukee suburb.

Joe and Tami ran into the house, where their daughter, Kelly, was having a party with some friends. In a few days, she would be leaving for Spain as part of a study-abroad program with St. Louis University. Tami excitedly told everyone about the developments of the last hour. They then listened on speakerphone as the tension built until there were just two tickets left in the hat—and Joe's name was one of them.

"The school wants to know what you want to do," Mary Beth said over the raucous background noise. "The person with the other ticket says he'll split the $10,000 prize. That way you'll each get $5,000."

Tami tugged at his arm. "Take the $5,000, Joe. I just charged five airline tickets to go to Spain to see Kelly over Thanksgiving, and it's costing us around $5,000." Joe's shoulders slumped from the news that he was $5,000 deeper in the hole than he thought. "You're right. It would be prudent to take the five thousand. Did you hear that, Mary Beth? Tell them I'll split the prize."

"Dad, don't!"

Joe turned to see his oldest son, Kyle, standing in the kitchen. "I can't believe it, Dad. You always told us to go for it in life, and now you're wussing out!"

"You know what? You're right." Joe held his cell phone up to his mouth. "Listen, Mary Beth. You tell 'em I've changed my mind. I'm not splitting the $10,000. It's all or nothing!"

"You sure, Joe? A bird in the hand..."

"I'm all in."

A huge roar could be heard as the emcee informed the audience that it was all or nothing. The emcee appealed for calm as he pulled the winning ticket out of the hat.

Joe Sweeney won $10,000 that day, the same day he paid Randy Bennett's tuition at Marquette University High School.

Three years have passed since Randy enrolled at Marquette University High School. He played on the undefeated freshman soccer team and was named co-captain. Randy was a key contributor on the Marquette football team that captured the Division I State Championship in 2009, and in the spring, he ran the 200- and

400-meter sprints on the track team. On campus, he's known as a hard-working student-athlete.

Alton Taylor, the football team's assistant coach known on campus as Mr. T, has taken Randy under his wing and mentored him. Tina says she doesn't know where she would be without Marquette University prep school in Randy's life, especially after his younger brother had several brushes with the law and was arrested.

Compelling stories like these reveal the character of Joe Sweeney, who has authored a tremendous resource in this book. As Joe will tell you in the coming pages, networking isn't about tapping into another guy's contact list so you can pitch them with annuity deals. Networking is about working with others to meet their needs, and when you give in life, something magical happens, as in the case of Tina and Randy Bennett. It truly is more blessed to give than to receive.

Joe's solid advice about how networking can enrich your life is a must-read for anyone during these tough economic times. As you'll discover, Joe is a master networker with more than three thousand solid contacts in his BlackBerry, including me. In fact, Joe networked with me to get me to write the foreword for this book. Our paths crossed in 2007 shortly after he learned that he didn't get the Green Bay Packers CEO position. Even though he came up short, Joe wanted me to know that my book, *Success Principles*, had inspired him to adopt my Rule of Five during the Packers interview process, so he tracked me down via e-mail to thank me. The Rule of Five means doing five things every day that will move you toward your goal.

I e-mailed Joe back and returned the thanks for his kind words and invited him to come to a workshop that I was doing in San Diego in February 2008. Milwaukee can be a pretty tough place in the winter, so I shouldn't have been surprised when Joe introduced himself to me in San Diego and handed me a copy of his Packers Business Plan, modeled after my principles.

I was touched. In fact, as our relationship has grown, I recently asked Joe to be on my board of advisors at the Jack Canfield Companies.

Joe's heart is not only in the right place, but as I've gotten to know this entrepreneurial-minded individual over the last few years, I would say he's the right man with the right message. Networking *is* a contact sport, and there's no better person than Joe Sweeney to get you in shape for connecting with others.

A Note to the Reader

from Joe Sweeney

THE THEME of *Networking Is a Contact Sport* is that when you truly give to others without any expectations or strings attached, you will receive much more than you ever could have expected.

Remember this main thesis as you read the stories in this book as well as the lessons that I impart in the coming pages. I've long believed that miracles—like the one I experienced with the Edgewood High raffle ticket (as noted in the foreword)—will happen when you give of yourself and allow life to work its natural course without manipulating the outcome.

I believe networking gives you confidence to interact with others, teaches resiliency, and helps you overcome challenges in life. The concept of engaging others with an attitude of giving, not getting, will enrich your relationships.

To help you become a better networker, keep these four themes in mind as you read *Networking Is a Contact Sport*:

1. Ask. You have to learn how to ask good questions. Since relationships deepen through face-to-face contact, the ability to make interesting and thought-provoking inquiries can turn you into an excellent conversationalist and strong networker. As you'll see in coming pages, I've learned how to probe creatively and persistently, which is part of the foundation of good networking.

2. Listen. When you engage in a conversation with someone—friend, associate, or business client—listen actively. Listen intuitively. Listen to that quiet voice within you. Listen closely to what is being said that could present you with an opportunity to offer help or advice, which is my core tenet of networking—looking for ways to give, not get.

3. **Take action.** Be the person who always follows up. Don't be someone who makes a vague promise to do something ("Sure, I'll give that vice president a call for you") and then not stay true to your word. Those who offer to take action and follow through are worth more than gold—and never forgotten.

4. **Believe and receive.** Have faith in yourself and what you're doing. When you're open to answers that you didn't know existed, great things will happen.

Networking Is a Contact Sport will help you understand these four themes and how you can apply them in your everyday life. My intent is that this book will teach you a process and methodology that will help you become better connected, grow your business, and give your life greater meaning.

Introduction
Networking
with Bob Costas

THE IDEA CAME as most great ideas do—from the chaise lounges parked on Seven Mile Beach in the Grand Cayman Islands, where the azure waters of the Caribbean lapped at the sand, and the setting sun dipped steadily toward an orange-hued horizon.

"What about Jim Nantz or Dick Enberg?" I offered to my buddies, Craig Leipold and Mark Leopold. "Either one would make a terrific master of ceremonies."

For the last twenty minutes, the three of us had been throwing out the names of someone I could ask to host the Wisconsin Sports Hall of Fame dinner seven months away.

At that time in 1995, I was president of the Wisconsin Sports Authority (WSA), the nonprofit organization hosting the Hall of Fame dinner, while Craig Leipold was the chairman of the board governing the WSA. My other close friend, Mark Leopold, worked for the family of Craig's wife at a large corporation back in our home state of Wisconsin. The Leipold and Leopold connection caused no shortage of confusion among our friends, who called us "The Three Amigos" after the Steve Martin comedy from the 1980s.

Basking in the warm glow of a Caribbean sunset, our threesome agreed that we needed to go after a well-known personality who could draw hundreds—better yet, thousands—of Milwaukee-area sports fans to an expensive gala dinner and Wisconsin Sports Hall of Fame induction ceremony scheduled for a Tuesday evening the following November. Tickets would be in the $125 range, a tidy sum in the mid-1990s.

Craig sat up in his lounge chair. "I know whom the people of Milwaukee would love," he said, pausing for dramatic effect.

"Come on, Leipold, spit his name out." I was thinking that Craig would bring up Bob Uecker's name again. He was the hilarious Milwaukee Brewer play-by-play radio announcer on WTMJ 620 who had parlayed a .200 lifetime batting average and seven uninspiring seasons as a journeyman catcher into a successful career as a comedian, actor, and broadcaster. Bob joked that his batting slumps lasted into winter and that he led the league in "Go get 'em next time."

But Bob Uecker was too local. We needed someone with a national presence in the sports world, someone who would create a buzz in the Cream City.

"I think our guy is Bob Costas." Craig waved his sweating gin and tonic for emphasis. "Wisconsin folks love him because every chance he gets, he's telling the country that Brewers baseball fans enjoy the most unbelievable brats and Secret Stadium Sauce at County Stadium. He's talking up our Brewers brats every time he talks about ballpark food. He'd be perfect."

Craig, Mark, and I clinked glasses from our beachside hacienda in the Grand Cayman Islands. "To Bob Costas," I toasted, but as soon as the adult libation touched my lips, a sense of foreboding overshadowed the reverie. Convincing the superb and highly sought-after NBC broadcaster who'd hosted Super Bowls, Olympic Games, World Series, NFL pre-games, and NBC's baseball "Game of the Week" to actually get on a plane and fly to Milwaukee for a Hall of Fame dinner was going to take every ounce of my networking skills.

Starting the Search

The beachside brainstorming happened in late March 1995, the same year that Larry Page and Sergey Brin, a pair of Stanford computer science grad students, began collaborating on a search engine named Google—a play on the word "googol," a mathematical term for a number represented by the numeral 1 followed by 100 zeros.

I felt like I had about the same chance—one in "googol"—of enticing Bob Costas to Milwaukee during the month of November, a dispiriting time when the days are short, nights are cold, and the late autumn sky is draped in a dreary gray blanket. But I had to give it a shot. The selection committee for the Wisconsin Sports Authority, which I chaired, had come up with what I thought was our greatest Hall of Fame class ever, and they deserved a first-class emcee. Our inductees were five legendary sports celebrities who could grace any Hall of Fame dais:

- Baseball Hall of Fame member Robin Yount, who spent his entire twenty-season career with the Milwaukee Brewers, collecting 3,142 hits;
- basketball legend Oscar Robertson, who guided the Milwaukee Bucks to their only NBA World Championship in 1971;
- former Marquette University basketball coach Al McGuire, who led the Warriors to their only NCAA Championship in 1977; and
- speed skaters Dan Jansen and Bonnie Blair, who earned gold medals at the 1994 Winter Olympics in Lillehammer, Norway.

These amazing stars all shared something in common: a deep-rooted connection with Wisconsin sports. As president of the Wisconsin Sports Authority, I was in charge of a nonprofit, quasi-government agency that promoted sports-related activities in the Badger State through a statewide network of community partnerships.

One of my ideas was to have the WSA take over the Wisconsin Sports Hall of Fame, which had been suffering from institutional neglect in the late 1980s and early 1990s. Since there had been only one Hall of Fame dinner since 1988, I felt the time was ripe to "go big"—do something that would get Wisconsinites talking around the water cooler about something other than Brewer baseball or whether the Green Bay Packers would field a playoff-caliber team.

Bob Costas as emcee would do the trick. But first I had to find him, and tracking him down wasn't going to be easy. I knew he worked for NBC Sports but a cold call to some underling in a mammoth media conglomerate would likely net me zilch. The Internet was basically the province of nerds in 1995, and nothing like Google existed, where today searching "Bob Costas contact information" would land you all sorts of helpful information.

But I didn't let the difficulty bog me down. My mindset was that if he was anywhere on God's green earth, then I could find him. I started by rifling through my personal "Rolodex"—three rectangular boxes containing every business card I had received in the last fifteen years, all filed alphabetically. I also had a three-ring binder containing page after page of typed contact information for those who hadn't handed me a business card. At the time, I had amassed probably eighteen hundred names, addresses, and telephone numbers.

I flipped through my business cards until I collected several names and phone numbers of Milwaukee media types who could have crossed paths with Costas. Then I began dialing for dollars, a phrase I used to pump up my adrenaline. I didn't have any luck, though, until I reached Bob Wolfley, a reporter at the *Milwaukee Journal Sentinel* newspaper whose beat included writing about TV and sports.

Wolfley, an experienced hand, told me that Bob Costas lived in St. Louis, the same city where he broke into broadcasting as a play-by-play announcer for the Spirits of St. Louis of the now defunct American Basketball Association. He explained that Costas had gotten his big break in 1983 when NBC hired him at the age of thirty-one to be the lead announcer for the "Game of the Week" baseball games every Saturday afternoon. From there, the sky was the limit: a high-profile broadcasting job with NBC Sports, syndicated radio, and well-paying speaking gigs. Even though he had established a national reputation and could live anywhere, Bob Wolfley said Costas maintained his residence in St. Louis.

Once I learned that Bob Costas lived in the Gateway City, I had a starting point. Dialing information in St. Louis was rather straight-forward in those days because the entire state of Missouri shared just three area codes. The operator had a listing for Bob Costas—the unusual last name helped. It was for a business entitled "Bob Costas Enterprises."

A woman named Pam answered my call. I explained that I was representing the Wisconsin Sports Hall of Fame dinner this coming

November, a gala event with a stellar induction class, and we'd love to have Bob—

"Oh, he's *very* busy," interrupted Pam. "Very, very busy."

"But do you think he could at least consider—"

Pam cut me off a second time. "I'm afraid Mr. Costas is too busy to consider your request, but we thank you for your interest."

I hung up, disappointed that I had struck out—with the bat still resting on my shoulder. I didn't even get the chance to take my best swing.

My thoughts were interrupted when my secretary buzzed me. Craig Leipold was on the line, no doubt seeking news. I punched in and heard Craig say, "How did we do with Costas?"

"Ah, he can't come. He's really busy." Keep in mind this phone call took place in April asking for Bob Costas to speak on a Tuesday night in early November. It wasn't like I was trying to book him during the baseball season or on a Sunday afternoon when he would be hosting an NFL pregame and halftime show.

"That's bull@#$%," Craig said. "Try him again in a few weeks."

A short time later, I dropped in on a Brewers baseball game, which is a great place to run into folks in Milwaukee. One of them was Dave Andera, a stockbroker and investment manager, and a close friend. I don't know what Dave liked more—taking in a baseball game or devouring one of Milwaukee's famous "brats"—bratwurst sausages slathered with Secret Stadium Sauce.

That night, after watching Dave wolf down his third brat, we watched the "Sausage Race" take place in the middle of the sixth inning. "Sausage racing" had begun in Milwaukee a few seasons earlier when mascots donned oversized foam sausage uniforms that stood more than seven feet tall from the top of the head to the knees of the runner. Their "race" was a sprint starting from the third base dugout to the outfield warning track and all the way around to the first base dugout. It was hilarious watching three sausages and a wiener—the Bratwurst, the Polish Sausage, the Italian Sausage, and the Hot Dog—charge for the finish line. Whoever finished first was the "wiener," and whoever finished last was the "wurst."

Wait a minute. What did Craig say about Bob Costas loving the "brats" at Milwaukee County Stadium?

An idea formed in my mind—an idea to ship Bob Costas a box of bratwursts. These couldn't just be any bratwurst sausages—they had to be the real thing from Milwaukee County Stadium, the famous brats that Costas had sung hosannas to on national television.

I told Dave what I was thinking. He said an outfit named Sportservice ran the concessions at the stadium. Sportservice? I was sure I knew a couple of guys who worked there.

The next day, I couldn't wait to arrive at work. My first phone call was to a contact at Sportservice. When I told him my plan, I received an enthusiastic response. "We can pack a box of brats in dry ice and ship them overnight to St. Louis—today, if you'd like," he said.

"That'll be great," I replied, adding that I would drop off a cover letter, formally inviting the NBC broadcaster to be the master of ceremonies at the Wisconsin Sports Hall of Fame dinner on Tuesday, November 14, 1995.

I was secretly hoping that a box of brats would soften Costas's heart, but when I didn't hear anything from his office after a week, I fired off a second salvo. I called my new buddy at Sportservice and said I needed to up the ante. "Can you send Bob Costas a case of Secret Stadium Sauce?" I asked. The Secret Stadium Sauce was developed back in the 1970s by a Milwaukee County Stadium vendor who—after running out of ketchup and mustard—mixed barbecue sauce, a little ketchup and mustard, and smoked syrup into a unique flavor that tastes like a combination of barbecue sauce and sauerkraut juice.

The Sportservice rep laughed and grunted his approval. That afternoon, I dropped off a second cover letter to Costas explaining that he couldn't enjoy Milwaukee brats unless they're smothered with Secret Stadium Sauce. Oh, and by the way, we'd still love to have him emcee our Wisconsin Sports Hall of Fame dinner.

Bob Costas still didn't bite.

Time to turn up the heat. In June, I was called by Bob Trunzo, the Secretary of the Department of Development, to a meeting at Governor Tommy Thompson's well-appointed office in Madison, the state capital. The governor and Secretary Trunzo had requested a status report on the Wisconsin Sports Authority, which had several plates spinning in the air. One of our initiatives was to entice NFL teams to move their preseason training camps to the relatively cooler summer climate of Wisconsin. Practicing in full pads and helmets in our 80-degree days in July and August was far better than dealing with triple-digit temperatures and stifling humidity back home.

"I'm happy to report that the Jacksonville Jaguars can't wait to get here next month," I reported to Governor Thompson. "When the Jags arrive, that will make five NFL teams training in our state." The "Cheese League," as the media had dubbed it, consisted of the Chicago Bears, Kansas City Chiefs, New Orleans Saints, and the pride and joy of every Cheesehead in the great state of Wisconsin—the Green Bay Packers.

"That's super," the governor said. "What else is going on?"

"Well, we have this big event down at the MECCA, set for November." I was referring to Milwaukee's twelve-thousand-seat indoor arena, which was officially known in those days as the Milwaukee Exposition Convention Center and Arena—or MECCA. (These days the MECCA facility is known as U.S. Cellular Arena, thanks to a naming rights deal.)

"Is this the Hall of Fame dinner I read about in the papers? The one with the Big O, Robin Yount, and the skaters?"

"That's the one. We've got quite a class coming in, but we can't get Bob Costas off the dime. He would make a great emcee for the event."

I could see the wheels turning in the governor's head. "How can I help make that happen?"

I had anticipated the question. "A letter from you, personally inviting him on behalf of the state of Wisconsin, would help our cause."

"Consider it done. Scotty, can you handle that?"

Tommy Thompson's aide, Scott Fromader, who had joined us in the governor's office, looked up from his legal pad. "Joe and I will get together after this meeting," he said.

Scott and I crafted a letter over Governor Thompson's signature declaring that Bob Costas's presence would add a "touch of class" to an evening that the entire Wisconsin sports community had been looking forward to for months.

That wasn't my final shot. All summer long, I followed up the brats, secret sauce, and Governor Thompson's plea with phone calls to my new best friend—Bob Costas's secretary named Pam. I spaced out my inquiries so as not to appear obtrusive, but they were regular enough to send the message that we still hoped Bob Costas would find the time to grace the Wisconsin Sports Hall of Fame event with his wit and charm.

A Turn for the Better

Still no response by August, and I was headed on summer vacation with my family. One day I picked up a *USA Today* and saw a front-page story about the funeral for New York Yankees legend Mickey Mantle.

The news of Mantle's death shocked me, even though I had heard that he'd been very ill. The story noted that years of heavy drinking had left Mantle with hepatitis as well as liver cancer, which led to a liver transplant several months earlier. Unfortunately for Mantle, the cancer had spread to his other organs.

My eyes popped out when I read that Bob Costas had delivered a eulogy to the two thousand mourners at Mantle's funeral in Dallas, including actor Billy Crystal, teammate Bobby Richardson, and Yankees owner George Steinbrenner.

"I'm here, not so much to speak for myself as to simply represent the millions of baseball-loving kids who grew up in the fifties and sixties, and for whom Mickey Mantle *was* baseball," Costas said. "For a huge part of my generation, Mickey Mantle was the most compelling baseball hero of our lifetime. Always so hard on himself, he finally came to accept and appreciate that distinction between a role model and a hero. The first, he often was not; the second he will always be."

As a speaker, this guy's a class act, I thought. *No wonder he's so busy.*

I was still clutching my copy of *USA Today* when I called my office in Milwaukee to pick up any messages. My secretary, Katie, was nearly hyperventilating. "You need to call St. Louis," she said. "Pam at Bob Costas's office is looking for you."

My heart skipped a beat. Why would Pam call *me*? Unless—

I dialed Pam's number by memory. I'll never forget her first words to me: "Bob says he'll show up."

Three months later, I greeted his flight at Mitchell International Airport six miles south of downtown Milwaukee. The boyish-looking Costas looked just like he did on TV. He hopped in my car, and off we drove to the Milwaukee Hyatt, where I had reserved the penthouse suite for this member of broadcasting royalty.

To make small talk, I told him I really enjoyed the eulogy he gave at the Mickey Mantle funeral. He said he loved Mickey Mantle and had carried a Mickey Mantle baseball card in his wallet since he was twelve years old.

I sensed a story coming, and I was right.

"The night before the memorial service, I still hadn't written the eulogy," Costas said. "I couldn't make the words come, so in the middle of the night, I called Billy Crystal, who was staying at the same hotel as I was. Billy said sure, he'd come down and help me, and together we knocked out the eulogy."

After getting him checked into his suite, I walked Costas through the program while he peppered me with questions about the Wisconsin Sports Hall of Fame dinner. How many people were coming? Where was it being held? How were the inductees feeling? Was Bud Selig, the Milwaukee Brewers owner and interim commissioner of Major League Baseball, going to be there? I knew why Costas asked that question. He had ripped Selig's leadership during the baseball strike the season before, which resulted in the cancellation of the 1994 postseason, including the World Series.

"Yes, Bud will be there," I said. "The Brewers general manager, Sal Bando, is also coming. Bob Uecker will be at their table, too. He'll be introducing Robin Yount."

I briefed Costas as best I could, and he took copious notes. I told him the reason we were having the dinner inside the MECCA was because that indoor arena had been the site of some of Wisconsin's greatest sporting moments. The MECCA complex was where the Milwaukee Bucks played their only NBA championship season back in 1971. Playing that season was a beefy point guard named Oscar Robertson and a skinny seven-foot, two-inch center named Lew Alcindor, who hadn't yet adopted his Muslim name of Kareem Abdul-

Jabbar. Later, Al McGuire's Marquette Warriors called the MECCA their home court during their championship 1977 season.

"We're expecting seventeen hundred to attend the dinner, and they'll be seated at one hundred and seventy tables spread out on the arena floor," I said. "The demand for tickets was so great that people are paying to sit in the grandstands and *watch* people eat their dinner and listen to you and the Hall of Fame inductees."

Costas whistled his appreciation and thanked me for my time. As I got up to leave, we shook hands. "I have to tell you, Joe, that you're one of the most persistent characters I've ever met."

I took that as a compliment.

I didn't sit down the entire evening of the 1995 Wisconsin Sports Hall of Fame dinner. In my mind, I had seventeen hundred of my closest personal friends in the house, and I worked the tables the entire evening. I made it a point to shake hands, pat backs, and say thank you to as many people as I could.

After the dinner dishes were cleared away, the house lights dimmed inside the cavernous indoor arena, and Bob Costas strode to the podium under the glare of a bright spotlight.

A standing ovation greeted his arrival, and the cheering sounded like the roar of a crowd after a Marquette player hits a game-winning buzzer-beater during March Madness.

After thanking the appreciative audience for the enthusiastic welcome, Costas grabbed the podium with both hands and gave the audience his most deadpan, serious expression. "I have to say that Joe Sweeney, one of the driving forces behind this dinner, was a most persistent and persuasive man," he began. "He calls me in March and says, 'Can you come to Wisconsin in early November?' I said, 'Gee, I'd love to, but I'm very busy.' The next day, a shipment of bratwurst from County Stadium arrives in St. Louis. I'm trying to resist; I haven't committed yet."

By this time, Costas has the audience in the palm of his hand. "The next day, a vat of Secret Stadium Sauce arrived," he continued. "A couple of days after that, a *pleading* letter from Governor Tommy Thompson. I'm just about at the edge, and then Sweeney calls and threatens to give Uecker my home phone number. Fine— I'm coming!"

The stars were aligned in Milwaukee on a special evening in November 1995 when the Wisconsin Sports Hall of Fame inducted (from the left) Robin Yount, Al McGuire, Oscar Robertson, Bonnie Blair, and Dan Jansen. Host Bob Costas (third from left) told me afterward that this was the "greatest sports induction ceremony I've ever attended."

The audience howled, and standing in the back of the arena, I split a gut as well. Not only was Bob Costas a master raconteur, but it also appeared that he never let a few facts get in the way of a good story.

Networking Makes Things Happen

If my experience with Bob Costas proved anything, it's that networking is a contact sport. Sometimes you get pushed aside or knocked down, but if you persevere, remain focused, and look for ways to engage people—ways that are fresh, clever, and persistent—networking will make things happen and take you where you want to go in life.

As a hustling entrepreneur, successful business owner, and present-day investment banker, networking is something I *love* to do. I hope what I've learned in the trenches over the last twenty-five years will convince you to think proactively and *intentionally* about connecting with others because networking means getting out there and making yourself known. When you're willing to network, you'll find life richer and more meaningful when you connect with friends, acquaintances, business colleagues, and even strangers.

Why do I say that? Because my definition of networking is the opposite of what most people think the practice is all about. The classic definition is that networking is the process of establishing beneficial relationships with other business people and potential clients and customers, or a way for like-minded confederates to exchange information, ideas, and support. This latter concept dates back to Roman times, when the Latin phrase *quid pro quo* meant "something for something," which indicated a more-or-less equal exchange of goods and services. In other words, you ask for a favor with the knowledge that you'll be asked to do something for the other person sometime down the road. It's the idea of tit for tat: *You scratch my back, and I'll scratch yours.*

If you think *Networking Is a Contact Sport* is about how to scratch the backs of business contacts so that they'll scratch yours, then please allow me to disabuse you of that notion. Networking is not about figuring out how to use business contacts for your personal gain. People can smell an agenda from one hundred paces, and if you strike up a loaded conversation with someone you barely know with the end goal of developing some sort of business relationship that lines your pockets, you'll burn a bridge and never build a meaningful relationship with that person.

I see networking in an entirely different light. I view networking as an opportunity **to** *give*, **not to get**, a way to make myself available to friends and contacts without any expectation of reciprocity.

Sure, there have been occasions when I've called someone I barely know seeking a favor—like the time I asked Bob Wolfley at the *Milwaukee Journal Sentinel* how I could get in contact with Bob Costas. He was glad to help me out, just as I would have been happy to help him out. What really gets me going is receiving a phone call from someone needing a hand, seeking a word of advice, or asking for direction—and I don't need anything in return.

Sometimes I don't even wait to get that phone call. When I find an awesome book, I'm that author's best friend because I'm liable to purchase hundreds of copies. I've probably given away three hundred copies of *Half Time: Changing Your Game Plan from Success to Significance* by Bob Buford, who reminds guys broaching midlife that whether you are a millionaire, a manager, a teacher, or whatever, one day you will have to transition from the struggle for success to a quest for significance. Another book I hand out like party favors is *Body for Life* by Bill Phillips, because I'm a fitness nut and think that others could benefit from his well-organized fitness program.

Whenever I ask my wife, Tami, if she wants to accompany me to our local bookstore, she rolls her eyes, knowing that I'll walk out of the store with an armful of books that I'll give away to others. I keep a credenza full at my office because whenever I talk to someone and find out he's dealing with a certain issue or could benefit from a self-help book, I make sure I get a copy into his hands. My buddy Craig Leipold is constantly teasing me about this, saying to friends, "How many books did you get from Sweeney this week?"

Why have I purchased literally thousands of books and mailed them off to others—including business contacts I hardly know? Because a wrapped book says, *I care about you. I hope this helps your predicament—or gives you some insight or clarity.*

Buying books, returning phone calls and e-mails, being a good listener, and asking the right questions ("Tell me, Brad, how are you *really* doing?") are the bricks and mortar for building relationships. Relationships are what make the world go round, and I shudder to think what life would be like without the interactions I enjoy with my family, my friends, my acquaintances, and even my business contacts. (And contacts forged in business can often become your best friends.)

Relationships heighten the human experience, magnify our participation with others, and give life its ultimate meaning. When English clergyman and poet John Donne wrote that "No man is an island" in the seventeenth century, he was declaring in a poetic way that we all hunger for connection with others—and thirst for significance. We should matter to others and have them matter to us. Networking helps us do that.

The Runt of the Litter

You'll learn more about how my upbringing shaped my extrovert personality in the next chapter, but for now here is a little background. I, Gary Dean "Joe" Sweeney, was born the ninth of ten children to Raymond and Marian Murphy Sweeney. I was practically the runt of an Irish-Catholic litter growing up in Madison, Wisconsin.

My earliest memories are of sitting around an enormous circular table in the kitchen, back when I was five or six years old. Sometimes thirteen, fourteen, or even sixteen kids gathered around to wolf down Mom's famous spaghetti or homemade goulash.

Why the extra mouths to feed?

Because my parents always told my eight older brothers that they could invite anyone they wanted over for dinner, so the Sweeney home at 4306 Waite Circle was the happening place. When Mike (fifteen years my senior) and Jack (a year younger than Mike) headed off to Notre Dame, they often returned on weekends with a friend or two looking for a home-cooked meal and a welcome break from the "Animal House" of college life. I can assure you that the energy level kicked up a notch whenever we welcomed college kids or neighborhood "strays" to sup with us. Dinners at the Sweeney household were raucous demonstrations of male testosterone that were fun!

Compare my boisterous upbringing to how many kids are raised today. If I can play armchair psychologist for a moment, there have been colossal societal changes since I was born in 1958. Smaller families, working parents, and sedentary kids inhibit the natural flow of interaction, much like a governor on a golf cart. The stratospheric rise in the number of single-parent homes correlates to a corresponding increase in latchkey kids (those coming home from school to an empty house). There's no chance for them to have interaction with a parent—or even a sibling, since some older brothers and sisters work to pay the bills in single-parent homes—until they get off work.

Any after-school contact for children flows mostly one way and is media-driven: watching TV, texting classmates, listening to the iPod, surfing the Internet, or engaging in their favorite pastime—Facebook or other online communities.

I'll have a lot more to say about social networks like Facebook, LinkedIn, and Twitter in Chapter 11, but tapping out "RU bored?" on your cell phone will never substitute for hanging out with a peer or two. On the business side, you can't discount the incredible value of looking someone in the eye and giving him a firm handshake or an embracing hug. Touch triumphs over technology every time. The hunger for human contact is universal and eminently more satisfying.

That's why I hate to eat alone when I'm on the road. I don't know about you, but I'm the type who seeks out mom-and-pop diners so I can sit at the counter and kibitz with the short-order cook scrambling my eggs or make small talk with the salaryman settled on the stool next to me. I like people. I like their stories. I like the contact.

From my perch at the counter, though, I see way too many young men—and young women, to an extent—pass up opportunities to engage others or reach out beyond a tight circle of acquaintances. Young people have become more insular, more content with going home to an empty apartment, turning on ESPN, MTV, or Bravo, and "vegging out" while texting and watching TV.

Everyone's free to live life the way he wants, but that's not the recipe for a relationship with others. In *Networking Is a Contact Sport*, I hope to convince you about the importance of reaching out. Networking does many things that can help inside and outside the office cubicle: it gives you confidence, teaches resiliency, and helps you overcome life's challenges. My concept of networking—where you engage others with an attitude of giving, not getting—will enrich your life and open up avenues for personal enjoyment and advancement. When you make networking a contact sport, you'll find that the wonderful idea of what "goes around comes around" certainly applies in these type of interactions, and any personal gain that comes as a result of networking is just icing on the cake.

A Confidence Builder

You might be reading this book because you've been recently laid off, and you're wondering if "networking" can help you land your next job. If that's your situation, then your instincts are correct.

Networking is often the *only* way you can get hired again. The cliché that *who* you know is more important than *what* you know is certainly true when you're on a job search.

Think about the last time you got hired. Did you get the job because someone told you about the opportunity? Did a friend open some doors by making a call or two on your behalf? Did a contact inside the company tip the scales in your favor? Did a golfing buddy actually hire you? As any human resources director will tell you, résumés are a dime a dozen these days.

More often than not, networking is the name of the game when it comes to finding a job, and it's needed more than ever in these times of adversity. Since 2008, more than eight million workers have been laid off or handed a pink slip—many of them forever. Others have had their positions "downsized" or been forced to take unpaid furloughs, which is tantamount to a wage cut. In Chapter 4, I'll discuss networking for a job in length.

I make my living as an investment banker, and the mergers and acquisitions market—the sandbox I play in—has been frozen since the fall of 2008, so I've had my challenges as well. What's kept the doors open has been working with folks that I've developed a long-standing relationship with built on mutual trust. While I understand that business is tough, many of you are facing the most gripping hardships of your life.

If you're straining to keep your business afloat, save your home, and not go into deeper debt, I understand. I travel a great deal throughout the Midwest, and it breaks my heart to see our country's manufacturing base erode like a sandcastle at high tide. Shuttered factories and assembly lines in Michigan, Ohio, Illinois, and Wisconsin—along with the mighty General Motors being forced to "reinvent" itself— do not bode well for our country's economic future. We could be headed for a long, severe recession. Double-digit unemployment is likely to be with us for many months, if not years.

Networking Is a Contact Sport can help you reinvent yourself if you've lost your job or are waiting for the axe to fall. If you've found yourself in the unenviable place of looking for a job, here are ten points that I'll be referring to time and again in *Networking Is a Contact Sport*.

1. Be clear about your objectives and outcomes.
2. Do your research.
3. Don't be afraid to ask.
4. Get comfortable with traveling outside your comfort zone.
5. Try, try, try—and then try again in a creative way.
6. Do your best to connect the dots.
7. Seek out in-person contact—there is no substitute for the personal touch.
8. Take 100 percent responsibility for your networking.
9. Treat others as you would want to be treated.
10. Present an offer to help others before you ask for anything.

Let's look at how I did with these ten points when it came to enticing Bob Costas to come to Milwaukee:

1. **I had a goal, but it took a while to come up with a plan.** My goal was to convince Bob Costas, one of the most recognizable personalities in sports broadcasting, to come to Milwaukee on a Tuesday evening in November, which was going to be uphill sledding the entire way. The good news is that I had some time to work with, which gave me wiggle room to come up with different approaches.
2. **I did my research.** In 1995, I had to work the phones to even find out what *city* Bob Costas lived in—information that today is a few keystrokes and .38 seconds away via a search engine.
3. **I wasn't afraid to ask Bob Costas to come to Milwaukee.** Okay, maybe some of you living on the Eastern Seaboard or the Left Coast view Milwaukee as a blue-collar burg where the only thing to do is sit around, drink beer, snack on cheese, and talk about the Green Bay Packers, but I'm a Milwaukee booster who's seen the city revitalized with a dazzling array of fabulous restaurants, museums, theaters, and festivals. Besides, Bob had been to Milwaukee many times, so he knew where he was going.

4. **I got comfortable with traveling outside my comfort zone by thinking outside the box**—with a box of Milwaukee County brats, that is. I added a box of Secret Stadium Sauce, too.

5. **I tried, tried, and tried again to land Bob Costas.** How many times did I call Pam, his secretary, to check in, even though I had been told that he was "too busy"? Probably a half-dozen times. I could have given up after the initial rebuff, but I remained persistent—in a friendly sort of way. I could have asked Bob Costas a hundred times, but it wasn't until I got creative and sent him a box of Milwaukee brats and a case of Secret Stadium Sauce that the logjam was broken. Without being creative, persistence can be a turnoff to others.

6. **I connected the dots.** Organizing a Hall of Fame dinner for seventeen hundred people was a logistical tangle that involved networking with dozens of people to pull it off. At the end of the evening, former Marquette coach Al McGuire sidled up to me. "Sweeney, you really know how to connect the dots," he said. What McGuire meant was that I used my networking skills to bring people with divergent backgrounds together to complete a task.

7. **There's no substitute for the personal touch.** Every attempt to engage Bob Costas was done through a personal phone call or a direct letter (and package) from me—and I personally picked him up at the airport.

8. **I took responsibility for my networking efforts to reach Bob Costas.** As the guy in charge of the Wisconsin Hall of Fame dinner, it was up to me to bring in Bob Costas for a landing. Sure, I needed help to find Costas or ship him some brats, but I stayed persistent because I was the guy standing in the batter's box.

There are some people who say, "I work for Microsoft, so I don't have to network," or "I work for the feds, so networking isn't important to me." No matter where you work—even if you have a public-sector job—you'll still profit from having a networking mindset. That's the mindset I've always tried to have in life, and you should, too.

9. **Treat others as you would want to be treated.** The Golden Rule never goes out of style and may prove to be critical in networking. Sure, I treated Bob Costas like a king, but I try to treat everyone I come into contact with—from the parking lot attendant to the waitress to the personal assistant to the CEO—with the same respect and attention I afforded the NBC broadcaster.

10. **Present an offer to help others before you ask for anything.** I never had the chance to offer Bob Costas anything—unless you count a Milwaukee bratwurst dripping with Secret Stadium Sauce—before I asked him if he could do the sports fans of Milwaukee a huge favor by coming to our Hall of Fame dinner. The ideal situation is offering to do something for others before you ask anything yourself.

These are quick-hitting principles that distill the larger message of *Networking Is a Contact Sport.* In the coming pages, I'll tell you how you can take small networking steps. I'll share my 5/10/15 networking exercise that will give you a framework to reach out and touch people. I'll urge you to find a "wingman" who can watch your back as well as serve as a sounding board and accountability partner. I'll help you determine your personality type, and if you're an introvert, I'll give you some tips on how you engage others and what it means to get out of your comfort zone. I'll sort through the rapidly changing ways that technology is making it easier—but sometimes more difficult—to network.

If you've been laid off, I'll describe how networking can get you back on your feet, and if you're a woman, I'll show you how you can network even if you're not playing in the corporate golf outing.

The main thing I've found in life is that success—and failure—leaves clues. I've studied successful people, and they invariably have one thing in common: they saw themselves involved in something bigger than themselves.

I hope you come to view networking in the same light. When you network to give and not to get, you open yourself up to networking with even *more* people and living a life well-lived.

Not convinced? Ask anyone at the sunset of life, when he knows the final whistle is about to be blown. The cliché is that no one on his deathbed ever said, "I wish I spent more time in the office" or "I wish I could have put one more deal together."

Those who are dying often have a simple request: to be surrounded by loved ones and friends as they stand on the doorstep of eternity. Relationships and memories are what give life inestimable richness and clear-headed purpose. I'm doing my best to keep that thought centermost in my mind, and I hope you will, too.

Thanks for joining me as you learn why networking to serve others will help you stay connected, grow your business, expand your influence, and even land your next job.

Remember: networking is a contact sport.

The Art
of Networking:

As Natural as
Wisconsin Cheese

I'M A PHYSICAL FITNESS NUT, someone who believes that intense bouts of exercise are absolutely crucial for keeping mind, body, and spirit in top shape, especially now that I'm in my early fifties.

Sometimes I combine exercise *and* networking by blowing off steam at the Milwaukee Athletic Club during the noon hour. This grand and venerable fitness club has a long history, having been around since 1882 and occupying all *twelve* stories at its imposing location in the heart of downtown Milwaukee.

Within these dozen floors, you'll find a formal dining room, seventeen private meeting rooms, sixty guest rooms, two cocktail lounges, a library, barber shop, child-care facility, racquetball and squash courts, a co-ed fitness studio, private men's and women's athletic facilities, and lap pools. The Milwaukee Athletic Club is where the local business community goes to break a sweat, take a sauna, and perhaps knock down a salad and an iced tea before heading back to the office. This private club is also a great place to run into business people of all stripes, which is why I love the Milwaukee Athletic Club's motto:

Workout. Network. Have Fun.

Now that I've given you a thumbnail description of the Milwaukee Athletic Club, perhaps you can picture me standing inside the well-furnished men's locker room, dressing after a noontime swim and bracing shower. An insurance guy I knew—not well but he was part of my three-thousand-strong networking list—approached me as I was slipping on my loafers. Without preamble, he got right to the point. "Hey, Joe," he bellowed. "I left my insurance company, so I'm out on my own. What do you say if I take you to lunch and we do a little networking?"

I understood the coded message. What the insurance fellow was saying was this: *Hey, Joe. Can I steal ninety minutes of your valuable time so that you can give me your database and contact list so I can market my services to them?*

That is a classic example of networking to get, not to give. The insurance man's rather bold request left me feeling underwhelmed and rather put out, which is human nature. It would have been far better for the insurance guy to have quietly approached me, asked how my kids were doing or some other innocuous small-talk question, before saying something like, "Hey, Joe, I know you're an investment banker and I also know that business is soft out there because of the lackluster economy. I looked at your website and saw that you do primarily four things: one, sell companies; two, help people buy companies; three, raise capital; and four, invest in private equity deals. I know your market targets companies in the $10 million to $200 million range. I think I know two or three CEOs who are looking to raise some capital and could use your services. I'd be glad to call them, if you think that would be a good idea."

Whoa, talking about turning the tables. If the insurance guy had taken that offer-to-help approach, maybe the next time I ran into him at the Milwaukee Athletic Club, I would favorably respond to his request to do a "little networking" with him over a pastrami sandwich.

That's how I was raised to view networking. My Irish-Catholic parents reared me in a crowded home that fostered give-and-take and working things out with others. If you didn't "network" in my family of twelve—give in order to get—you weren't going to be a happy camper.

Following my arrival on April 23, 1958, the Sweeney family was front-page news in our hometown of Madison, Wisconsin. After all, how many families have nine consecutive sons—enough to field a baseball team? What's interesting about the story in the *Wisconsin State Journal* is that the reporter never mentioned the person who delivered all nine boys—my mom!

My orderly and loving parents, Raymond and Marian, set the tone in the Sweeney household by stressing cooperation and working together. Good thing they did because otherwise there would have been total mayhem. You could also say that Dad and Mom stayed the course and were a persistent team. When they set out to have a family, they always said they wanted a baby girl, but Mom kept having boys until the Sweeney clan could field a baseball team.

> If you didn't "network" in my family of twelve— give in order to get—you weren't going to be a happy camper.

I joined the fold in 1958, the ninth of nine boys. Even back then, this was a remarkable feat. Two months after my birth, the *Wisconsin State Journal* printed a photo of Dad sitting on our grassy front yard, cradling me in his right arm and hanging on to Brian, sixteen months old at the time, in the crook of his left arm. "Ninth Son Gets in the Sweeney Lineup" announced the boldface headline. The long caption noted that the "Sweeney baseball team" had recently "signed" its latest member—me—but that my father would continue playing right field until I got a "little more seasoning."

Give my parents some props. Even though their lineup card was full, they didn't give up their dream of having a girl. You could say that Dad and Mom went into extra innings, and on January 12, 1960, their first, and only daughter, Mary Beth, was born. With her arrival, Dad and Mom finally threw in the nursing towel.

What was life like growing up in the Sweeney household? The best term I can come up with is "organized chaos." If you've ever seen the old sixties movie *Yours, Mine, and Ours* with Henry Fonda and Lucille Ball (he's a widower with ten children who marries a widow with eight children), then you might have an idea of how our home life bordered on bedlam and constant turmoil. But there was tons of love surrounding me, and growing up in a large family taught me the value of working things out with my eight older brothers and one younger sister. You had to go along to get along. Whenever I sat down at our outsized table at dinnertime, there was a built-in audience to "network" with.

Looking back, I'm confident that being born ninth in the batting order shaped my personality in ways that prepared me to become an outstanding networking individual. I couldn't slink off to my bedroom and shut the door because I shared that bedroom with two or three brothers! Heck, we boys often slept two or three to a bed, which is why I often joke that I didn't sleep alone until I got married.

Life in the Sweeney family was always about interacting with others, whether you wanted to or not. From these early childhood experiences, I learned the value of communication and not being afraid to introduce myself or interact with others. In fact, I can remember the first time I "networked" like it was yesterday.

A Trip to Notre Dame

My family likes to tell me that growing up, I was a rambunctious, good-hearted kid who was always looking out for my older brothers. I know they looked after me.

In late December 1966, when I was eight years old, we took a long driving trip to the shrine of Catholic college education—Notre Dame—where my second-oldest brother, Jack, was in seminary studying to become a Catholic priest. (My oldest brother, Mike, was in Ecuador as part of the Peace Corps.) The banter in our household was that Moreau Seminary didn't let their seminarians go home over Christmas because they feared they wouldn't return.

So we needed to visit our homesick brother, but getting to South Bend, Indiana, from our hometown of Madison involved a daylong drive in my parents' 1962 Ford Falcon station wagon. Notre Dame was also home for my older brother, Tim, who had just finished playing a strong season on the freshman football team as a "walk-on"—meaning he had been invited to try out but was not given an athletic scholarship.

In those days, "frosh" athletes weren't eligible to play on the varsity teams, so Tim was hoping that his stellar play at quarterback would win him a spot on the varsity squad as well as an athletic scholarship, which would greatly ease the financial burden on my parents. I'm sure that Dad and Mom worried mightily about how they would ever put ten children through college. Tim wasn't in the Ford Falcon that morning, though; we left him back in Madison since he was still on Christmas break and wanted to hang out with his old high school buddies.

We didn't have room for Tim anyway because we had to squeeze nine Sweeneys into our small Ford family cruiser, which had the disturbing habit of coughing and misfiring every few miles or so. The three youngest boys—Pat, Brian, and myself—drew the short straws and were assigned the very rear bench in the station wagon. During the eight interminable hours on the road, I managed to only have five bruises and two welts from my older brothers by the time we arrived at Notre Dame.

When we pulled up to my brothers' seminary, Father Superior took one look at us and muttered under his breath, "Holy Mother of Jesus, here comes the Sweeney clan. God give me strength and patience to endure this test." The priest would soon realize how much he underestimated the challenge he was about to endure.

A few days into our collective destruction of Moreau Seminary, Jack said, "Let's go swimming at The Rock," referring to the student gymnasium building named after legendary football Coach Knute Rockne. Jack hoped that a group swim at the indoor pool would dissipate our pent-up energy. I'll never forget the ugly cloth swimsuits they made us wear, which felt like I was swimming in a diaper. I didn't stay in the plunge long. I slipped out of the pool, changed back into my regular clothes, and snuck out into the lobby of Notre Dame's main athletic building, looking for something exciting to do.

That's when my eyes spotted a building directory on a nearby brick wall. I walked over and scanned the names, and one leaped out at me: Ara Parseghian.

Ara Parseghian? I knew all about him. He was the Fighting Irish head football coach for the top-ranked football team in the country. Just five weeks earlier, Notre Dame and Michigan State—ranked No. 1 and No. 2, respectively—had fought to a 10-10 tie in the "Game of the Century," which even today is called one of the greatest games in college football history. The tie (college teams didn't play overtime in those days) meant that Notre Dame would finish the 1966 season with a 9-0-1 record and be awarded with its first NCAA National Championship since 1953. From the perspective of a third-grader, though, I thought Notre Dame and Ara Parseghian were as close to God as I would ever get.

Over the Christmas break, all Tim had talked about was whether Coach Parseghian would award him a spot on the varsity squad the following fall. If Tim made the team, a scholarship offer would certainly follow.

Maybe I could help Tim's cause by talking to Coach Parseghian.

I sprinted up three flights of stairs until I found a glass door with his name inscribed in gold lettering. I confidently opened the door, where a middle-aged, prim-and-proper secretary sat behind a desk, tapping away on an electric typewriter.

She looked over the glasses perched on the tip of her nose. "May I help you, young man?" she asked.

"I would like to see Coach Parseghian," I announced in the most grown-up voice I could muster. "Is he here?"

A warm smile came over the secretary's face as she looked me over from head to toe. After the longest pause, she said, "Let me see if Coach Parseghian is available."

You may be wondering why Coach Parseghian was even in his office in late December, instead of preparing for a bowl game. Notre Dame had a policy of not playing in bowl games until 1969, which meant that the 1966 season ended on November 26 with a 51-0 thrashing of the USC Trojans.

The secretary stepped into a hallway behind her desk while I stood in place and rocked on my heels. I wasn't nervous at all, which may sound odd. Most eight-year-olds would be shivering in their shoes, as if they were standing next to the Scarecrow, Tin Man, the Cowardly Lion, and Dorothy while they waited to be ushered before the mighty and powerful Wizard of Oz.

Not me. A plan had formed in my mind, and that plan involved asking Coach Parseghian whether he was going to award my older brother an athletic scholarship. I wasn't afraid because I had some serious business to conduct.

I cooled my heels until the secretary returned with the verdict two minutes later. "Coach Parseghian will see you now," she announced, beckoning me to step into the hallway and follow her. "And who may I say is calling?"

A few years before I, as an eight-year-old boy, walked into Coach Ara Parseghian's office on the Notre Dame campus, he appeared on the cover of *Time* magazine for leading the Fighting Irish to the top of the college football rankings. My older brothers presented me with this magazine cover at my fiftieth birthday.

I wondered if I should give her my real name—Gary Dean Sweeney—or what everyone called me, which was Joe Sweeney. I chose the latter.

I walked into Coach Parseghian's well-appointed office and he offered his hand, which I shook. He then ushered me toward a burgundy leather coach to sit down.

"Tell me, Master Sweeney, what's on your mind?"

"That was great, Coach, that you won the national championship. Our family was really excited," I began.

"Thank you, young man. I think we proved that Notre Dame football is the best in the country," replied the famous coach.

The initial exchange bolstered my confidence. "Do you think we can win next year?" I asked.

"I sure do. We have a lot of fine players coming back. Now that we've had a taste of what it's like to be number one, there's no reason why we can't win the national championship next season."

I saw my opening. "Coach, I have an older brother who goes to school here. His name is Tim. He's the best athlete in our family. He was All-State in football, basketball, and baseball in Wisconsin, but he really wants to continue playing football for Notre Dame."

"Oh, yes. I heard of your brother. He did a good job for us on the freshman team this season."

"I know. So are you going to give my big brother a scholarship?"

The great coach suppressed a smile and answered, "Joe, all I can promise is that we're looking at a lot of quarterbacks, but I'll make sure your brother gets a good look."

Satisfied that my mission was over, I stood up to leave. "Thank you, Coach," I said, extending my hand for him to shake. "Thank you for your time."

I departed the office and nearly floated down the stairs as I worked my way back to the indoor pool entrance. Instead of hailing my return, however, my grumpy brothers were quite angry, the loudest being Jack, who informed me that he and several other brothers had been looking for me for almost a half hour.

"We were just about to call the campus police," Jack complained. "Where were you?"

"With Coach Parseghian. In his office," I stammered.

"What were you doing up there?"

"Asking him to give Tim a scholarship."

A chorus of derisive laughter filled the hallway. Jack and my brothers thought this was the most hysterical thing they had heard in a long time. "And the next thing you'll tell me is that John Lennon was there, too, and he wants you to join the Beatles," Jack scoffed.

"It's true. I saw him. I really did see Coach Parseghian."

My earnest defense earned me another round of ridicule.

"If you don't believe me, I'll show you myself," I declared with total confidence.

Six brothers followed me up the three flights of stairs. I knew exactly where to go. When I opened the door to Coach Parseghian's office, the secretary's face lit up in recognition.

"Hello, Joe," she smiled. "Back to see Coach again?"

The looks on my brothers' faces were priceless.

"I was wondering if I could introduce my brothers to Coach Parseghian," I said.

"Let me see if we can make that happen," she replied with a conspiratorial wink.

Thirty seconds later, Ara Parseghian—a mythic presence in my brothers' minds—strode into the foyer and shook hands with a suddenly very quiet and very respectful gathering of Sweeney sons. After five minutes of small talk about the championship season, he wished us the best and bade us goodbye. As we walked back to the seminary, Jack kept saying over and over that he couldn't believe what I had just pulled off.

Several months later, Tim Sweeney received the outstanding news that he would be receiving a Notre Dame athletic scholarship. He ended up playing just one season as a defensive back—Notre Dame had a surplus of great quarterbacks—because he blew out his knee. When Tim recovered, he turned his attention to baseball and played on the Notre Dame varsity team, but he will always be able to tell his grandchildren that he ran up and down the hallowed field of Notre Dame Stadium before sellout crowds of Irish faithful.

Lessons Learned

Although I couldn't have known it at the time, the way I established a relationship with a tough, famous football coach—who ranked right up there with the Pope Paul VI in our Irish-Catholic home—was an illustrative piece of networking.

When it comes to making connections, you can't be afraid to introduce yourself and make new relationships. I don't know what possessed me, at the tender age of eight, to walk into Ara Parseghian's office on behalf of my brother, but if I hadn't asked for an audience with the "pontiff" of Notre Dame football, Tim would have never collected that coveted athletic scholarship.

At least, that's what I prefer to think, even though I know Tim still had to earn his spot on the Notre Dame football team.

> When it comes to making connections, you can't be afraid to introduce yourself and make new relationships.

As I look around at today's work environment, though, too many young men and women, middle managers, executive types, and even the unemployed have a skewed idea of what networking should look like. Many view networking as a commercial version of "What can you do for me?"—much like the insurance salesman at the Milwaukee Athletic Club who wanted to tap into my contact list so that he could pitch new insurance clients.

Instead, networking starts with introductions. I *love* introducing myself—not because I think I'm anything special—but because I've learned the value of connecting with others ever since I walked into Coach Parseghian's office as a young boy. But don't get the idea that I search out only the well-connected and well-heeled. In many ways, I enjoy being on a first-name basis with breakfast waitresses, office janitors, and the guys at the street corner hot dog stands. Treating these folks with respect is not only the right thing to do—because I'm treating them the way I would want to be treated—but I've learned that the people you meet while moving up the ladder will be the same people waiting for you if you ever have to make your way down the ladder.

Networking is not a place to play favorites. We need to network with everyone, from famous football coaches down to the parking lot attendants. Sure, it helps to have friends in high places, but it never hurts to know a smiling face at a downtown parking lot just before a Fourth of July fireworks show.

Networking is like cultivating a garden: nothing will ever bloom if you don't take time to water and weed, to give plants the proper amount of attention. People are the same way. We all hunger for recognition, an aching desire that somebody knows us in this impersonal world. Going out of your way to introduce yourself—with an attitude of *How can I give, not get?*—is what good networking is all about.

Good networking is also about being a good listener because if you wait long enough, people will leave clues about how things are really going with their lives—like Tina Bennett, the single-parent mom who wrung her hands when I asked her whether her son would be attending Marquette University High School that school year.

You may be thinking, *What could Tina Bennett do for you, Joe?*

Perhaps she couldn't do anything, at least in the world's eyes. But the way I responded to her need is the attitude I try to have when I am in the company of business peers and acquaintances, and I'm certain that kind of attitude shows.

To drive home this point, I'm going to offer a short multiple-answer test on the next page. Let's see how you do.

QUIZ

1. **When you're in a social setting that's related to business, which statement sounds like you?**

   a. Within a minute of meeting someone, you're sizing up whether a person can help make a sale or advance your career.
   b. You're polite, and while you show some interest, you still play your cards close to the vest.
   c. After shaking hands, you start asking questions that will help both of you establish common ground—background, family life, neighborhood, and what he or she does for a living.

2. **When attending a business mixer:**

   a. You look for familiar faces and end up hanging out with them the entire evening.
   b. You hand out a few cards to some new acquaintances, but you're careful to keep things superficial and not too "deep."
   c. You make it a point to introduce yourself to at least ten new people before the evening is over.

3. **If you lost your job tomorrow:**

   a. You'd panic because you've been a "lone wolf" ever since your first job.
   b. You would be concerned, but figure that your well-rounded résumé will open doors.
   c. Start going through your contact list of people you know to see if they can help you get your next job.

Even a slow-minded Irishman such as myself can tell that the "c" answers are where you want to be when it comes to networking.

Networking is more than getting to know people or investing in others without expecting anything in return. Networking is about acting with confidence and exuding a self-assurance that you belong and are comfortable in your own skin. The reason I say this is because your networking efforts won't get very far if you remain in the shadows instead of stepping into the spotlight—or, at least, where the action is happening.

Which brings me to my final point in this opening chapter on networking: **Act like you belong, no matter where you are.**

When I walked into Ara Parseghian's office, you may think I was a precocious kid acting beyond his years when I asked to see the Notre Dame coach. I don't view things that way at all. Instead, I walked in as a confident kid—not as a smart-alecky third-grader—who respected Coach Parseghian for who he was and what he did. At the same time, though, I understood that he was the decision-maker regarding whether my older brother received a football scholarship. I needed to make a play for Tim, so I wasn't about to act like a squeamish kid terrified at the prospect of being in the same room with the head coach of the Notre Dame football team. I showed some moxie that December day in 1966 because really, what did I have to lose?

When you go through life with self-confidence—and by self-confidence, I mean a quiet assurance that you belong in the room—people will be attracted to you. They will want to spend time with you. They will want to be part of your "network." If I had been ushered into Coach Parseghian's presence and mumbled something about him being the closest thing to God in our family and that I wasn't worthy to tie the shoelaces on his football cleats, I don't think he would have given me those fifteen valuable minutes of his time.

I used to be Brett Favre's marketing agent (more on this in Chapter 8), and it used to bother me whenever Packers fans would warily approach Brett like he was some god, barely making eye contact when asking him for an autograph. I always respected the fans who looked Brett in the eye, asked if they could shake his hand, and wished him the best for the coming season. You can respect someone who's accomplished something in life, but you don't have to idolize sports heroes, business leaders, and leading politicians. Talk to them like you would with your next-door neighbor.

These days, whether I find myself at a business mixer or in a boardroom staring at a bunch of faces I've never met, I act like I belong there. You should, too. I'm not saying that you should throw your weight around or act like you have to be the middle point whenever you're with a group. I'm just saying that acting like you belong is the personification of a confident demeanor, the unshakable belief that you can associate with anyone and fit in anywhere. Acting like you belong means you're willing to get into the game, not sit on the bench.

Sometimes acting like you belong has ramifications outside of a business setting—in a good sort of way.

Let me explain. Back in the early 1990s, when I was president of the Wisconsin Sports Authority, we formed a group called Hockey Wisconsin that lobbied the NCAA to bring the 1993 collegiate national championship hockey tournament to Milwaukee. Called the "Frozen Four" after the March Madness "Final Four" on the basketball side, I was sure that the national collegiate hockey tournament would be a big draw in Milwaukee. The University of Wisconsin Badgers were a perennial threat to win it all.

We won the 1993 bid, so in late March 1992, I flew to New York City with three directors from the Wisconsin Sports Authority to attend the 1992 Frozen Four tournament being held a few hours north in Albany. We wanted to check out how another city was handling this collegiate sporting event.

Since we had a free night in the Big Apple before we had to drive to Albany, I called a friend, Gary Brokaw, who worked in the NBA office to see if he could get us four tickets to the Knicks basketball game at Madison Square Garden.

Gary was a good buddy of mine, dating back to my MBA years at Notre Dame when Gary was an assistant to head basketball coach Digger Phelps. Gary had moved on and was working as the NBA director of operations in New York City. When he took my phone call, he assured me that four seats for a Knicks game wouldn't be a problem.

You can imagine how I bragged on Gary as my three friends and I approached the Will Call line at Madison Square Garden. "Wait until you see these seats," I boasted. "We'll be sitting right behind Spike Lee." Filmmaker Spike Lee always sat courtside, and the TV cameras loved focusing on him as he cheered for his beloved Knicks.

Our seats weren't behind Spike Lee. Not even close. As we trudged higher and higher in the cavernous Madison Square Garden, my buddies started teasing me about the "quality" seats.

"The players look like ants," said one as we settled into our mezzanine seats, the highest of six levels.

"Typical Sweeney, sticking us in the nosebleed section," chimed another.

"Yeah, Sweeney, some networker you are," said the third. "You must be really connected. Look at these great seats."

They kept it up while I slowly steamed. My eyes weren't on the game, though. Instead, I looked down toward where Spike Lee was sitting and spotted four unoccupied courtside seats. I kept my eye on them the entire first quarter. With a minute to go, I made an announcement.

"That's it, guys. I've had it with your bellyaching. Grab your stuff and follow me." I stood up to leave.

"Hey, Joe, where are we going?" asked the most belligerent one.

"You'll see. Just shut up and follow me. And act like you belong."

I led them down to the entrance of the floor-level seating. When the first-quarter horn blared, I marched us toward the four empty seats right next to Spike Lee—when a Madison Square Garden usher spotted me.

As he approached, I spotted the nameplate on his red-and-blue uniform. Before he could ask me for my ticket, I bellowed, "Jimmy, where the hell have you been lately?" I really got into his face and gave him a slight shoulder tap.

I could tell the usher wasn't sure what I meant or how to respond. "Ah, I had surgery about six weeks ago, and I'm just getting back on my feet—"

"Let me tell you what, Jimmy. It hasn't been the same down here at courtside without you. Gosh, it's great to see you again."

I could see the wheels turning inside Jimmy's cranium, trying to place me. Naturally, he couldn't. "Hey, thanks, and enjoy the game," he murmured.

We took our seats, and the three guys trailing me had their jaws hanging open.

Of course, that was a real seat-of-my pants moment, just like the time I stepped into Ara Parseghian's office. Most of the time, though, networking takes more forethought and planning.

But the fact of the matter is that networking is just plain hard work, as you'll see in the next chapter, when I introduce a system that will help you network with purpose and give you the confidence to start acting like you belong.

The Art of Networking: As Natural as Wisconsin Cheese

1. Act as if you belong, no matter where you are.
2. Always offer something in a networking encounter—seek to give, not get.
3. Combine networking with one of your passions, which will make networking much easier for you.
4. Follow the Golden Rule: treat others as you would want to be treated.
5. Understand the value of clear communication, and *always* look people in the eyes.
6. Stay persistent.
7. Never be afraid to introduce yourself first.
8. Know your objective. Wait for the proper time, and then strike.
9. Don't be infatuated with another's success. Your über admiration will show and lower your credibility.
10. Take time to cultivate relationships, which is the heart of networking.
11. Be a great listener and ask open-ended questions. Remember, God gave you two ears and one mouth, so use them in proportion.
12. Treat service providers—maids, parking lot attendants, and bartenders—with the utmost respect, and always over-tip breakfast waitresses.
13. Understand the difference between real self-confidence and artificial confidence.
14. Sometimes you need to fake it until you make it.

The Nuts and Bolts of Networking:
Working a Room

I KNEW IT WOULD BE a helluva birthday party, and I was right.

Christopher Doerr was celebrating his sixtieth birthday and two hundred of his closest friends were invited to his manicured, two-acre estate in an upscale Milwaukee suburb. Underneath a massive white canvas tent in the backyard, live music played while beautiful young women in black dresses held trays of hors d'oeuvres. We're talking elegant, sophisticated, and classy.

Chris certainly had every reason to celebrate in style. He and an older brother had grown up working in the electric motor manufacturing business, and when they started LEESON Electric in 1972, they didn't have much cash or experience—Chris was just twenty-three years old—but they had plenty of confidence on hand. Fast forward nearly thirty years, by which time LEESON Electric had become a very large company, attracting numerous corporate suitors. In 2000, Regal Beloit, a maker of gearboxes, motors, and generators, acquired LEESON Electric for $260 million in cash. Since then, Chris had turned his energies to running Sterling Aviation, an aircraft management and charter company that he purchased.

I had known Chris for some time through the Milwaukee business network. We sat together on an advisory board for Accents—a manufacturer of craft goods sold in retail outlets like Michaels—after he accepted the LEESON buyout. We clicked and became fast friends.

I liked Chris because he was an unpretentious guy, especially given his incredible wealth. His adult kids and girlfriend decided that he should commemorate his sixtieth birthday in a big way, including two energetic bands providing the evening's entertainment. The first band, a nine-piece group called Dynasty, drove up from Chicago to rock the joint. The other entertainers, Jason D. Williams and his backing ensemble, came in from Nashville. Jason D. Williams was a dynamic, enthusiastic piano player with a rockabilly edge who reminded me of Jerry Lee Lewis.

Great balls of fire.

That was my initial reaction as my wife, Tami, and I stepped into the backyard patio. Sometimes you go to a party and can slice the tension in the air, but not tonight. Everywhere I looked, lighthearted couples were enjoying themselves, with trays of French champagne and exquisite appetizers. The party had an easy-going vibe. Five minutes in, I knew we were in for a good time.

> *There's a fine line between casually meeting new people in a fun social setting and turning every social event into a networking opportunity.*

There's a fine line between casually meeting new people in a fun social setting and turning every social event into a networking opportunity. I certainly didn't want to cross that demarcation. At the same time, I sensed that this gala evening would be a favorable occasion to really connect with others. That's why three items were burning a hole in the front right pocket of my black dress slacks: a birthday card, a piece of leftover stationery from Capital Investments, and a golf pencil. The birthday card contained a dollar bill because Grandma Sweeney always gave us grandkids (and she had more than forty) a dollar on our birthdays. In keeping with Grandma Sweeney's memory, I scribbled the following message on the card: "Dear Chris: As part of growing up, we knew our grandmother loved us because she always sent her grandchildren a buck on our birthdays. I am personally delivering this card with a single dollar to say how much you mean to me. Best, Joe."

Tami and I made the rounds on the expansive patio before descending into the backyard and party tent. We shook hands and exchanged hugs as we ran into people we knew, saying hello and swapping the latest news. What I like to do at these affairs is ask questions *to* and *about* the other party. Practicing these techniques makes it easier for me to be an active listener and keep the conversation moving along.

THE ART OF MAKING GOOD CONVERSATION

Good networking begins with the ability to start and carry on a good conversation.

You won't get very far in this world if you can't make eye contact, act confidently, and engage in an intelligent conversation punctuated with give-and-take, back-and-forth dialogue. Think about it: conversation is an essential element in nearly every relationship we have. If you can't hold a conversation—and be a good listener—then very few will want to network with you. They'll look for ways to cut short their interactions with you, which leaves a negative impression in their minds the next time you run into them—and are looking to do a "little networking."

The ability to engage in small talk speaks well for you—and leads to engrossing exchanges that deepen a relationship. According to a study at the Stanford Graduate School of Business, the most successful students weren't the ones with the highest grade-point averages. Those who were the most successful were the ones most comfortable with having friendly conversations with others, particularly strangers.[1]

But you're an off-the-chart extrovert, Joe.

You may say that because I come from an Irish-Catholic family of twelve, but that's just so much blarney. Yes, the talking part came easily for me, but there's another side of the equation, and that's being a good listener. Staying engaged as an active listener is hard work but well worth the effort. When you're a good listener, you improve your ability to win friends and influence others—and perhaps avoid a misunderstanding that can set relationships back years.

I may not be a perfect listener, but it's a discipline that I've improved upon over the years. Every now and then I have to remind myself to be attentive when someone tells a long-winded story, but that's like reminding myself to keep my head down when I stroke a putt.

Actively listening is just part of the discipline it takes to become a top-notch networker.

About forty-five minutes after our arrival, Tami and one of her golf buddies got lost in conversation. Knowing that she wouldn't mind my absence for a short time, I quietly excused myself to meet some more people.

Free to Roam

After leaving Tami and her golfing friend, I made my way to the lengthy bar underneath the white canvas tent. I had already sipped my way through one vodka tonic, so I switched to water on the rocks to keep my wits about me. When I start making the rounds at a social event, I act like a cop on the beat, saying hello and tipping my proverbial cap to people I recognize as I pass by. If I want to engage a specific party—someone who's already having a conversation with someone else—I know better than to butt in. What I do is stride by and perhaps grab a shoulder for an instant to make eye contact, and then I keep moving. What I'm basically doing is sending a signal that says, *I know you're tied up. I'll reconnect with you later.*

Those I don't know well enough to tap a shoulder must be handled differently. In those cases, I exercise patience and wait for the right moment to make my approach. What works even better is having a mutual acquaintance make the introduction, which often allays any awkwardness on either party's end.

I zigzagged around with a glass of water in my hand until I saw the first person I wanted to "bump" into. Darrell owned a medium-sized business that just might need the services of an investment banker like me. I am the "rainmaker" for Corporate Financial Advisors, and it's my job to bring new business to our investment institution, and that almost always comes through my concentrated networking efforts. As I'm fond of telling others, 50 percent of what I do is a waste of time; it's just that I don't know which 50 percent that is.

From the bar, I got within five or six yards of Darrell and kept my eyes on him until he glanced my way. When we made eye contact, I nodded and raised my glass of ice water, which Darrell acknowledged before he returned to the conversation he was carrying on with two other guys.

I waited several minutes until one of the fellows excused himself, which I used as an opportunity to approach Darrell and the other gent. Since the two of us had already exchanged that coded look, he interrupted his one-on-one conversation to welcome me into the fold. An introduction was made to the guy he was with, and I did my best to get into the flow of their conversation.

I've found that when I'm brought into a conversation—and I don't know the third party—I need to clam up and listen. No one likes someone who pokes his nose into the middle of someone else's chat fest. I've also found that when three, four, or five guys are engaged in a circular conversation, sooner or later one of the parties will feel like a third wheel and quietly excuse himself to go find someone else to speak to. There's nothing wrong with that. That's the nature of human interaction, and that's what happened on this evening when our third conversation partner dropped out.

Now it was just Darrell and myself, but it wasn't the time for me to launch into a soliloquy, something on the order of, "Hey, Darrell, howyadoing, didyouknowIclosedthreedealslastweek?"

That would have been an instant turnoff. What I try to do is ask a compelling question that goes beyond a predictable conversation starter like "How 'bout them Packers?"

CONVERSATION IS A TWO-WAY STREET

The art of good conversation is very much like playing a game of backyard catch. After you utter something, you're tossing the "ball" of conversation to the other person, meaning it's his (or her) turn to say something. If you continue holding on to the ball, however—by giving a long-winded, play-by-play description of your recent vacation to Lake Okoboji in Iowa—then you're gripping the ball of conversation too long and not allowing your friend or business acquaintance a chance to "play." Do this too many times, and you'll be dismissed as a pompous, full-of-himself bore.

Pay attention to how long you're holding on to the ball, and then toss the ball back in his direction, which signals it's *his* turn to talk. In time, he'll toss the ball right back to you.

That's what the art of good conversation is all about.

I knew Darrell was in the plastics industry, but asking him open-ended questions like, "How goes it in the plastics world these days?" wouldn't engage him much. From past business dealings with contacts in the plastic industry, I had picked up some particulars about the manufacture of plastic, so I searched my mind for a penetrating question to ask—and remembered that resin was an important ingredient in the production process. Since resin was separated from crude oil during the refining stage, that meant the cost of resin was directly tied to the price of a barrel of crude oil.

"Hey, Darrell, what's going on with the price of resin these days?" I asked.

Darrell nearly did a double take. He knew I was an investment banker, meaning I was just another money-grubber who doesn't know the first thing about plastic, including the fact that resin played a vital role in its production.

"Steady as she goes," Darrell replied as he regained his equilibrium. "But you never know what will happen with the crazy price of oil these days. It looked like it was going down a few weeks ago—"

When Darrell paused for a half-second, I finished the sentence for him. "Until China recently completed a new strategic storage facility and started buying up oil. Up five bucks a barrel in the last few weeks, right?"

"Yeah, the oil producers got us over a barrel, but what else is new?"

In that short exchange, I had established a connection with Darrell, the owner of a plastics manufacturing firm. We continued to kick around the high cost of resin and what it was doing to the plastic business. I listened as Darrell unloaded months of pent-up frustration about the yo-yoing of oil prices and how that volatility made it difficult to project the future contract pricing of plastic.

Even though Darrell rambled a bit because he was in his realm, I certainly didn't want to interrupt his train of thought. Nor did I want to bring up *my* business with Darrell—unless he inquired about how things were going in the investment banking world. A soft-sell follow-up with Darrell would come the following Monday, as part of my 5/10/15 program that I'll introduce in my next chapter.

We continued kibitzing a few more minutes until another friend of Darrell's interrupted and joined the conversation. After introductions and a round of hearty "How ya doing's?" were exchanged, I took the opportunity to grasp Darrell's hand and tell him how much I enjoyed running into him. "Hasta la vista," I joked, using up half my Spanish vocabulary.

As I mentioned earlier, it's easier for me to be an active listener when I'm the one asking questions. If I know the person at all, I'll rifle through my memory banks and try to come up with an interesting question or observation, usually about his profession or take on something in the news.

But what about those situations where you don't know much—or anything—about the person that you're starting a conversation with?

I've found myself conversing with captains of industry, big-time athletes, and famous politicians and chitchatting with supermarket cashiers, breakfast waitresses, and security guards. Unless there's a specific question burning on my lips, I know two topics they all love to talk about—themselves and their kids.

I'm not pointing any fingers here. If you were to ask me something about my life or family—"Hey, Joe, you got kids?"—I could speak without notes for a long time. Unless you're the wallflower type, you should have no problem talking about yourself either.

That's why, after I meet someone for the first time and someone I know nothing about, I'll usually say something like, "Tell me something about yourself, Rodney. You got a family or any kids?"

You should see their eyes light up. Everyone loves a freestanding invitation to wax eloquent about himself or his family. If you're an active listener and have a good memory, you can put that information to good use the next

> *Everyone loves a freestanding invitation to wax eloquent about himself or his family.*

time you see him or her. You wouldn't believe the great service I get whenever I ask my favorite breakfast waitress how her son played in last Friday night's football game. I know to ask because I remember

her telling me that her son was the starting running back from a previous time I dropped in for a bagel and cream cheese.

While conversation-starting questions are as numerous as a blanket of stars on a Wisconsin summer night, you have to be careful.
I won't bring up the two taboos—politics and religion—unless I'm
absolutely sure my networking contact and I are on the same page.
But anything work-related, plus the always reliable kids, sports, and
weather, are safe places to start a conversation.

The best, of course, is if you can come up with a thoughtful lead-
in question that goes beyond the basics. That opens up all sorts of
avenues—and makes you more interesting to others.

HOW DO YOU REMEMBER NAMES?

Have you ever been introduced to someone, been told his or her name,
only to blank out fifteen seconds later when you try to recall that name?

Some people say the toughest part of networking is remembering the
names of people they meet. Others say that they're amazed at those who
can repeat their names with ease and control after an introduction has
been made. Either way, remembering names is a valuable asset to have in
the business world. You build instant rapport and make a strong impression with new contacts. "A person's name is to him or her the sweetest
and most important sound in any language," said Dale Carnegie, who
authored the seminal classic, *How to Win Friends and Influence People*, in
1936.

A popular book back in the 1970s and 1980s was *The Memory Book* by
Harry Lorayne and Jerry Lucas, which described in detail several memory
techniques that would help you remember anything you wanted—including the name of the last person you were introduced to. Lorayne was a
magician and card shark who had no problem memorizing a fifty-two card
playing deck in order. Jerry Lucas was a professional basketball player
with the New York Knicks who wowed *Tonight Show* host Johnny Carson
by memorizing large portions of the New York City phone book and with
his ability to instantly recall the names of audience members whom he
had met just before the show.

The Memory Book authors recommended visualizing a feature about
the person that you've just been introduced to. For "Bill Dougherty," you
might picture a dollar bill wrapped around the midsection of a Pillsbury

doughboy. A "Susan Hightower" might be a lazy susan spinning on top of a clock tower.

After reading *The Memory Book* I gave it a shot. One time before a community event, I was introduced to a fellow named Ted Brooks and was asked to introduce him to a lunchtime audience. *Ted Brooks...Ted Brooks...*I pictured a teddy bear playing next to a brook. *That should work.*

Five minutes later, I strode to the podium to introduce "my good friend Ted Rivers," and howls of laughter erupted from Ted's friends. Brook...river...well, at least I was close.

These days, I use movies and music to "associate" a new name to the person I'm trying to remember. A "Dan" might be Lieutenant Dan from *Forrest Gump*, a Max from Maximus in the movie *The Gladiator*. Arnold is easy—Ah-nold Schwarzenegger from *The Terminator*. If I meet a Steve, I'll associate him with Motown musician Stevie Wonder. Memorizing first names is usually good enough in my world.

This technique—associating the person you just met with someone you already know—is what works for me, but there are other things you can do to remember names. Here are a few more ideas:

- concentrate and listen closely when the introduction is made and *immediately* repeat the name to verify it;
- repeat his or her first name two or three times during the first few minutes of conversation;
- use an association technique that works for you...for instance, the next Gerald you meet reminds you of President Gerald Ford, or the next Lynn reminds you of country singer Loretta Lynn;
- ask for a business card when you make your goodbyes, and then read the name several times (this especially works if you're a visual learner and not an auditory learner); or write his or her name down on a piece of paper when you get back to the office.

If this seems like work to remember names, remember that it *is* hard work to make people feel important. The time and energy you put into remembering people's names will win you a ton of goodwill and open the door to successful networking relationships.

Besides, no one wants to go through life like baseball legend Willie Mays, who was known as the "Say Hey Kid." How did he get that nickname? Because when Willie first came up to the big leagues, he had a lot of trouble remembering names, so when somebody spoke to him, he would say, "Say...hey you."

Making the Rounds

I connected with about ten people that evening at Christopher Doerr's luxurious crib. One was a corporate lawyer in the merger-and-acquisition arena whom I found filling a plate with seared ahi tuna at the hors d'oeuvres table. Instead of opening with a basic-but-boring "How's your M&A practice?", I remembered hearing an attorney friend say that a lot of the merger-and-acquisition attorneys working in Milwaukee's largest law firms were being moved to the "workout" area.

"Workout" is insider lingo that means working out terms with creditors that both sides can live with. It's the equivalent of ditch-digging work in legal circles, however; no one wants to do it, and the pay's not that great.

I knew this corporate attorney was the leading partner in a major Milwaukee law firm, so my conversation starter was this: "Good to see you again, Jeremy. Tell me…are you moving a lot of M&A attorneys over to the workout areas?"

Again, a quizzical look from this attorney that said in so many words: *How did you know that?*

"Heck, yes," he replied. "Our transaction business is dead, but our workout area and bankruptcy people have been swamped since spring." For the next five minutes, I listened closely as the attorney expounded upon the subject of how the legal trade was adapting to the new economic realities. I received an excellent tutorial because I had asked a good question.

When it comes to networking, you want to use *any* scrap of information flying around your brain to formulate an interesting question, which can cut through the clutter that typifies human discourse these days. Here's another example of what I mean: I met a steel rep at the Doerr party, not a manufacturer, and I knew that steel reps were paid three or four "points"—or percent—as their commission. When steel prices are rising, their incomes rise accordingly. When steel prices fall from weak demand, their commission billings evaporate.

"What's going on with steel pricing these days?" I asked one steel rep. "Are you getting any relief?"

A large smile came to the rep's face as he took another swig from his cocktail. "Happy days are here again," he said. "Just had a $10 million order. I like the way the market is moving."

And so it went—a fascinating evening meeting interesting folks and making worthwhile connections. One of the last people I ran into was Tom Sonnenberg, who runs a sales rep business. I wanted to chat him up because investment bankers like myself need to stay connected with folks like Tom. Does he own a big company? No, he's a hustling, aggressive business-type like myself who calls on hundreds of businesses each year. He has his ear to the ground, which means he knows which companies are doing well, which ones are struggling, and which ones are on life support. In other words, Tom can refer me to companies that need to get sold, and that's where the services of my investment bank can come in. We facilitate the merger and acquisition of companies in the $10 million to $200 million range.

Tom belongs to my informal network of "bird dogs"—my eyes and ears in the community. If one of his tips leads to a deal, we're more than happy to pay Tom a referral fee for his trouble. Tom and I have a great relationship, but saying, "Hey, Tom, got any business for us?" would have been awkward for both sides.

SET UP YOUR SCOUT TEAM

Since I can't possibly have my finger on the pulse of the entire merger-and-acquisition market in the Midwest, I need scouts who provide great recon on what's going on inside the companies within our target market. That's why I've assembled a team of networking-minded individuals— culled from the ranks of sales reps, bankers, accountants, and insurance reps—who can tip me off to companies that need to be bought, sold, or merged. It's a win-win for everyone: they receive a referral fee, I make a commission for putting together the deal, and a business that was on the block gets sold.

No matter what your business is, you should be setting up a scout team that can bird-dog business opportunities for you. With an incentive-based referral program, you'll make it a win-win for your networking team.

As I approached Tom to say hello that evening, I suddenly remembered the last time I saw him. It was four or five months earlier at the Wisconsin Athletic Club, where he was sitting in the dressing room, rubbing his tender right shoulder. When I asked him what was the matter, he replied, "My doc says it's my rotator cuff. I must have torn it pretty badly. I'm scheduled for surgery next week." He could barely lift his right arm above his shoulder that day.

Enough time had passed for Tom to have undergone the rotator cuff surgery and received post-op therapy. When I saw him at the Doerr party, the first thing I asked him was, "Tommy, how's that shoulder doing? Did they get you some good rehab?"

Tom grimaced. "I still got a ways to go," he said, but I could tell in his eyes that he was touched that I remembered his injury.

Then my mindset of networking—a place to give, not to get—kicked in when I remembered a set of exercises that could help Tom rehab that shoulder.

"Tell you what," I said. "Let me walk you through some great shoulder exercises I learned. You got time next week?"

"Sure. Send me an e-mail," Tom said.

> *I didn't want to forget a single name because come Monday morning, I planned to follow up with each one of them using my 5/10/15 plan.*

From there, Tom and I slipped into small talk about what he was seeing out there on the street, and then it was time to move on. Within one hour at the Doerr party, I connected with nine or ten people, more than I thought I could in a relatively short time period.

I knew Tami would soon be waiting for her escort to return, but I couldn't go find her just yet. First, I had to locate a bathroom to deal with two glasses of water—and do a little homework. I took out the golf pencil and the leftover stationery and I began scribbling the names of every person I had connected with that evening. There was Darrell, Tommy Sonnenberg, a couple of lawyers, a biotech entrepreneur...

I didn't want to forget a single name because come Monday morning, I planned to follow up with each one of them using my 5/10/15 plan, which I'll describe in detail in the next chapter.

The Nuts and Bolts of Networking— Working a Room

1. Any time you're out in public, especially at a social event, it is a favorable time to make connections with others.

2. Always keep your eye out for networking opportunities, whether you're at work or at play.

3. Be intentional about trying to meet the right people, especially in a social setting.

4. When you attend a party, reception, or networking opportunity, act as if *you're* the host. Take time to introduce people to each other. Make sure others are having a good time. Those at the party will gravitate toward you because they want to be near the "host."

5. Understand the difference between networking at a business event—a community luncheon or after-hours mixer—and making connections at social events. The former is conducted in a business environment where you're *expected* to glad-hand; the latter calls for keeping your cool, showing an interest in others and who they are, and developing deeper relationships based on an attitude of giving, not getting.

6. Don't "try" to network when you're at a social event. Any overt attempts to hand out business cards like a waiter delivering hors d'oeuvres from a silver platter is apt to backfire and be met with disdain.

7. No matter what style or "trick" works for you, become good at learning names. Never forget that one of the most impressive things you can do to become a good networker is to remember someone's name.

8. Resist the urge to butt into someone else's conversation. However, make eye contact, and patiently wait for the contact to draw you into his or her circle.

9. Think of interesting questions that you can use to start off a conversation. What do you know about the person that can help you formulate an intriguing inquiry?

10. Become the type of interesting conversation partner that you would enjoy talking with.

11. Be an active listener who readily tosses the "ball" of conversation back and forth.

12. Develop a loose network of "bird dogs"—business associates, contacts, acquaintances, and friends—who can tip you off on leads that result in deals. Consider paying a referral fee, which is an incentive that often drives even *more* business your way.

Networking 101:
The 5/10/15 Program

MEETING PEOPLE and establishing a connection is the nuts and bolts of networking—the relational side, as I call it—but there needs to be a tangible component that will give you the right framework to succeed in networking. I call this element the 5/10/15 program, and if you faithfully incorporate this plan of action, you'll see your networking efforts propel into the stratosphere.

The 5/10/15 program, an idea that I came up with years ago, is basically an organized system that provides structure and personal accountability. It doesn't matter which business you're in; the 5/10/15 program works for everyone. If you want to network like a pro, then you should adopt the 5/10/15 program—or a variation that works for you—into your business life.

Here's a thumbnail description of how the 5/10/15 program works for me:

- The "5" means that I try to have five "meetings" or "encounters" a day. This doesn't mean sitting down in a conference room and having a formal meeting. A "meeting" means making some sort of contact with a person, even if it means you're both standing in a Starbucks line. On the other hand, an "encounter" is a another rung up the networking ladder and means you have a meeting where you're able to describe who you are and what you do.

- The "10" means I send out ten letters or pieces of correspondence, on corporate or personal stationery, every single day. Personal e-mails can count in this area, but not impersonal e-blasts.
- The "15" means I make a minimum of fifteen phone calls a day. In the world of networking, my BlackBerry is my friend—and one of my strongest assets.

At the end of the day, the goal of 5/10/15 is to get five business-related engagements that keep the chains moving down the field. In other words, the complete way to write this networking equation would be 5+10+15=5, as in five business engagements netted from my efforts. Our boutique investment banking likes me to have five engagements going at all times, and the 5+10+15=5 ensures we always have that number in our inventory.

I know—the math doesn't add up, but the numbers do, and it's all about getting those five engagements where a friend, acquaintance, or referral says, "Hey, Joe, I was wondering if you could speak with my brother-in-law. He's thinking of selling his business."

That's one of the things our investment banking firm does. We're financial intermediaries who perform a variety of services: raising capital; aiding in the sale of companies; facilitating mergers and corporate reorganizations; and basically acting as the middleman in the sale and purchase of businesses. Ever since the American economy went into the tank in 2008, though, I've had to hustle to bring business through the front door. Hence my full-court networking press at the Doerr summer soirée, especially with folks like Tom Sonnenberg, who can give me leads on businesses headed for the auction block.

If you're looking at how to expand your networking horizons, my 5/10/15 networking plan will put you on a straight-and-narrow road that can get you results. My focused and disciplined approach will help you stay on track, grow your business, and give you a sense of accomplishment. If you're currently unemployed, then the 5/10/15 plan will help you pick yourself up off the mat and greatly increase your chances of landing that next job. And I have some good news for you: when you need a job, you don't need five deals. You need just *one* person saying yes.

I'm a visual guy, so let me show you what the 5/10/15 plan looks like on paper. I have an Excel file that I print out and place in a separate three-hole binder, one for each day of the workweek, Monday through Friday. (See the following page for a sample blank page.) For more sample pages, please go to NetworkingContactSport.com and get our *Networking Is a Contact Sport Playbook* (or make your own 5/10/15 pages).

Mari, my assistant, prints out a 5/10/15 plan for each day and sticks it in my binder. In case you're wondering, I keep my binder next to my Day-Timer throughout the day, writing down whom I've called, contacted, and met that day. That's where the accountability comes in.

I haven't gone totally virtual with the 5/10/15 program because I prefer to put pen to paper as I list all the meetings, letters, phone calls, and engagements I conduct throughout the day. I'm a bit old school in that way because I'm also writing down any future appointments or pertinent information—like directions on how to get to a certain meeting—into my Day-Timer. But there's nothing stopping you from making your own 5/10/15 Excel file and using your computer or smart phone to record your meetings, letters, phone calls, and engagements.

When I arrive at my office each morning, I'll study my 5/10/15 plan for the day and write down any meetings or encounters I've already had *before* work—someone I ran into while getting my morning coffee, for example, or bumped into in the office parking lot. These chance encounters could develop into a lead or engagement, even if our conversation never gets deeper than the Packers' playoff chances. And if I make any business-related phone calls on the drive into my downtown office, I certainly count those toward my goal of making fifteen phone calls per day.

My next move is to open up my laptop and sort through my e-mails. If they are important enough to warrant a snappy business-related reply, I might count them toward my ten letters for the day. It depends on my mood and how much actual correspondence I send out later that day. This is also the time to generate some e-mails, like following up with people I networked with at the Chris Doerr party.

Once my immediate e-mail correspondence is out of the way, and it's after 9 A.M., I reach out and touch someone. (I generally wait

5+10+15=5 Engagements

5 MEETINGS/ENCOUNTERS

1. _____
2. _____
3. _____
4. _____
5. _____

10 CORRESPONDENCES

1. _____
2. _____
3. _____
4. _____
5. _____
6. _____
7. _____
8. _____
9. _____
10. _____

15 PHONE CALLS

1. _____
2. _____
3. _____
4. _____
5. _____
6. _____
7. _____
8. _____
9. _____
10. _____
11. _____
12. _____
13. _____
14. _____
15. _____

5 ENGAGEMENTS

1. _____
2. _____
3. _____
4. _____
5. _____

until 9 A.M. before I start making "unexpected" phone calls since I personally dislike early morning calls and figure others feel the same way.) If I owe anyone a phone call from the previous day, those get dialed first since I pride myself on returning calls ASAP. (And in case you're wondering, I'm not into cold-calling on behalf of Corporate Financial Advisors because my time is better focused on people inside my networking universe rather than "prospecting" with people I have no connection with.)

Once I'm caught up with e-mails and return phone calls, what I do next is more unusual in the Information Age: I read newspapers. Not online. Real newspapers. In my ink-stained hands. And glossy magazines as well.

I start with the *Milwaukee Journal Sentinel*, which, as Wisconsin's largest newspaper, gives me a good sense of what's happening in the community. I then move on to *The Wall Street Journal*, which provides the national perspective that I need. My last two newspapers are the *Business Journal of Milwaukee* and *BizTimes*, which shed important light on downtown business news, contain feature stories about noteworthy businesspeople, and report announcements of the latest promotions and reshuffling in upper management ranks. I also skim several national merger-and-acquisition publications to get a pulse on the national state of affairs. And for good measure, if I have some extra time, I'll catch up on some national sports magazines (*Sports Illustrated*, *The Sporting News*, etc.) since I used to run a sports-management firm.

One reason I like to read actual newspapers and magazines is that the practice gives me a chance to clip articles that can be used to make a networking connection. For instance, if I read that a Billy Joe Jackson was kicked upstairs to CEO or a Sue Ellen Smith was named "Entrepreneur of the Year," I'll clip out the story and attach it to a quick letter of congratulations with one of my business cards—and give myself credit for one of the

> *One reason I like to read actual newspapers and magazines is that the practice gives me a chance to clip articles that can be used to make a networking connection.*

ten pieces of correspondence that are part of my 5/10/15 program for the day.

My ten correspondence "touches" are my favorite part of the 5/10/15 program. When I see that Sue Ellen Smith won "Entrepreneur of the Year" and mail her the clipping along with a quick personal note, my underlying message is this: *It was nice to see you get the recognition you deserved. That's why I thought enough of you to go to the trouble to send this newspaper article to you.*

I love keeping my eyes peeled for articles that relate tangentially to potential networking contacts. Let's say I'm perusing the sports section in the *Milwaukee Journal Sentinel* and I see that high school senior Matt Angel was named "Player of the Week" for scoring six touchdowns in his last game at Ashwaubenon High. Since I'm aware that Matt is the son of Gary Angel, a big wheel at a Green Bay tech firm, I'll clip the story and put it in the mail to Gary with a quick note of congratulations. Even if Gary and I met only one time at a business mixer, I know he'll be busting out with parental pride.

I know what it means to be on the receiving end of a letter like this. A few years ago, *BizTimes* did a feature story on me as the managing director at Corporate Financial Advisors. "The Deal Maker" was how the boldface headline read, and the subhead line said, "Sweeney Began Career as Daring MBA Student." The thrust of the story was that after more than twenty years in the trenches, I was making deals to buy and sell companies at CFA and doing well.

After the *BizTimes* story came out, I received two extremely heart-touching and meaningful letters from Peter Sommerhauser and Dick Van Deuren, two of the finest M&A attorneys in Wisconsin. What I found compelling about their correspondence was that they were in their seventies and eighties but still had the energy to send me a pair of heartfelt letters. Was it any wonder why these two legal giants had enjoyed such successful practices over the last fifty years?

There's something else I enjoy doing besides sending newspaper and magazine clippings marking an achievement or an award, and that's sending out books, just for the heck of it. As I mentioned in the Introduction, I always have a bunch of my favorite books on hand at the office, ready to mail and share with others—and make a connection.

I love sharing *Halftime: Changing Your Game Plan from Success to Significance* by Bob Buford because it's a superb life-planning book that inspires business and professional leaders to look for a deeper significance in life. A couple of other books that have received a lot of love from Joe Sweeney are *Body for Life: 12 Weeks to Mental and Physical Strength* by Bill Phillips and *Success Built to Last: Creating a Life That Matters* by Jerry Porras, Stewart Emery, and Mark Thompson. The first book shows you how to get your body in shape and start living a healthy lifestyle; the second shares "life coaching" secrets that resonate with me. I've mailed out dozens of copies over the years, and they do make impressions.

Here's an example. A few years ago, I was invited to join Wisconsin Governor Jim Doyle on a trip to China as part of the Governor's Trade Commission. Jim Doyle, an attorney, grew up in Madison and knew all eight of my older brothers. I would run into Jim on the basketball court when I came home from college. I can't claim him as any close friend, however. The reason I got invited on the Governor's Trade Commission was because of another guy—Tim Sheehy, president of the Metropolitan Milwaukee Association of Commerce, who *was* a good friend.

While in Beijing and Shanghai, I got up early each morning to work out in the hotel fitness area. The only other members of our delegation to join me in those early-morning workouts were Governor Jim Doyle and Tim Sheehy.

Well, if you get three Irishmen in a room, watch the gloves come off. We ripped each other pretty good, all in good fun, but I also took the occasion to share some tips from *Body for Life*, including the pyramid workout devised by Bill Phillips. I could tell the governor appreciated the workout advice, so when we got home to Milwaukee, the first thing I did was go to my library, pull off a copy of *Body for Life*, and mail it off to the governor. My inscription read, "Governor Jim, It was great working out with you in China. Best, Joe." (I also sent a copy to Tim Sheehy.)

A week later, Tim Sheehy was called into a debriefing meeting at the governor's office, and he spied a copy of *Body for Life*. He looked at Governor Doyle and said, "Let me guess. Sweeney sent you the book, right?"

Three Irishmen at the Great Wall of China—I'm sure there's a joke somewhere. I was invited to join Wisconsin Governor Jim Doyle (center) and Tim Sheehy, president of the Metropolitan Milwaukee Association of Commerce, on a trade commission trip to China in 2004. In keeping with Irish tradition, we ripped each other pretty good.

On his drive back to Milwaukee, Tim called me from his car. "Were your ears burning a couple of hours ago?" he asked. "Doyle and I were giving you all sorts of crap for sending us those books."

Although Tim couldn't resist the urge to bust my chops, I'm glad I have a reputation as being that "book guy" who sends out hardbacks at the drop of a hat. So here's a bit of advice: purchase copies of *Networking Is a Contact Sport* by the dozen and mail them out to all your friends and business contacts.

No, you don't have to do that, but I know I will!

Landing Clients

Mailing out appropriate books is a nice touch, although I'll admit that it's an expensive investment in networking. In the long run, you'll do well by adopting the 5/10/15 program into your natural workday. If you work twenty days a month (figuring four weeks of Monday through Friday each month), then you'll have 100 meetings or encounters, write 200 letters, and make 300 phone calls using my 5/10/15 program.

It's too much, Joe. You don't know what you're asking.

All I'm asking of you is what I ask of myself. I've faithfully executed the 5/10/15 plan for more than twenty-five years and reaped the rewards. Have there been days where I didn't completely fill out the 5/10/15 sheet clipped in a binder? Of course. Have there been days when I was unmotivated and slacked off? Happens to the best of us. All I know is that I bounced back much faster when I put on the harness of the 5/10/15 plan and tilled the soil again.

I operate under no illusions. Since the 5/10/15 plan takes iron discipline and boatloads of time to execute, it helps to have an accountability partner asking how you're doing. That person can be your assistant, a fellow salesperson, or another manager. Even better would be enlisting your "wingman" as your accountability partner. (I talk about having a wingman in Chapter 6.)

Let's say you're a young investment manager, trying to get established. You've been told that you need to find 200 clients to have a solid career. Landing a client, as you've discovered, isn't an easy thing to do, especially in today's tough economic climate.

To land a paying client, you have to find a prospect. To find a prospect, you need a lead (also known as a suspect). I've found that you usually need ten leads to get a good prospect. Then you need ten prospects to land a client.

When you do the math, you can see that you'll need to contact 100 people to get one single client, and that can be a daunting task. So you take things one step at a time—one meeting, one letter, and one phone call at a time.

So if getting clients is your goal, and you're ready to get serious about networking, you need to adopt the 5/10/15 personal accountability program into your workday. It's the only way you'll get leads, which turn into prospects, which turn into clients.

NETWORKING FUNDAMENTALS IN REVIEW

Since networking is a contact sport, let's review the basics of good networking one more time:

- When you attend a business function, community mixer, or social event, identify whom you want to network with. If possible, try to view an attendee list online or arrive early so you can study the nametags on the welcoming table.

- Survey the room and make a mental list of the top ten people you want to connect with. Don't save the most important person for last. He (or she) may depart early or be fatigued from the "meet and greet" process by the time you introduce yourself. Instead, fix your sights on meeting this important person first—before he gets too tied up with others.

- Consider every encounter and touch point as an opportunity to learn, grow, or even land a new customer. You never know who will become that golden client, which is why you should treat all networking opportunities just the same.

- Be sure to identify what objective you want to accomplish with each "touch" you make at an event. Are they potential clients? Referrals? Connections? Having an objective can help you budget your time.

- Understand the difference between a lead, a prospect, and a client or customer. This is another idea that will help you budget your time and make the most out of a networking event.

- Don't interrupt a conversation, but connect with your eyes or a hand on the shoulder as you walk by. Sometimes it's not easy breaking into a conversation, but station yourself nearby without being intrusive. After you make eye contact, move a step or two closer, but remain patient. Sooner or later, the person you want to meet will "bring" you into the conversation.

- Have business cards ready in your pocket, but don't hand any out unless you're asked for one. Remember the last time someone offered you his business card unsolicited? You probably thought the guy was a schmuck. You'll elicit the same feelings if you hand out business cards like party favors—and those cards will get tossed like so much confetti.

- When you're introduced to a person for the first time, pretend you're an investigative reporter trying to obtain valuable information on a client or prospect. It's okay to "interview" someone. Most are flattered, especially if you're asking questions about themselves or offering their expertise. You usually can't go wrong by starting a question in this manner: "What do you think of—"

- Ask riveting questions that connect you with him (or her) and demonstrate knowledge and insight into his world. It helps to be well-read, which gives you a leg up on the competition. Don't forget that it takes practice asking good questions, so start practicing.
- After you've asked your question or made a comment, actually listen to the response. Then keep the conversation going by "playing off" something he said. I likened conversation to a game of catch in my last chapter, where you toss the "ball" of conversation toward him and he tosses it back to you. Keep the ball going back and forth so that there are no awkward gaps, which could prompt him to bring the conversation to a close.
- Soft sells work better than hard sells at networking events. Nobody likes to be arm-twisted into making a commitment, especially at a public or social event. Let your follow-up a few days afterward be your "hard sell," even though you should tread lightly here, too. One of the goals of networking is to make a friend, not a sale.
- Incorporate the 5/10/15 program into your everyday work schedule. It feels good to set daily goals and then meet them. The 5/10/15 plan will not only give you structure, but you'll also feel like you're making consistent progress in your networking efforts. Download my 5/10/15 plan from my Web site at www.NetworkingContactSport.com and give it a go—today!
- Know what's going on in the world by reading newspapers and magazines. I have four children in their twenties, and they're part of this first generation that hasn't gotten into the habit of reading the daily newspaper and other periodicals. There's something about taking a newspaper section or a printed magazine and flipping through it, scanning your eyes and attention to and fro, looking for interesting stories to read. But if you really aren't a newspaper reader, at least go online each morning and read your local paper and a national publication (*The New York Times, The Washington Post,* or *USA Today*) to get some perspective. (*The Wall Street Journal,* which is an excellent newspaper for those in the business world, costs a hundred dollars a year for online access, and we may be seeing more publications following suit, including *The New York Times.*)
- Be sure to clip newspaper or magazines articles about other people's successes and send them a quick note of congratulations. I've also

printed out stories I've read online and sent them on to the noteworthy person. Even though it only takes a few minutes of your time, people really respond to your thoughtfulness—and remember who you are.

- Finally, keep in mind that getting new business is tough, but what gets easier is taking care of clients once you have them in the fold. That's why I service the hell out of my clients using the PEACE principle: Persistently Exceeding All Clients' Expectations. You can do the same.

I urge you to study and review these fundamentals of networking and incorporate the 5/10/15 program into your daily work schedule, even if you're currently unemployed. In fact, if you are out of work, networking can help you land your next job, which is the topic of my next chapter.

Networking 101: The 5/10/15 Program

1. Incorporate the 5/10/15 plan into your everyday work life: five meetings or engagements, ten pieces of correspondence, and fifteen phone calls.
2. Get yourself a blueprint for the 5/10/15 program by going to NetworkingContactSport.com and ordering our *Networking Is a Contact Sport Playbook*.
3. Keep a running total of how you're doing with the 5/10/15 program throughout the day. A record of your meetings, letters, and phone calls will encourage you since tangible evidence of your efforts are documented.
4. Besides clipping and sending newspaper or magazine articles to those featured in the publication, be sure to write notes commending people for a recent promotion or new job. Since so few bother to send a short handwritten note to a colleague or business associate these days following a noteworthy event, your effort today could be remembered for decades.

Networking and the Unemployed:

The Difference Between Networking and Not Working Is Just One Letter

THE CALL CAME IN to my direct line at my office on the twenty-eighth floor, situated atop the Milwaukee Center skyscraper. From my bird's-eye perch, I took in a commanding view of denim-blue Lake Michigan, where a fall breeze raised a light chop.

I didn't recognize the name on my caller ID. When I lifted up the phone, the deep voice identified himself as Matt Morris—that's not his real name—and said he was a CEO in town. He mentioned that he had met with an attorney friend of mine who recommended that he give me a call.

"Nice to hear from you, Matt. So how can I help you?" I asked solicitously.

A pause came over the line. "I was wondering if we could meet for lunch this week. Maybe do a little networking."

There was that code phrase again. The way Matt said "do a little networking" sure sounded like there wasn't much upside for me. He obviously wanted to tap into my network, although I couldn't fathom what a corporate CEO would want from my contact list unless he was selling his daughter's Girl Scout cookies. His unadorned request left me nonplussed and reminded me of the insurance salesman at the Milwaukee Athletic Club who hit me up for a "little networking" after a noontime workout.

I rubbed my temples. Perhaps it was time for a tutorial. "You know, Matt, whenever someone calls me out of the blue with a request to do a 'little networking,' it comes across as one-sided, like you want me to hand over every contact I have. I like to think of networking as a place you go to give, not—"

"@#$% you, Joe," he interjected. "If you think I'm going to listen to you give me a @#$% speech about networking, you can go @#$% yourself."

The f-bombs were falling fast and furious. "Whoa, hold on a moment," I said, backpedaling a bit. I was actually blown away since Matt went off on me even though we had no relationship. "Why are you bringing all the @#$% heat?"

(Sometimes you have to match fire with fire.)

There was another long pause on the line. "Because I just got let go. Never happened to me before." Matt sounded contrite. In a lowered voice, he said, "I called because I thought you could help me find another CEO position. I need a job, Joe."

Suddenly, I got it. Matt had been laid off from one of the top corporate jobs in Milwaukee. A well-paid CEO was out of work. Unemployed.

Startling phone calls like Matt's were coming my way with increasing frequency, and they didn't surprise me. I had been paying close attention to unemployment figures since the summer of 2008 when a sudden surge of layoffs signaled the start of the worst recession since Black Tuesday activated the Great Depression in 1929. The ensuing economic downturn swamped the banking industry, which became one of the hardest-hit sectors of the American economy. Even with all the government bailouts and TARP money flooding Wall Street and the monetary system over the last couple of years, my world—the investment banking business—has experienced tremendous challenges.

The ripple effect of bank failures, as well as factory closures, losses at the retail level, and small business cutbacks, has caused a tsunami loss of millions of jobs in this country. As *Networking Is a Contact*

Sport goes to print, more than eight million Americans have been laid off since the start of the recession. The number of people who have been out of work six months or longer—known as the long-term unemployed—adds another six million, or 42 percent of the total jobless.

Many despair over ever finding decent-paying work again, and those perusing the employment classifieds know that the competition to get hired again borders on the insane. There are six times as many workers looking for jobs as there are job openings, according to a Labor Department report, meaning that it's very difficult to get rehired these days.[2]

HAVE YOU LOST HOPE?

I've counseled a lot of depressed men the last couple of years, and I can see the absence of hope in their eyes. But you have to find hope in something, whether it's in your belief system, your family, or yourself. There's a famous saying: You can live thirty days without food, three days without water, and three minutes without air, but you can't live three seconds without hope.

What's fueling all the competition is the United States' high unemployment rate, which has hovered around 10 percent since the last quarter of 2009. But more worrisome is the soaring rate of the unemployed and the *underemployed*—workers who have seen their hours whittled back—which now tops 17 percent. Everywhere hours are being cut by employers. Teachers, government employees, and hourly employees from Portland, Maine, to Portland, Oregon, are being furloughed two or three days a month, without pay, to combat budget problems. With the ensuing loss of salary and benefits—or wondering if their position is the next to go—there's an incredible amount of angst out there in the public and private sectors.

If you're among the millions who've lost their jobs during the Great Recession, as the media is calling it, I can feel your pain. Why can I say that when I still have a job? Because even though I still put in Monday-through-Friday workweeks at Corporate Financial

Advisors, paychecks had been few and far between. As we say in the investment banking industry, you eat what you kill.

There haven't been many kills in the last two years because I'm part of an "event-driven" business that works on a commission basis, meaning I have to wait until a business has been bought or sold using the services of our investment banking team before I receive my slice of the pie. Since I'm one of Corporate Financial Advisors' owners and managing directors, the few deals I've cobbled together the last couple of years have gone straight to offsetting CFA's overhead—employee salaries, office rent, capital expenditures, and utilities. Bottom line: I've never seen the investment banking industry in such horrible shape.

It's not just what's happening in investment banking that has me concerned. Serving on eight boards of directors, being involved in two operating companies, and investing in three private equity companies has given me another window into how bad things are out there. Of the thirteen organizations in the diverse industries that I just listed, ten have been struggling since 2008. Most of our work at Corporate Financial Advisors has been in restructuring balance sheets and trying to keep banks from foreclosing on many of our clients.

Here in Wisconsin, we have seventy-seven publicly traded companies. In the spring of 2009, 57 percent of the companies' stock values were down more than 50 percent from the previous twelve months. I've seen $72-a-share stocks tumble to $1 and dozens of wealthy individuals lose everything. Many days, I feel like I'm a doctor, advising very sick patients what to do next.

It's bad out there. Whenever I attend a social event in town—like the Christopher Doerr party—I can't tell you the number of experienced business people who've told me that this hurting economy is unlike anything they've seen in the last thirty years.

Listening to knowledgeable people say these scary things has caused more than a few sleepless nights for me. I'm sure the impending fear of economic disaster caused a seasoned executive like Matt to unload on me that morning. When he exploded at me for pontificating about the oh-so-proper way to approach someone for networking, I realized: *He's never been through this before. He's scared spitless.*

But there was another raw edge to Matt's voice, and it was anger. His rage boiled over when he thought I was feeding him a spoonful of sanctimonious crap about networking. This wasn't my intent, but that was his perception. Since anger is often a secondary emotion, that meant something else was deeply bothering Matt—probably the loss of status in the community.

Think about it: he was a highly regarded CEO, used to being master of the universe. Now he was unemployed and tossed onto the streets, looking for a job for the first time in decades. Matt was no doubt wondering how he'd provide for his family, keep his house, and hang on to any valuable assets—cars, vacation homes, and the like. Feelings of insecurity bubbled up from underneath the surface of his emotions, and that's why he lashed out at me.

Instead of firing back, though, I absorbed his verbal blows and offered to meet with him to do a "little networking." Our lunch meeting went well, and we patched things up. I gave him a few leads and wished him all the best.

All this happened six months ago, but last I heard, Matt was still looking for the right position.

The Difference Between One Letter

When I was working on an outline for *Networking Is a Contact Sport*, I knew I wanted to include a chapter about how networking can relate to getting a job, but when I worked on the Table of Contents with my writing partner, Mike Yorkey, we originally slotted "The Difference Between Networking and Not Working Is One Letter" toward the back of the book.

As the floodwaters of unemployment remained high, however, my thinking changed. We moved the "unemployment chapter" up toward the front of the book because I wanted to speak more directly to the fears and anxieties of millions of Americans' needs. The subject is that important.

BUT WHAT IF I ALREADY HAVE A JOB?

Even if you're gainfully employed, I don't want you to skip this chapter. First of all, you never know what tomorrow brings. We're sailing through uncharted economic waters, and if the events of the last couple of years can teach us anything, it's that nothing's guaranteed in life—including your job today or your benefits tomorrow.

In addition, we're living in an era when you're almost *expected* to change jobs. The median years a person stays in one job has dropped to 4.1 years, says the Bureau of Labor Statistics at the U.S. Department of Labor. Between the ages of eighteen and forty-two, you can expect to hold 10.8 different jobs, says the Bureau of Labor Statistics.[3]

How many times does the average worker change careers? Statistically speaking, no one knows since the U.S. Department of Labor doesn't col-lect that data, but everything I've heard says that people change careers about seven times in a lifetime. Sounds about right to me . . . I'm on No. 5: book author.

I want you to look at this chapter—"The Difference Between Networking and Not Working Is One Letter"—as an investment for the future: you nev-er know when you may be calling on a friend or business acquaintance to land that next job.

It was also my sense that we would have many jobless readers eager to find out how networking could help them land their next job. If I've just described your situation, then my instincts are good. Networking, I believe, plays a *huge* role in whether you'll get hired or where you'll land your next job. The oft-said axiom is frequently true when it comes to a job search: it's not *what* you know but *who* you know.

I want you to think back to your last position. How did you get the job? I would lay good odds that you were hired because of one of these following reasons:

1. You had a relationship with the person who hired you.
2. A friend or acquaintance in the firm recommended you for the job.
3. A networking contact gave you glowing recommendation or made a phone call to the right person on your behalf.

4. You heard about the job opening from a friend or business contact.

Hiring is often a relationship-based arrangement, and while who you know won't guarantee you'll get hired, networking can certainly jam a size 12 wingtip into the doorjamb of the human resources director's office. Sixty to 90 percent of jobs are found through friends, relatives, and direct contacts, according to the Career Playbook Web site. The U.S. Department of Labor says that nearly two-thirds of all workers "knew someone" to find their job. *The Wall Street Journal* reported that 94 percent of successful job hunters claimed that networking made all the difference for them.[4]

> The Wall Street Journal *reported that 94 percent of successful job hunters claimed that networking made all the difference for them.*

Again, I'm writing from the perspective of someone who has never been laid off, although there have been periods in my life when I was "between" careers and was looking for my next opportunity. Even though I technically didn't have a job during those times, I never stopped working because I bought into the idea that you're always working when you're networking.

In your situation, this is not the time to pull down the shades and retreat into the shadows of your home. Layoffs are happening with such regular occurrence that the shame sometimes associated with losing your job isn't there anymore, at least in my mind. It's not your fault or a reflection of your job skills; it's the marketplace reacting to the reality of today's economy, which acts in unpredictable ways and is subject to the whims of economic policies emanating from Washington or your state capitol.

If you've had the cold water of unemployment splashed in your face, it's time to tell people that you're looking for a job and enlist them in your job search. A quick job search on Monster.com and sending out a few half-hearted résumés won't cut the mustard, as we say in the Bratwurst Capital of America. Now that you're looking for work, this is the time to take a deep breath, look around at your options, and then develop an effective networking strategy to land that next job.

A Checklist to Follow

So, are you ready to get started? I hope so. Let's go through the following checklist step-by-step:

✓ **Begin by taking inventory.**
Where are you at this moment?
You're unemployed.
As tough as that notion is to embrace, you have to accept it. Losing your job happens. Take heart in knowing that you're not alone.
I think the hardest thing to do at this time is count your blessings and realize no matter how bad it gets, everything's going to be okay. My parents and grandparents survived the Great Depression at a time when the "safety net" was the corner soup kitchen. Today, state governments provide benefits for up to half your earnings, up to a maximum amount, for at least twenty-six weeks. And as we've seen time and time again, Washington does not have the political will to end unemployment benefits for many of the jobless, which is why we read about the latest "extension" in the newspapers.
Believe me, I'm not trying to gloss over the difficulties that lie ahead. You probably have a mortgage or monthly rent staring you in the face. You may have orthodontist bills to pay and a family minivan running on bald tires. And your wife's (or husband's) admonition— "When are you going to get a job?"—creates more stomach-churning stress. An unemployment check only goes so far.
This is where faith comes in—faith in yourself, faith in the future, and faith in God, if you have a belief system. The only job security you'll ever have is the faith and confidence you have in your abilities: it's no longer with a big company; it's no longer with the government; and it's not with a rich parent.
There's another thing to keep in mind. Bleak as any long-term outlook appears to be, remember that with all the downsizing, plant closures, mergers, and layoffs, complaining about your fate will get you nowhere.

You have to confront reality, and one of those realities is that the days of working for one company and receiving a pension and a gold watch after four decades of faithful service are over. My father, Ray Sweeney, was among the last of the Wisconsin Mohicans. For forty-five years, he worked the same job—running a plumbing, heating, and wholesale business. As a small-business owner, he treated his forty or fifty employees like family. I can remember the same set of sunny faces every time I visited Dad at his business on Main Street in Madison.

That type of long-term employment ended with the eight-track player. Here's the deal: the Industrial Age, signified by manufacturing giants like General Motors and U.S. Steel, has given way to the computerized Information Age. Thomas L. Friedman, author of the bestselling book *The World Is Flat: A Brief History of the Twenty-First Century*, contends that technology has "flattened" our world—in other words, leveled the playing field—and therefore change will happen faster and faster in this era of globalization.

People in my father's generation thought that working for a big company provided security. Well, you can officially toss that idea on the scrapheap of history. What the events of the last few years teach us is that there is no security. With all the downsizing, mergers, and raft of companies who are here today and gone tomorrow, the only security you have is yourself and your faith community. And if you think you can rely on the government, sooner or later the bureaucrats will run out of other people's money.

We're in the midst of a shakeout for American workers, and who knows what the long term looks like. The structural changes in the labor market have economists fearing that a recovery from the current recession will not produce strong unemployment numbers. In fact, political pundits are predicting a "jobless recovery," which is another way of saying that the economy will continue to sputter and the jobs picture won't improve any time soon.

So basically, you're on your own—until you tap into your network and/or expand your networking horizons. But before that can happen, though, you need to:

✓ **Get in the right frame of mind.**

Your thoughts create feelings inside you, and those feelings lead to behaviors, which lead to results—good and bad. What you want to create is good results from positive thoughts. If you're thinking your next job is just around the corner, you're more likely to engage in behavior that will lead you to your next job. Every time a hill or mountain presents itself, you'll figure out a way to climb over it.

Some people see insurmountable hurdles everywhere they turn. One of them was Richard Neureuther, who agreed to let me tell his story. Richard is a retired FBI guy who loves speaking to kids about drugs and peer pressure. He has that tough-guy FBI swagger that makes him a compelling speaker, as well as a good pitch to young people about how and why acting responsibly about drugs is for their benefit.

> *Your thoughts create feelings inside you, and those feelings lead to behaviors, which lead to results—good and bad. What you want to create is good results from positive thoughts.*

At any rate, Richard called me up to do a "little networking" with me, and I told him to drop by my office. The tenor of the conversation was this: Richard was looking for a financial angel to put $150,000 in seed money to take his speaking career to the next level. He said his goal was to speak about the dangers of drugs to school assemblies in elementary and high schools around the country, but he felt his primary market was Milwaukee. He added that he was looking for $600 to $800 per day or per school assembly.

I asked him a series of questions, and when I thought I had a good handle of the situation, I said, "Instead of trying to get someone to give you money so you can go do your thing, why not approach the MPS?" I was referring to the Milwaukee Public Schools, which is the largest public school district in Wisconsin with 198 schools serving more than 85,000 students. We both knew drugs were a huge problem on high school campuses, especially in the inner city.

"Joe, there's no money in the MPS system."

My jaw nearly hit the floor. "That's a bunch of crapola, Richard. The annual budget is $1 billion. You and I know that. You just have to figure out a way to get to it. They have to have a huge budget for assemblies. Or perhaps there's a way to make your talks part of their anti-drug curriculum. The money's there, Richard—you just have to get to the right people."

"I guess you're right, Joe."

"Here's another thing," I said, warming to the subject. "Are there only public schools in Milwaukee? No, of course not. There are plenty of private schools that need to hear this message. My wife, Tami, is on an advisory board at Marquette University High School, and they're always bringing in drug and alcohol people to speak."

"That's a good idea. I'll go to the private high schools," Richard said.

"What about the Catholic grade schools or private grade schools?"

"Joe, they definitely don't have the money."

"Wrong, Richard," and I proceeded to explain to him that even St. Eugene's, our parish's elementary school, had a five-figure budget to bring in outside speakers.

I blew all of Richard's objections out of the water just by getting him to reframe his situation. You need to get in the right frame of mind as well.

To begin, I want you to visualize several dream jobs. Write them down. Let them marinate in your thoughts, which will create feelings, which will lead to behavior changes, which will land results.

Psychologists tell us that we have thousands of thoughts each day. What is your mindset? Is it positive or negative? Research shows that a positive mindset will produce the feel-good neurotransmitters serotonin and dopamine, while negative thoughts trigger a fight-or-flight response that dumps stress chemicals into our brains, leading to more negative thoughts and perhaps depression.

That explains why if you're stewing on negative thoughts—*I'll never get a job...I'm no good...No one will hire me*—then you're listening to thoughts that make you feel hopeless, worthless, and powerless. These feelings lead to behaviors that... well, let's just say you don't feel like going the extra mile.

So get in the right frame of mind, focus on the positive, and then be willing to:

Study these three charts, which were provided to me by Susan K. Wehrley, a communication empowerment expert from Milwaukee whom I've consulted with. Do you now see better why your thoughts end up affecting your results?

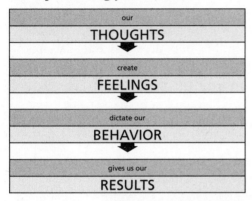

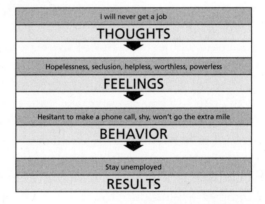

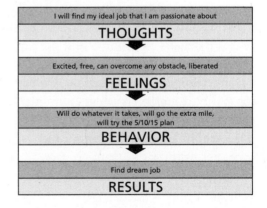

✓ **Change your mindset.**

How many times have you ever seen the FedEx logo? Hundreds of times, right? Maybe thousands of times over the years, if you think about every single time you received a FedEx package, saw a FedEx truck in your neighborhood, read a print ad in a magazine, or viewed the FedEx Cup standings on a Sunday afternoon golf broadcast of a PGA tournament.

John Assaraf, a good friend of mine, is the founder of OneCoach, a provider of small business coaching services. He pointed out something to me in one of his books, *Having It All*, in which he directed readers to take a look at the FedEx and find the arrow.

I would like you to do the same. Do you see the arrow?

I didn't until John pointed it out to me. Look at the space between the E and the X. Do you see the white arrow? Keep looking.

Got it? I bet you never saw that white arrow before, even though it's been there all along. What I'm giving you is a new way of looking at something you've seen hundreds of times because when you change the way you look at things, those things change in response.

I want you to look at your unemployment situation in a new way, perhaps even as a once-in-a-lifetime opportunity to do something that you've never done before. You're a free agent, ready and willing to pursue your dream job. Sign with a new team.

If you've been hanging on to a job that you've never liked, here's your chance to reshuffle the deck. A layoff notice might be just the kick in the butt you need to try something new, which leads me to my next point:

✓ **Be willing to reinvent yourself.**

I mentioned earlier that I've had to play the role of doctor attending to a very sick patient, meaning that my investment banking team and I come in, we go through the books, dissect the business plan, and look for a way to turn around a company that's headed for bankruptcy court.

Many of these firms are small manufacturing businesses—the mom-and-pop shops that found a manufacturing niche decades ago in the Midwest. The trouble is their market has steadily eroded because a Chinese or Vietnamese manufacturer figured out how to make the same widget for a fraction of the price. Buyers these days prefer to purchase the cheaper commodity or product, and that puts the small manufacturing company under all sorts of pressure. Orders dry up, workers are laid off, and the company falls into a death spiral.

When I'm asked to help reverse a company's fortunes, I'll come in and do my due diligence. More often than not, I'll sit before the board of directors and soberly deliver the bad news: it's over. "Unless you—" and I let the thought hang for a moment.

"Unless we do what?" the company president will ask.

"Unless you change your core business from manufacturing to distributing," I might say. "You've got to start importing your product from China, Taiwan, or some Far East country and form a distribution firm. People could care less where your product is manufactured. They still want to buy it from your company, but at a price that matches the competition."

You wouldn't believe the pushback I receive. It's like I let a skunk loose in the boardroom. "My grandfather was a manufacturer! My father was a manufacturer, and I'm a manufacturer!" one company president thundered as he pounded the conference room table for emphasis. "Don't tell me how to run my business!"

CEOs and presidents who pounded the table are now pounding the pavement. One after another, I've seen these respected manufacturing companies close their doors because they failed to reinvent themselves.

Unless you have a skill that is readily employable, you may have to reinvent yourself and your career. For instance, let's say you were laid off from a factory job and have always been intrigued by surveying but never felt you could become a surveyor. Well, now's your chance. This is the time to enroll in technical school to learn a new trade and pursue a career you might never have considered but could see yourself doing. This is the time to reframe and readjust your work situation.

More likely than not, you're going to have to go a totally different direction—a direction to where the jobs are. *Money* magazine looked at the jobs with the highest ten-year growth rate (as estimated by the Bureau of Labor Statistics) and ranked them in this fashion:

1. Telecommunications network engineer
2. Systems engineer
3. Personal financial advisor
4. Veterinarian
5. Senior financial analyst
6. Business analyst, information technologies
7. Software development director
8. Physical therapist
9. Physician assistant
10. Computer/network security consultant[5]

See anything that appeals to you? You may have to go back to school for training, but you'd be putting your energies (and tuition fees) toward jobs that should be in high demand for the next decade.

Another part of reinventing yourself could be reinventing where you live. Would you consider a move? You may have to in order to get a new job, especially if you want to remain in your trained field.

I understand that pulling up stakes may sound impossible for some people because of their family situation, where their kids are in school, or what part of the country they live in. However, if moving to another part of the country is what you need to do to get your career back on track—and get a positive cash flow for the family finances—then I think you should be at least willing to consider a move.

If you're single and in your twenties, then your commitments are few and an out-of-state move is easier to contemplate. Married with children complicates things, especially if you're part of that "sandwich" generation that finds themselves caring for elderly parents as well as your growing-like-saplings youngsters. Only you know what is doable and what is a pipe dream, but serious times invoke serious measures.

Which leads me to another aspect to reinventing yourself, and it's this:

✓ **Realize that you're not above any position.**

I know a lot of guys in the Midwest advertising world who were used to making six figures, but when they were laid off, they turned up their noses at taking an advertising position with another company for a $50,000 salary. "I'm a six-figure guy," they say. "I'm not going to take that job."

It's too bad they harbored that attitude because they could have been back up to six figures by now after proving their mettle. Instead, they felt the initial salary offer was beneath them, and today they remain on the outside looking in—or have had to chuck their careers in advertising. This attitude is shortsighted because if you're good at what you do, managers will notice and move you up the ranks.

I enjoy playing and following golf, and I know the PGA golf tour is based on meritocracy: only the top 125 in money earnings each season get to keep their "card," or playing privileges, for the following year. Play poorly and don't make enough cuts, and you'll find yourself relegated to the second-tier Nationwide Tour. (That's unless you can somehow get through the terrifying "Q School"—the end-of-the-year qualifying tournament where a small number of golfers earn PGA Tour cards for the following tournament season.)

Whatever path pro golfers take, "dropping down" to the next tour is not the end of the world. You can bounce back. (In fact, the PGA Tour has a statistic known as the "Bounce Back," which tracks how often a player follows an over-par hole [like a bogey or double bogey] with an under-par hole [birdie or eagle], which is an interesting real-world example of resiliency.) You can start playing better and gaining confidence. Play well on the Nationwide Tour, and you'll graduate to the PGA Tour and be rewarded with playing the same tournaments as Tiger and Phil, along with a chance to earn big bucks.

The same scenario works in the everyday work world. Do a good job, and you'll be promoted. Show management what you're capable of, and you'll be rewarded. But you can never put your job skills or experience on display if you never get off the driving range or the practice putting green. You need to be out there on the course, and the same holds true in the workaday world. You need to be inside the ropes, not in the gallery.

Sometimes, though—and especially if you're just out of college and you're looking for that first job—you should:

✓ **Consider working for free.**

I hear the gnashing of teeth all the way in Milwaukee. *Are you telling me, Joe Sweeney, that I have to work for nothing?*

You don't have to, but it might be the best thing you ever did.

Résumés are falling out of the sky like snowflakes these days, especially for entry-level positions. Human resource directors and department managers, who are snowed under by the sheer number of job applicants, can afford to be very picky. Offering your services gratis may get you the break you were looking for. Besides, if you're collecting an unemployment check, it's like playing with house money. Why not volunteer and do something productive that could lead to your next job?

Shortly after Tami and I got married, we moved to South Bend, Indiana, because I was enrolled in Notre Dame's MBA program. Tami, then in her early twenties, had to leave behind a good position as a promotions producer at the Madison, Wisconsin, public television station.

We moved to South Bend without a job for Tami, but we both thought it was auspicious that our graduate-student housing landed us next door to WNDU, the NBC affiliate. One night around dinner, Tami mentioned that she'd love to be an on-air reporter some day. She had always been behind the camera in Madison as one of the producers.

"You should apply for a reporter's job," I said one evening. "Maybe WNDU has something."

"They'd never hire me," she replied. "I've never done any on-air work."

"Just go hang around. Tell them you'll work for nothing. Tell them you'll carry cables around on the newsroom floor."

A few days later, Tami rolled up her sleeves and walked confidently into the WNDU studios. She eventually pigeonholed the news director, Mike Collins, and made the following pitch: "Listen, I just moved into town. I'm a TV producer from Madison, so I have experience. I know you probably don't need anybody, but I'll work for nothing. I'll carry cords or do anything you want. I just want a chance to prove myself."

Mike rubbed his chin. What did he have to lose? After all, Tami said she'd work for free.

"Fine. You can intern for us," said the news director. "The last time I checked, at that salary, you're in our budget."

For six weeks, Tami did nothing but grunt work, but she had a great work ethic and never complained about being a glorified gofer. Then two reporters gave notice: one took a job at another station and the other quit after getting pregnant.

Within days, Tami Sweeney was WNDU's latest on-air reporter, assigned to the soft-news beat. Everyone loved her outgoing personality and on-camera work, and within months, she became a WNDU weekend reporter and even hosted a half-hour talk show on Sunday mornings called *The Michiana Report*, which was about the goings-on in southern Michigan and northeastern Indiana.

> *Something good happened when Tami said, "I'll do anything for nothing." You may have to make the same offer, especially if you're interested in making a career U-turn.*

Granted, this incident happened in a different economy and would be unlikely to occur today in some markets, but something good happened when Tami said, "I'll do anything for nothing." You may have to make the same offer, especially if you're interested in making a career U-turn.

When I started my sports management company, SMG, our front door resembled a revolving door for all the just-out-of-college, eager-beaver males who envisioned themselves as the next Jerry McGuire. We used to joke in meetings that we should beat back this horde with a baseball bat.

When we were in the hiring mood, I would tell applicants, "Here's the situation: I've got a hundred guys who want this position, but I think you could help us. Here are thirty things I want you to do over the next thirty days. I'm not paying you anything, but if you're really good, I'll give you a job."

I had these guys do everything from answering the phone to writing reports to going out on calls with me. Most didn't make it, but I did hire seven or eight guys over a five-year period under those parameters.

IS THIS YOU?

Many people hang on to jobs they never liked in the first place, oblivious that their unhappiness—which they mistakenly thought they could hide—hurts their performance and attitude. Andrea Kay, the author of *Life's a Bitch and Then You Change Careers*, said, "Typically, not until someone is forced out of what they've been accustomed to doing do they feel the need to change."[6]

Which leads me to my next point:

✓ **Realize that networking is your best chance to get hired again.**
This is not the time to retreat behind closed doors or lick your wounds away from public view. This is the time to tell everyone you know that you're looking for work. Don't be bashful. Make phone calls. Send out e-mails. Even admit your need on your Facebook page and other social networking outlets. If you've never done the 5/10/15 program, there's no better time to start. Try to meet or engage with five people a day. Send out ten e-mails. Make fifteen phone calls.

Do you have a friend or a spouse who'll let you work for free for a couple of hours a day? If so, you won't have a gap in your résumé so it doesn't look like you're on the street. But don't feel that you have to devote eight hours a day to a job search, and I say that because you'll go nuts if you do. Show some balance. In fact, I would add another "5" to your 5/10/15 plan by creating a "Victory Log" that lists large and small successes. Some examples:

- You joined your wife (or husband) for a brown-bag lunch at her office.
- You read a book to each of your young children.

- You went to the library and perused trade journals and professional publications for jobs you might want to pursue.
- You had a great workout at the gym.
- You started blogging about your industry as a way to stay involved.
- You prepared yourself for a job interview by doing online research about the type of questions that human resources often ask.
- You vacuumed, straightened up around the house, and even cleaned the toilets!
- You did the grocery shopping, cooked dinner, and did the cleanup.
- You gave the kids their bedtime baths and put them down for the evening.
- You turned off the TV and talked with your spouse until it was time for bed.

Taking on these types of tasks will lift your spirits because you are doing something meaningful with your time.

But there's something else you can do besides contacting everyone you know or scouring Craigslist want ads, and it's this: use some shoe leather.

What I mean is that I would literally knock on a few doors unannounced at employers of interest, just like Tami did with WNDU. This idea only works at smaller companies because a small business owner is apt to be an entrepreneur who'll like to see some spunk from a job seeker making an in-store appearance. If you go to a large company and present yourself at the reception desk, the best you'll get is, "The personnel department is down the hall. Go talk to them."

At the end of the day, though, finding a new job becomes a numbers game, which is why it's important to embrace the discipline of the 5/10/15 program. Even if you only have twenty-five or fifty contacts or people you know (meaning, you have a relationship with them), they can pass along your résumé to *their* contacts.

MEET JOE SWEENEY: BAG BOY

Maybe I can don a blue vest and become a Walmart greeter when I'm in my spry eighties.

Or maybe I could bag groceries today—if I had to earn some money.

That's what I learned when I lost a bet a few years ago. It all began when I dropped by my neighborhood Sendik's Food Market, Milwaukee's family-owned and -operated grocery stores that have been around for more than eighty years. I was picking up my usual morning coffee at the Sendik's Market in Bayside when I ran into John Sendik, the store owner.

It was a bright Friday in June, and the news of the morning was that Tiger Woods had shot a 76 in the opening round of the 2006 U.S. Open at Winged Foot the previous day.

"Did you see what Tiger shot yesterday?" John asked. "He's going to miss the cut."

"Baloney," I replied. "He'll make the cut. He always does." Tiger Woods had never missed the cut in a major tournament in ten years as a professional.

"You wanna bet?" John plastered a wicked grin across his face. He had been my partner in

I bet John Sendik, the owner of Sendik's Market in Bayside, Wisconsin, that Tiger Woods would still make the cut after shooting a 76 in the opening round of the 2006 U.S. Open. Well, I lost that bet, and for my penance, I had to work an entire day bagging groceries and stocking shelves at John's store. Naturally, he chose December 23, the busiest day of the year, but I figure I got a chance to network with 200 people that day. Talk about turning lemons into lemonade!

some best-ball competitions, but John was a terrible golfer, a real hacker.

I took the bait. "Sure, what you do you want to bet?" I asked.

When John paused to think about it, I filled in the vacuum.

"Tell you what," I said. "If Tiger makes the cut, you'll deliver $300 worth of groceries to my house, and if he doesn't make the cut, you pick the busiest day of the year, and I'll work all day as a bag boy at Sendik's."

We shook on it, and lo and behold, Tiger posted another 76 on his scorecard and missed his first cut in a major as a professional.

John—no dummy—chose December 23 to bring me in, which had to be the busiest grocery-shopping day of the year as families stocked up for Christmas Eve parties and Christmas dinners. When I reported for work, John handed me an apron and a nametag that said: *My name is Joe Sweeney. I lost a bet to John Sendik, so that's why I'm working at Sendik's today.*

Nothing like rubbing it in.

I did everything: bag groceries, stock shelves, replenish the produce stocks, and help little old ladies as the carryout boy. (Thanks, Mrs. Rooney, for the $5 tip.) It seemed like I knew half the people that came in that day, and I overheard more than a few say, "Oh my God, Joe Sweeney must have lost his job. He's bagging groceries."

Listen, that day at Sendik's was one of the most fun workdays I've ever had. Better yet, I probably networked with 200 people that day. Because I was at the bad end of a bet, I realized that a lot of folks hit a patch of bad luck with serious consequences. I learned that if I had to bag groceries at Sendik's to put food on the table, I could do it. I didn't let outside circumstances affect my thinking, and neither should you if you're out of a job.

When it comes to networking to find a new job, you may have more contacts than you think. How many teachers, coaches, business associates, and high school and college friends do you know? Unless you've been cloistered in a rectory all these years, research shows that most people know upward of 250 people. So if you know 250 people and they know 250 people...

You may know more people that you realize—or more than you give yourself credit for. One of my favorite movies is *It's a Wonderful Life*, the 1946 black-and-white classic starring Jimmy Stewart as George Bailey, who spent his entire life giving of himself to the people of Bedford Falls.

George has always wanted to travel, but he stays put to prevent a rich skinflint and evil banker named Mr. Potter from taking over the town. The only thing standing in Mr. Potter's way is George's modest building-and-loan company, founded by his generous father. On Christmas Eve, George's Uncle Billy loses the business's $8,000 while on his way to deposit it into Mr. Potter's bank. Mr. Potter finds the misplaced money and hides it from Uncle Billy.

When the bank examiner discovers the shortage, George realizes that he'll be held responsible. The future looks bleak: his company will collapse, he'll be sent to jail, and mean-spirited Mr. Potter will be granted his wish—taking over the town of Bedford Falls.

A getting-more-desperate-by-the-minute George Bailey wishes he was dead and contemplates suicide. The prayers of his loved ones prompt a gentle angel named Clarence to come to George's aid, but when Clarence sees that he's unable to persuade George from ending it all, the angel decides to show George what life in Bedford Falls would be like if George had never lived. In a nightmarish vision in which the Potter-controlled Bedford Falls has sunk into a den of sex and sin, those who George loves are either dead, ruined, or miserable.

George sees the light and concludes that he had touched many people in a positive way, and it has indeed been a "wonderful life."

Sure, the example of George Bailey from It's a Wonderful Life sounds corny nearly sixty-five years later, but I would hazard a guess that you've touched more people than you've ever realized. Reaching out to others through the 5/10/15 plan is probably the best thing you can do to find your next job.

I mentioned how the 5/10/15 plan is a numbers game when it comes to finding a job, but the odds are far more in your favor. Why do I say that? Because in my line of work, I need to turn five engagements twice a year in order to close ten deals. That's always been my goal—ten deals a year.

But when you're looking for a job, all you need is one "deal."

I would be shocked if you didn't get a job within four months using my 5/10/15 plan. After a one-month effort (twenty workdays), you will have had one hundred meetings or encounters, typed out two hundred letters, and made three hundred phone calls. Even if you completed all these tasks in *two* months, I'm confident that you could land that next employment opportunity.

If you are serious and committed to this process, I would do something else: engage an accountability partner—or what I call a "wingman"—to encourage you, inquire how you're doing, and ask for a progress report. Having wingmen in your life can make all the difference, and I'll talk about them in my next chapter.

The Difference Between Networking and Not Working Is One Letter

1. Take action because action cures fear. The Chinese have a great proverb for this: *Man stand long time with mouth open before roast duck fly in.*
2. Meditate and pray each day—even if it's only for five minutes. Have a time of quiet self-reflection, which will feel like chicken soup for the soul.
3. Although the phrase "God helps those who help themselves" can't be found in the Bible—Benjamin Franklin uttered it in 1736—do as the Amish do, which is to "pray with busy feet." In other words, pray *and* make it your job to find your next position.
4. Realize that you're not your money, not your house, not your car, and not your toys. Don't let "stuff" define who you are or what you are.
5. Don't let outside circumstances beyond your control affect your thinking, which is really hard to do and easy for me to say.
6. Don't listen to naysayers who cluck, "There are no jobs out there." Sure, there are fewer employment opportunities these days, but to make a blanket statement that there are *no* jobs available is a defeatist attitude and simply not true.
7. Understand life's rhythms because life is a series of highs and lows. Nothing in life is as good as it seems, and nothing in life is as bad it seems. Somewhere in the middle is where reality falls.
8. Focus on what you can achieve—today. Many times when you're unemployed, you feel powerless and without control. Engage in an activity that you can completely control, like gardening in the backyard, sweeping the steps, or walking the dog. Starting and finishing one chore or errand will give you a sense of accomplishment and perhaps propel you further in your job search.
9. Write down on a piece of paper, "What a difference a year makes." Then focus on where you want to be a year from now.

10. Take some time each week to help others with their problems. What this does is take the focus off your problems.
11. Use this "down time" to improve your health—exercise and eat better than you might have when work interfered with meal times. You'll feel better about yourself, which will lift your self-esteem.
12. Also take time to do something every day that you love to do, like reading, going for a scenic walk, playing your guitar, or riding a bike.
13. If you have any friends who are also unemployed, give them advice just as I'm doing. Then follow your own counsel.

Networking Is All in Your Personality

I'VE ALWAYS FOUND the topic of human behavior and personality types fascinating, and you should, too. When it comes to networking, you need to consider what kind of personality—or temperament—your friend or acquaintance has so that you can better understand how to connect with that person. If you understand his or her personality type, you'll be able to better calibrate what you say and how you relate to that person. Learning how to recognize certain personality traits will help you network better, manage people more efficiently, and sell to others more effectively. Business is not about managing money; it's about managing relationships and personalities.

If you've ever wondered why people do the things they do, or if you've ever wondered why you get along with some people and not with others, it's because personality traits affect the way people think and act. It's the reason why certain friends can rub us the wrong way and the reason why we consider some people obnoxious.

I would imagine that you have me pegged me as the consummate extrovert who finds networking as natural as shooting a free throw. I plead guilty as charged, and that's because of my personality type, which is a combination of inborn traits that subconsciously affect my behavior. You have personality traits as well, which are passed on by genetics, although intelligence, race, birth order, sex, and other factors add to the mix.

Through the years, psychology has narrowed down all human behavior into four basic types: choleric, sanguine, phlegmatic, and melancholy. I would imagine that you find those four words mystifying unless you've read extensively on personality types from psychologists like Carl Jung and Carl Rogers. I prefer the descriptions by authors and speakers Greg and Michael Smalley, who say the quartet of personality types can be likened to four positions on a cruise ship. They are:

- **Captain** — the leader type
- **Social Director** — the social, fun-loving type
- **Steward** — the loyal and relational type
- **Navigator** — the quality-control type

Let's take a closer look at each personality type.

Which Shipmate Are You?

You can find plenty of personality tests online, but the Smalleys have prepared the following survey that will show you specifically what your traits are so that you can better understand who you are. In the following test, circle each word or phrase that seems to describe you. When you're done, add up the number of words and phrases you circled in each box.

CAPTAIN

Takes charge	Determined	Bold
Purposeful	Assertive	Firm
Decision-maker	Leader	Enterprising
Goal-driven	Competitive	Self-reliant
Enjoys challenges	Adventurous	

Enter the number circled: _____

SOCIAL DIRECTORS

Takes risks	Fun-loving	Visionary
Likes variety	Motivator	Enjoys change
Energetic	Creative	Very verbal
Group-oriented	Promoter	Mixes easily
Avoids details	Optimistic	

Enter the number circled: _____

STEWARDS

Loyal	Adaptable	Non-demanding
Sympathetic	Even-keeled	Thoughtful
Avoids conflict	Nurturing	Enjoys routine
Patient	Dislikes change	Tolerant
Good Listener	Builds deep relationships	

Enter the number circled: _____

NAVIGATOR

Deliberate	Discerning	Controlled
Detailed	Reserved	Analytical
Predictable	Inquisitive	Practical
Precise	Orderly	Persistent
Factual	Scheduled	

Enter the number circled: _____

Which category did you score the highest in? I scored thirteen points for Captain and twelve points for Social Director, which means I'm a fun-loving leader, right? Those results mirror more formal personality tests I've taken over the years.

Looking at Your Personality

Now I think it would be instructive if we go over the following charts describing the four personality styles, their communication styles, and the best ways you can network with them. The descriptions for each are adapted from *Don't Date Naked*, Chapter 3: "It's All In Your Personality," by Michael and Amy Smalley.

THE CAPTAIN

Captains are usually the bosses at work, used to acting decisively. They are in a hurry to get things done and don't wait for things to happen. They are blunt, bottom-line people who can come across as insensitive at times. They are the types who'd stiff Grandma if that's what it took to close a deal. If Captains aren't in charge, they'll figure out a way to be in charge.

MOTIVATORS:
- Need personal attention and recognition
- Need to be put in charge
- Want opportunity to solve problems
- Need freedom to change
- Seek challenging activities

COMMUNICATION STYLE:
- Direct or blunt
- One-way
- Not known for being good listeners

RELATIONAL STRENGTHS:
- Takes charge
- Solves problems
- Is competitive
- Enjoys change
- Is confrontational

STRENGTHS OUT OF BALANCE:
- Too direct or impatient
- Cold-blooded
- Impulsive, too big a risk-taker
- Insensitive to others

How Best to Network with Captains

If you're a Captain, you need to back off a little when relating with another Captain. Don't be so competitive. Let him be the alpha male in this conversation. Besides, two bulls can't roam inside the china shop at the same time.

If you're a Social Director, you need to ask him about his adventures and goals. Have some fun and talk to him about the great possibilities you see happening in the future.

If you're a Steward, you need to let her know that you're reliable. (People in charge—controllers—like to hear that.) Talk in terms of bottom-line results and put your analytical skills on display.

If you're a Navigator, let him lead you and show that you're a good employee.

SOCIAL DIRECTORS

Social Directors make great networkers. They seem to know everybody, and they're always up for a party—because then they get to know more people! Social Directors motivate others ("Let's take on that project!") but tend to avoid details. They also tend to be disorganized, but they are usually well-liked because of their contagious enthusiasm and inspiration.

MOTIVATORS:
- Need approval
- Need opportunities to verbalize
- Want visibility
- Yearn for social recognition

COMMUNICATION STYLE:
- Contagious enthusiasm
- One-way
- High energy
- Can manipulate others

RELATIONAL STRENGTHS:
- Optimistic
- Energetic
- Motivating
- Future-oriented

STRENGTHS OUT OF BALANCE:
- Unrealistic
- Daydreams
- Manipulative or pushy
- Avoids details
- Lacks follow-through

How Best to Network with Social Directors

If you're a Captain, you need to show energy, optimism, and an appreciation for risk-taking when you network with a Social Director.

If you're a Social Director, you need to connect with each other's energy and ideas.

If you're a Steward, you need to ask inquisitive questions about the Social Director's ideas or plans. Try not to be too analytical or reserved. Work to be open to his big ideas.

If you're a Navigator, you need to be the good listener and nurturer that you are.

STEWARDS

Stewards are so loyal that if you laid one off, they would tell all their friends what a great boss you were. Since loyalty ranks high, they're willing to absorb emotional pain and punishment in relationships because that's their nature. Stewards are calm, predictable, deliberate, consistent, and tend to be unemotional and poker-faced, so you wouldn't want to play Texas Hold'em with them.

MOTIVATORS:
- Need emotional security
- Desire an agreeable environment

COMMUNICATION STYLE:
- Indirect
- Two-way
- Great listener
- Talks too long
- Provides too many details

RELATIONAL STRENGTHS:
- Warm and relational
- Loyal
- Enjoys routine
- Acts like a peacemaker
- Is sensitive to feelings
- Avoids conflict

STRENGTHS OUT OF BALANCE:
- Attracts the hurting
- Misses opportunities
- Stays in a rut
- Sacrifices own feelings for harmony
- Holds a grudge

How Best to Network with Stewards

If you're a Captain, you need to talk to a Steward about the importance of planning and procedures. Try to listen. You will be temped to say "get to the point." Resist that urge.

If you're a Social Director, you need to reinforce his emotional security and let him know that he is accepted. Don't talk about big flowery ideas.

If you're also a Steward, you need to be your agreeable self. Be sensitive to her feelings, which should be easy for you.

If you're a Navigator, you need to be warm and focus on relationship issues. Tell stories in a precise and factual manner.

NAVIGATORS

Navigators do things "by the book." They will even read Windows 7 User Guides! Navigators are forever analyzing things because they love being accurate and precise. Rules are big with them, but they are often too critical and too negative regarding new opportunities. Peek inside their cubicles, and you'll find a clean workstation, neat as a pin.

Motivators:
- Need the highest-quality effort and output in whatever they do
- Must perform to high expectations

Communication Style:
- Factual
- Two-way
- Great listener
- Desire for details and precision can frustrate others

Relational Strengths:
- Loves accuracy and precision
- Does quality control
- Discerns well
- Analytical

Strengths Out of Balance:
- Too critical
- Too strict
- Too negative about new opportunities
- Loses overview

How Best to Network with Navigators

If you're a Captain, you need to talk to a Navigator about quality-control issues in your company and your love for analytical thinking.

If you're a Social Director, you need to need to talk about facts and details. Do not tell your usual long-winded stories. If you tell one, keep it short and factual.

If you're a Steward, you need to realize that you're both analytical, so connect on that level.

If you're a fellow Navigator, you need to get into precise and detailed discussions on the topic. Since he or she is just like you, this should be easy.

So there you go, an introduction to personality types and how to network with others. This chapter just scrapes the surface, of course, so I urge you go to the Internet and learn more about personality types so that you can recognize and value other people's strengths, as well as your own.

With experience, as well as a greater understanding of particular personality traits, you can learn to calibrate what approach is best to network with others. Captains will want to see your determination and willingness to take ownership if you're networking together on a project. Social Directors, who are natural promoters, will want to see you join in their parade. Stewards are looking for you to be as loyal and as even-keeled as them because they like to form deep relationships. And Navigators, who are practical and predictable, don't like to hang around flakes.

So get out there and meet people—of all personality types!

Networking Is All in Your Personality

Examine your personality type. Which traits describe you? Does the result from the test in this chapter mesh with other personality tests you have taken in the past?

Study how you can network with each personality type, as well as manage and sell to each type. Doing this will help you significantly throughout your career.

Who's Your Wingman?

I SLIPPED ON MY Nike running shoes and zipped up my track sweats, complete with hoodie and gloves. Going out for a long run in the freezing drizzle wasn't easy to gear up for, but I needed to get out of the house on that blustery Sunday afternoon in January 1988.

My goal was to click off eighteen miles along Milwaukee's picturesque Lake Drive, which fronted Lake Michigan. The lingering edges of a nasty winter storm whipped up frothy whitecaps, and the churning of the lake's normally placid surface matched the churning I felt in the pit of my stomach. I thought I was going on a training run for the Boston Marathon, but what I was really doing that Sunday afternoon was running away from my troubles.

And I didn't know where to go.

As I settled into a workmanlike cadence along the lakeshore, I reviewed my precarious situation at work, which was worsening with each passing day. I was twenty-nine years old, the 50 percent owner of Arkay, a manufacturing firm that produced photographic and graphic arts film-processing equipment for in-house photo labs. My job was running the sales and marketing side of the business, servicing 800 dealers around the country, plus a handful of international accounts.

Sales and cash flow were strong enough to keep the company afloat, but we were highly leveraged. Truth be known, we were in hock to our eyeballs, owing several million dollars to our banking partners. While I was fine with our exposure, there were times when the mass of the debt felt like someone had strapped ankle weights around my calves and a ten-pound dumbbell to my shoulders.

What weighed even heavier was our next move. Through networking in the Milwaukee business community and the photographic industry nationwide, I had managed to tee up a multimillion dollar offer to purchase Arkay. Hallelujah! After paying off the banks, there would be several million dollars left over to split 50/50 with my partner.

The tidy sum of seven figures sounded like the riches of Croesus to me. I was taking home around $50,000 annually back then, which meant that Tami and I—she was a stay-at-home mom with three children ages four and under—were under constant financial pressure. We were living the proverbial paycheck-to-paycheck existence; I don't think we had more than a few thousand dollars in our rainy-day account.

Since certificates of deposit were paying north of 10 percent in those halcyon days of the late 1980s, the thought of earning six figures a year *just on interest alone* was causing me to toss and turn at night. Sell Arkay, and I'd be financially independent, perhaps set for life. I could breathe easy, knowing my family would be taken care of financially. That's why I was gung-ho to cash out.

So why didn't we sell Arkay in a New York minute?

Because my partner, Richard Johnson—not his real name—thought we were sitting on a goldmine that would be worth many more millions of dollars in a couple of years. Bottom line: he didn't want to part with the company.

Let me tell you about my partner, twenty-five years my senior with a head of gray hair and tons of business experience. Richard handled the manufacturing and research and development side of Arkay. He had gone hog wild on a new pollution-control device for the photographic industry, throwing millions of the company's precious capital into chasing this opportunity. "When we bring this new device to market, Arkay will be worth tens of million of dollars in no time," he declared with fervent and absolute confidence.

I wasn't so sure. I was out in the field, flying around the country and meeting with the lab techs and mom-and-pops running the processing labs, and what I was learning was that there wasn't any strong grassroots demand for Richard's pollution-control device. Maybe we could sell a few here and there, but this invention wasn't going to revolutionize the photo-processing industry.

There was another factor in play. Remember, I'm an Irishman, which means I'm not very smart, but back in the late 1980s, I kept hearing about another invention called "digital cameras" that would one day render 35mm film—and photo-processing equipment—obsolete. I didn't know if digital cameras were one year, five years, or fifty years away from making physical film outdated as the Latin Mass, but I could see the handwriting on the wall. Sooner or later, the demand for 35mm photographic-processing equipment would dry up.

I feared I was hitching my financial future to a dinosaur industry. That anxiety spurred me to shop Arkay to potential buyers. Because I could show a healthy annual cash flow, I landed a multimillion-dollar offer to buy us out. From my vantage point on the field, this unexpected purchase bid was looking more and more like a Hail Mary pass into the end zone just before the play clock expired.

"C'mon, Richard, we have to take this offer. We'd be crazy to pass this up," I said in my office.

"There's no @#$% way I'm selling out for a few million bucks," he thundered.

There you have it: we were at loggerheads, and that's why I needed to go for a long jog that Sunday afternoon. A zillion thoughts danced around my head as I pumped my arms along Lake Drive: Was there a way I could convince Richard to sell the business? Or should I rely on the wisdom of my partner, who had twenty-five years of corporate experience on his résumé, and stay the course?

Running south along Lake Michigan took me into the posh neighborhoods of Whitefish Bay and Shorewood. I glanced up at the gabled Victorian mansions and red-bricked Tudor manors set back from the street with long sweeping driveways. This was Millionaire's Row in Milwaukee, the environs where the captains of industry and the blue-blood country club set lived life large in their exclusive digs.

Powerful CEOs from companies such as Miller Brewing, Allen-Bradley, Briggs & Stratton, and Joseph Schlitz Brewing lived here, I reminded myself as my feet pounded the wet pavement. These top executives oversaw large companies with a board of directors who kept them on the right track—sounding boards that could offer them an outside perspective to the problems and issues they were confronting at that very moment.

A board of directors…experienced executives to bounce ideas off…wait—didn't I need a sounding board at the most pivotal time in my young business career? Wasn't I in desperate need of someone to talk to—a wise mind who would give me a fresh look and add level-headed advice for the challenge I was facing?

I certainly needed someone that I could pour out my heart to. I had been running through life like I was jogging along Lake Drive— all alone. I needed someone who would come alongside and listen to me, let me ask questions, and give me wise counsel.

> *I needed someone who would come alongside and listen to me, let me ask questions, and give me wise counsel.*

I was about halfway through my eighteen-mile run, inside the City of Milwaukee proper, when I saw the street where my cousin Bob Sweeney lived. I had known Bobby since I ran around in diapers, but I really got to know him back in high school when he hired me to paint houses with him. Three years my senior, Bob not only taught me how to properly paint trim and siding, but he also planted the idea for me to start my own home-painting business during my senior year of high school.

I hadn't seen Bob much in the last decade because he had moved out to Denver to get into real estate development. In the last year, though, he had moved back to Milwaukee when Faison Real Estate hired him to oversee the construction of a thirty-seven-story office building called 100 East Wisconsin. Only the forty-two-story First Wisconsin Center—the state's tallest skyscraper and now called the U.S. Bank Center—topped what Bob was working on.

Maybe my cousin could give me some clarity, I thought. I ran up to his well-appointed house and knocked on the front door. I was sopping wet from the light rain and cold to the bone.

"Hey, look what the dog brought in," Bob grinned. "You want a glass of water or something?"

"I'd love to stay, Bob, but I have another nine miles." I continued to jog in place to stay warm.

"You okay?" A look of concern came over Bob's face. Perhaps he could see the black cloud following me at five paces.

I stopped jogging in place. "Do you mind if I drop by after work tomorrow? I need to talk to you about something."

"Absolutely, Joseph. Come by my office around 5:30. I'll be there."

I ran home like my feet weren't touching the ground. I now had someone to talk to—someone who would have my best interests at heart.

A Sounding Board

The following evening at half past five, I stepped into Bob's office in downtown Milwaukee. We started out with small talk about our families, and Bobby filled me with the latest about his wife, Joan, and their five-year-old daughter, Erin.

Then Bobby met my gaze. "What's on your mind?" he asked.

"You see, Bobby, it's like this..." For the next hour, I laid out the crazy mess at Arkay—the multimillion-dollar tender, the obstinate partner, and the stalemate between us.

He occasionally stopped me to ask questions, but along the way Bob gave me free rein to lay out the scenario. We kept talking right through dinner time, past seven o'clock, past eight, and then nine. Then he held up his hand.

"Joseph, I've got something here. Why don't just go to your partner and say, 'Richard, I think you'd agree that you're not a great operator, but you've been a top financier for this company. Why don't you find investors to buy me out so you can keep your half of the company? That way, if your pollution-control device sweeps the industry, you'll be well-poised to reap the benefits.' "

I couldn't believe I hadn't thought of that option. My mind was fixated on investors buying us *both* out at the same time.

"If Richard could raise half of the total offer to buy out your 50 percent stake, would you take the money?" Bob asked.

"Hell, yes," I said, the enthusiasm rising in my voice. Buying me out also meant that any new partner wouldn't do the same kind of due diligence on Arkay as an outside company would when buying 100 percent of the company. My partner knew of the existing challenges that Arkay was facing; he just had a different opinion of the sales potential of the pollution-control devices.

Bob and I batted around this dilemma until 10:30 that evening, with every passing minute giving me greater vision on what to do. He showed me a different option, a new way of looking at things.

The next day, I approached Richard Johnson and delivered my rehearsed spiel. To make a long and complex story short, Richard found someone to buy my 50 percent interest in Arkay, and several months later I received a seven-figure check. A goal I had given myself back at Notre Dame—to bank a million dollars by the age of thirty—had surprisingly and wonderfully come to fruition, all because I listened to some great advice from someone watching my back.

Let me tell you how incredibly valuable Bob's advice proved to be to me and my family. After relinquishing my 50 percent interest in Arkay, Richard asked me to stay on, which I agreed to do with a reluctant heart. Mentally, I had checked out the moment that unimaginable check was thrust into my hands, but out of a sense of loyalty, I agreed to stay on during a time of transition.

Meanwhile, Richard poured even more resources into his pollution-control device while I tried to keep the sales and marketing side in high gear to fund his R&D efforts. After six months, though, my enthusiasm for the job had ebbed like low tide at the seashore. I had no incentive to stay on. No upside. I was just another employee, and expendable at that.

"You know what, Richard? You're a nice guy, and I've enjoyed my time here, but the fact of the matter is that I'm not a very good employee. I need to move on."

I resigned my position and walked away.

Two years later, Arkay folded when the flow of red ink could no longer be stemmed. The bank forced Johnson and his backers to close the doors and sell off the assets. Arkay was worth pennies on the dollar, and Richard walked away with zilch. He bet everything on the pollution-control system, and it didn't pan out.

The Value of a Wingman

You may be reading this and saying, *Shoot, Sweeney, you were smart to get out when you did.* Or you might be thinking I was lucky enough to win the Irish Sweepstakes.

The truth is that I wasn't smart at all. I had a hunch that the future didn't look bright and that I needed an exit strategy. But it was only with the help of a wingman that I was able to see the path ahead.

A wingman? What's that?

The term is military in origin. According to the U.S. Air Force, a pair of fighter jets always flies in formation with a lead aircraft while the other jet flies just off the right wing and slightly behind the lead pilot. This second pilot is called the "wingman" and is given the charge to watch the lead pilot's back.

In relational terms, a wingman is someone who'll fly by your side, prepared to watch your flank and see things that you don't see. A wingman is a sounding board, a strong listener who's available at any time to dialogue with you about what's happening in your life and what you're feeling.

A good wingman helps you avoid disasters, gives you vision to see matters with greater clarity, urges you to get out of your comfort zone, and stretches you in ways you never thought possible. He's not a self-centered type who has his radio always tuned to WIFM—What's in It For Me.

After I met with Bobby Sweeney that evening, I realized that I needed a wingman in my life. Many men have very few close friends to whom they can reveal themselves. Others don't have *anyone* they can get deep with—not even

> *History is filled with those who understood the importance of surrounding themselves with confidants.*

their wives. When you develop a relationship with a wingman, you free yourself to open up and express yourself honestly.

History is filled with those who understood the importance of surrounding themselves with confidants. In our modern era of politics, President Franklin D. Roosevelt relied on Harry Hopkins as his closest advisor. The thirty-fourth president, Dwight D. Eisenhower, looked to his brother Milton as his wingman. John Kennedy was inseparable from his brother Robert. But Richard Nixon, the only U.S. president to resign in disgrace, is said to have had no one he was close to.

Having a wingman is akin to having an "accountability partner," a term used in religious circles as well as by the Young President's Organization and The Executive Committee groups. When you have an accountability partner, you give permission for him to raise tough questions like:

- "How is it *really* going with your wife?"
- "How are you spending your free time?"
- "What's happening in your business that's keeping you awake at night?"
- "What are you doing to make sure you're raising your kids with good moral values?"
- "Do you have a difficult decision to make at work? What is it in regards to?"

Hearing those questions puts you on the spot, and no one likes to be placed under pressure—unless the environment is safe and non-judgmental. Confidentiality is a key component of having a wing-man. Integrity and trust are paramount.

When prompted to talk about themselves, many guys, however, keep their feelings bottled up because they were raised by fathers who told them never to let their guards down, lest they reveal a weakness. Others make an unconscious choice to keep friendships at arm's length. Some can't bridge the emotional distance with acquaintances because they never heard their fathers say, "I love you."

On that Sunday afternoon with my cousin Bobby, I was willing to open up about how nervous I was—actually, I was scared to death—regarding my future and my family's future. (If you're wondering why I didn't reach out to my father, Raymond, he had succumbed to lung cancer five years earlier.) It wasn't easy to admit for the first time—and especially to a family member—that I didn't know what to do about my unsettled situation with Arkay.

I liked how Bob listened patiently and asked leading questions. He didn't tell me that I was in a real mess or that I shouldn't have let the situation get out of hand—observations I already knew. After drawing me out, he understood the predicament I was in and offered solid advice from a perspective that I had totally overlooked.

So how about you? Do you feel isolated and lonely? Do you ever feel like you're going crazy, like you're Chuck Noland (played by Tom Hanks) in the movie *Cast Away*, stranded on a deserted island without anyone to talk to except a volleyball named Wilson?

You need a wingman, someone who knows you and likes you—someone you can trust to keep your conversations confidential. A wingman will pick you up when you fall down. A wingman will get in the foxhole with you when times are tough. A wingman will tell you to keep your head down until the offensive fusillade is over. A wingman will encourage you to leap into the unknown when the time is right.

If you don't have a wingman—someone you can trust as a confidant—then you need to go through your contact list and ask yourself whom you could approach. I would call this close friend and explain that you read about this wingman idea in *Networking Is a Contact Sport* and would like to give it a try. Say that you need a sounding board, someone with whom you can discuss what's happening in your life and who can help you see things or situations that you may be overlooking. If you can find someone who'd be a good wingman for your personal life as well as professional, even better.

If you sense a buddy has the right amount of ego and a kindred spirit—and things jell between you in face-to-face meetings—I would formally ask him, "Would you like to be my wingman?" If he says yes—and I've yet to meet the guy who didn't respond positively to such a request—then I would make it a practice to meet for coffee or lunch at least once a week. Phone calls in between are certainly fine.

I usually call a couple of my wingmen every day, but everyone knows what works for them.

You'll notice that I just used the plural form "wingmen," and I definitely think you should have more than one person watching your back. I have a core group of four wingmen that I call my "Inner

Circle," but those four are part of a larger group of wingmen that I call my "Twelve Apostles." I tend to go overboard on these types of things, and I have subconsciously added more wingmen to my life over the years, and I haven't regretted doing so one little bit. Having multiple wingmen can give you a variety of perspectives, and it never hurts to hear more than one point of view. That's why I have wingmen from different walks of life.

Generally speaking, you don't want to tell others who your wingmen are. Although that is not a hard-and-fast rule—you'll see why later in the next section about Archbishop Timothy Dolan—one of the worst-kept secrets in Wisconsin is my close friendship with Craig Leipold. I usually call Craig or someone in my Inner Circle every day because I want to keep them up to date with what's happening in my life, how work is going, and any challenges that I may have.

As I just mentioned, my wingmen are a varied bunch. I have a lawyer, three financial people, several business owners, and a couple of enterprising entrepreneurs. I have a Catholic priest and two older brothers, Mike and Mark. For the last twenty-two years, ever since that night I made myself vulnerable to my cousin Bobby, I've relied on my wingmen to watch my flank and tell me when they see me flying off course or headed toward an ambush.

"Plans succeed through good counsel" says the proverb. Don't wait too long to find your first wingman. Ask him to fly alongside you as you go through life.

If you do so, he'll keep you headed on the right course—and help you through turbulent times.

Keep Your Wingmen Under Wraps

When Bishop Timothy Dolan of St. Louis was appointed to become the tenth Archbishop of Milwaukee in 2002, he walked into a hornet's nest.

The Milwaukee archdiocese was embroiled in a horrific sexual abuse scandal. Archbishop Dolan's predecessor, Archbishop Rembert Weakland, was forced to step down after a former Marquette University theology student was paid $450,000 to settle a sexual assault claim he made against the archbishop stemming from incidents

Whom would you call on if you needed help—or someone to talk to—in the middle of the night? I know that I could dial up my closest confidants, whom I've nicknamed the "Twelve Apostles," any time of the day or night. Eleven of them are pictured here.

two decades earlier. It turned out that the Weakland affair was just the tip of the iceberg: dozens of pedophile priests in the Milwaukee archdiocese had sexually abused innocent children for decades. The Catholic community of Milwaukee, of which I consider myself a part, was rocked to its core.

I watched closely as Archbishop Dolan worked diligently and quickly to restore the archdiocese's reputation. My network told me that he was doing good things, and he certainly endeared himself to every Packers fan at an outdoor Mass when—on the opening day of the NFL season—he delivered his homily while wearing a bright yellow foam "cheesehead" hat.

I was thinking I'd like to get to know the Archbishop when my son Conor, who was attending Marquette University in downtown Milwaukee, said he had become friends with the Archbishop's niece,

Claire Hoffmeyer. One evening, the two of them attended an arch-diocese dinner, where Conor met Archbishop Dolan. My son came away impressed and said I had to meet him.

"I'd love to ask him out for dinner," I told Conor. "How do I get in touch with him?"

"Call Father Jerry at the diocese office. He'll put you through."

Nothing like networking with your son.

Father Jerry did patch me through, and when I had the Archbishop on the line, I mentioned how he had met my son and wondered if I could invite him out for a get-to-know-you dinner with the rest of my family.

"Joe, I'd love to," replied the Archbishop, "but I've given up drink-ing and going out to dinner during Lent."

"What about after Easter?"

"Wonderful," said the Archbishop. "Just let me know when would be good for you."

We settled on a date in May, and I told Archbishop Dolan that I wanted to take him to Mo's Steakhouse, an upscale Italian restaurant in downtown Milwaukee.

"Let me ask you something," said the Archbishop a bit conspirato-rially. "Does Mo's Steakhouse serve Bombay Sapphire Gin?"

I knew the answer without hesitation. "Absolutely, Archbishop. This is a top-drawer restaurant in every way."

The Archbishop's inquiry set my networking wheels in motion. The Rev. Timothy Dolan was obviously a fan of Bombay Gin when he was off-duty, so to speak, so the next day I sent him a fifth of Bombay Sapphire Gin and a small bottle of olives since he also confided that he was a martini lover. Similar to what I did with Bob Costas, I in-cluded a handwritten note that said, *Archbishop, I can't wait to have dinner with you. Enjoy the Bombay Gin and olives when Lent is over. Yours truly, Joe.*

When I met the Archbishop at Mo's that night, the first thing he said was, "My goodness gracious, Joe, I loved the Bombay Gin."

Nothing like networking through a man's gullet.

Let me tell you something: within fifteen minutes, I knew this guy had more charisma and personality than any human being I'd ever met. He was the type of guy who had me in tears laughing and five minutes later, listening to one of his moving stories left me with a huge lump in my throat. We just really clicked that evening, especially after the roly-poly prelate joked that he had to be sedated before he would submit to being weighed during his annual physical.

Halfway through the dinner, and after the third glass of an excellent Italian wine, I felt I could be bold with him. "Do you have a wingman?" I asked.

The term caught the archbishop by surprise. "What do you mean by a...wingman?" he wondered.

For the next fifteen minutes, I walked him step-by-step through who a wingman was and what he did.

The Archbishop turned reflective. "That's interesting to hear you talk about this wingman idea. I'm relatively new to Milwaukee, and I've had more than a few people offer to be my sounding boards. But I've been pretty busy—"

Archbishop Dolan let that thought hang in the air. We both knew the Catholic priest sex scandal had dominated his agenda after he was appointed to clean up the mess left by his predecessor.

"So what you're telling me, Archbishop, is that you don't have any wingmen."

The Archbishop nodded his head.

"Did you have any wingmen in St. Louis?"

"As you define wingmen, yes, I had four people that I could confide in and who looked out for me."

"Good, because you need wingmen here in Milwaukee. If you don't have anyone looking out for you in this town, you won't survive."

The Archbishop listened, and at the end of dinner, he pulled me aside. "Okay, Joe, you can be my wingman," he said. "You officially start today."

I thanked the Archbishop for his confidence in me, and I found him to be a gift from heaven. From that evening at Mo's restaurant, he let me ask him questions, enjoyed the back-and-forth, and allowed me to be another set of eyes and ears for him in the community.

Not long after we began our wingman relationship, I was standing around the lobby of the Milwaukee Athletic Club, where I like to work out during the noon hour, chatting up several friends and

Look—it's a bird, it's a plane.. no, it's a wingman! Here I surprise Archbishop Timothy Dolan with a special wingman T-shirt at a dinner given in his honor.

acquaintances. I heard someone walk in and turned to see a beaming Archbishop Dolan walking in my direction.

"Hey, there's my wingman!" he joked to the half-full lobby.

I pasted a fake smile to my face and approached the Archbishop. I grabbed his arm, stuck my fingernails gently into his flesh, and eased him out of earshot from the others standing the lobby.

"Don't you ever say that out loud," I growled.

"Say what?" The Archbishop had a look that said, *What have I done?*

"You know all the controversy surrounding the Catholic Church in this community. If people know I'm your wingman, they won't be straight with me. Part of my job is to get you recon. If I ask people, 'What's going on with the archdiocese?' or 'What's happening out there?', people won't give me the straight story if they know that I'm Dolan's wingman."

The Archbishop nodded his head in agreement. I think I did a pretty good job for him during his seven years as Archbishop of Milwaukee, but that's because our wingman relationship was kept between us, the way it should be.

As you bring wingmen into the fold, don't broadcast their identities to the world. You want them to pick up scuttlebutt, innuendo, and rumors that you could never learn on your own. They can report what they've heard on the street, which will help you become a better leader and perhaps make better business decisions. They need to be your eyes and ears in the community, just like I was for Archbishop Dolan.

In 2009, the Vatican kicked the Archbishop upstairs when he was appointed Archbishop of New York—the most visible job in the Catholic Church in America. My sources say that the appointment could soon bring the bright red Cardinal's hat to the young archbishop, who just turned sixty. And who knows what God has planned for Cardinal Dolan—the first American pontiff some day?

If that ever happens, just think about my networking possibilities inside the Vatican!

A TIME FOR TRANSPARENCY

For many men, having a wingman conjures up fears of having to tell all their secrets and setbacks about themselves—topics they don't want anyone else to know.

I don't doubt that it's extremely humbling to talk about how out-of-control credit card debt is gobbling up your paycheck like a rogue Pac-Man, or how you've missed two mortgage payments and the ninety-day foreclosure clock is ticking louder with each day. You may find it difficult to express your feelings about a boss who keeps threatening you with your job.

No one should make you share something you don't want to share, and I'm not here to say that you have to share *everything* in your life. But if you bring wingmen into your life, take steps toward transparency. Guys willing to open up about their feelings and struggles will often find a fellow traveler casting a listening ear—and may provide you with advice or observations that point you in the right direction.

Be willing to open up about what's important in life, just like I did with my cousin Bobby.

A Wingman and Success

When I speak on the topic of wingmen, I like to share three charts for success in life. The first one looks like this:

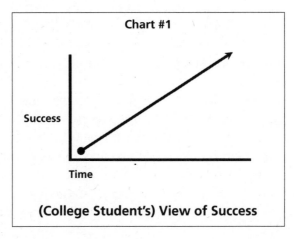

(College Student's) View of Success

This is how most people—especially college graduates—look at success: when you put in the time, success stays on a steady uphill trajectory. Of course, this is the theory, but the reality is often far different. More often than not, you move two steps up and fall down a notch. Success does not always rise in a clear-cut, 45-degree trajectory with the passage of time.

Then I show a second chart, which looks like this:

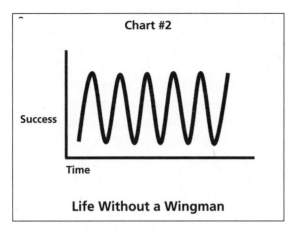

I explain that this is what life often looks like without wingmen by your side. The ups and downs are more pronounced because you're bound to make mistakes in judgment, mainly from a lack of experience and not having someone look over your shoulder.

My final chart shows what happens when you do have wingmen in your life. Success is a similar roller-coaster ride, but the peaks and valleys are not as pronounced because you have wingmen in your corner. Wingmen offer excellent advice, give you clarity, and either validate or pooh-pooh your plan or vision.

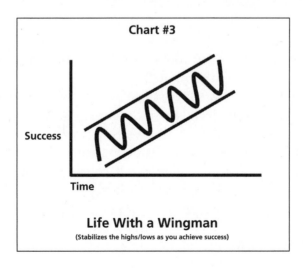

Wingmen help you realize that you are not alone. They help you avoid disasters. They help you figure out where you are at this moment and where you want to go tomorrow and beyond. Wingmen can help you reinvent yourself, your company, and even your relationships with others.

After meeting with my cousin Bobby back in 1988, I don't see how you *cannot* have friends you can trust watching out for your back. You need wingmen who will ask the right questions.

As I've said, I like to ask interesting, thought-provoking questions, especially when I'm chatting with people I've been introduced to in social settings. Sometimes, though, I've had guys tell me point-blank, "Shoot, Sweeney, you're nosy."

"Hey, I just want to get to know you better," I reply, and I mean that.

Most of the time, though, guys *love* to hear my questions, and before they know it, they're opening up a fire hydrant. They spill forth everything in their lives—work, marriage, kids, you name it. Before they catch their breath, I'm hearing details about the back-stabbing vice president, how the company stock is being manipulated, or which teen is threatening to run away—stuff that I wouldn't normally be privy to in a nice-to-meet-you-what's-your-line-of-work conversation.

After I've heard one hair-raising story after another, I'll say, "I bet you don't have a board of directors."

"How did you know that?"

"Because you're telling me way too much information."

An interesting thing often happens when I venture that opinion. The talkative executive invariably says, "I'm thinking of doing a board. Would you like to be on it?"

For the last twenty years, I've sat on twenty-three different boards of directors, including several private companies and a few nonprofits. Currently, I sit on seven boards, which is plenty, but I make room in my schedule because I see the value in them.

Do you need a board of directors? If you've been flying solo all your life, then you need wingmen to protect you from the flak that's sure to come. Look at wingmen as your personal board of directors—people who aren't afraid to let you know that you're flying off course or into a raging hurricane.

WHAT HAVING A WINGMAN HAS MEANT TO ME

by Ed Shanley, President of Drillmaster Tool Corp.

Drillmaster Tool—DMT—is a small company, with just twenty-five employees, that designs and builds custom machine equipment for engine manufacturers. Our end-users include Ford Motor Co., Mercury Marine outboard engines, Harley-Davidson motorcycles, John Deere tractors, and Briggs & Stratton lawn mowers. We like to think that Drillmaster Tool has been on the forefront of machine and tooling technology since 1974.

Several years ago, I was going through a sticky time buying out my partner. Unbeknownst to me, this partner approached several of our employees and negotiated their futures with the company, saying he was speaking on my behalf. I unexpectedly found this out after I called these employees into my office to discuss how we would move forward following the restructuring of the company. One said, "Well, that's not what the other guy said you were going to offer."

I felt that I was being undermined at a critical time in our negotiations, and that made me angry. But I kept my displeasure in check because Joe Sweeney, who was a friend of mine, told me two years earlier that I would one day have problems with my partner. He counseled me to be careful, and it turned out he was right.

All along, Joe was someone I could bounce ideas off, a wingman who provided the clarity I was looking for. I found his advice extremely helpful because he had gone through a similar trying period with a partner at Arkay.

Joe reminded me to stay calm no matter what happened. When feelings of trust evaporated between me and my partner, his words of advice were, "If you get mad, that's only going to cost you money. Think long term. Stay calm."

Joe's insights stopped me from saying something I would regret later, and I successfully completed the buyout of my partner. Joe is now part of my top-notch board of directors, and having him as my wingman made all the difference.

Let me put things on a more personal level, which is something I might do if we were introduced to each other at a business mixer. If floodwaters were rising in your neighborhood and you needed someone to help sandbag the perimeter of your property so that you could save your home, whom would you call?

Do you have anyone besides a family member that you're close to?

Here's another probing question: If, God forbid, you received a phone call at 11:30 P.M. from a policeman saying that your daughter's car was hit by a drunk driver and she's fighting for her life at the hospital, whom would you call? Who would get out of bed in the middle of the night to be there for you and your family?

> *Look at wingmen as your personal board of directors—people who aren't afraid to let you know that you're flying off course or into a raging hurricane.*

I know whom I would phone—someone in my Inner Circle like Craig Leipold or my older brother Mark. If they weren't available, I know that I could call one of my Twelve Apostles. Any one of them would rush down to the hospital at any hour to wrap an arm around my shoulder and give Tami a warm, embracing hug. They would be there in a heartbeat to hold our hands and shed a tear.

Back in 1854, the great American writer and philosopher Henry David Thoreau wrote that "the mass of men lead lives of quiet desperation."

His words ring true today, which is why I can't envision what life would be like without my wingmen looking out for me.

Ask someone to be your wingman today.

You won't regret it.

Who's Your Wingman?

Whom would you trust to bring into your confidence as a wingman?

Many captains of industry had wingmen. Thomas Jefferson, Henry Ford, and Harvey Firestone had confidants they could trust as sounding boards. Wingmen give you clarity on your dreams, your passions, your successes, your money, and what should be the most important aspect of life—your family.

Some tips for relating to your wingmen:

1. Give them permission to keep you accountable in these areas.
2. Get comfortable with being vulnerable and get used to speaking candidly with your wingmen.
3. Keep in mind that it takes time to build relationships—and trust. For the first month or two, expect things to be a little stilted until you get to know each other better.
4. Let them ask the "What if?" questions for every possible situation.
5. Follow the code of the locker room: *What's said here stays here.*
6. Never lie to your wingmen. There should be no games, no BS. Just straight talk with full disclosure on all issues.
7. Expect to become closer with your wingman (or wingmen). You'll often find that when you get real with a wingman, he feels emboldened to get real with you.
8. You should try to meet with your wingmen periodically, like four or five times a year. If you're a constant connector like I am, it's okay to touch base every day with a couple of wingmen. That's what I feel comfortable doing.
9. Just because a friend agrees to watch your back, though, that doesn't mean he has a full-time job of looking after you. Yes, regular contact is key, but developing a co-dependency relationship can be more harmful than *not* having a wingman.
10. When you feel a bond with your wingman, give him permission to ask the tough questions that everyone is thinking about but is reluctant to ask.

11. You don't have to be embarrassed about your dark sides or insecurities with your wingmen. They are present in your life to help you deal with your demons and tough situations.
12. Be sure to thank your wingmen for their emotional investment in you. While being in a wingman relationship is an enriching experience, it does take time and mental effort for both parties.
13. Lastly, remember the Wingman Credo, written by Rob "Waldo" Waldman, a former F-16 pilot and author of *Never Fly Solo*:

The Wingman Credo

I am your wingman
You can count on me
Integrity, service, and courage are at the core of all I do
Committed to excellence, accountable for results, and trustworthy
Mission ready and focused, I am always prepared
I will lend you my wings in the heat of battle
Leader. Confidant. Partner.
I will never leave you behind
And I will never let you fly solo.[7]

# Networking
from Scratch

NOW THAT YOU'RE FAMILIAR with the 5/10/15 program, have a handle on personality types, are ready to add wingmen to your life, and see networking as a place to give—not get—you may be thinking: *Joe, where do I start? How do I build my own networking network?*

I have a couple of quick answers:

1. You start wherever you are at this moment. The "past is prologue," as Shakespeare penned in his play *The Tempest*, meaning that it's up to you to decide what the future will bring. If you continue with a lackadaisical I-can-always-network-next-week attitude, you might miss getting connected with five, six, or even a dozen people between now and the weekend.

Networking, like shaving, is something you have to do every day. Never underestimate the power of networking; your success is directly proportional to the size of your social circle, be it at work or at play. Don't forget that you never know from whom or where the key contacts in life will come, including your next mentor.

2. You build your network by actively pursuing communication with others, by putting yourself in business and social situations that foster introductions, and by looking for ways you can serve others —or at least make their journeys through life go smoother.

It's been said that there's a time and a place for networking, but I've gone through life believing that there's no time like the present, a proverb that is certainly appropriate with regard to networking.

For better or worse, I have never differentiated my business and personal life. While we're all pressed to get everything done, there's always enough time to do the most important things, and that includes looking for ways to connect with others. Procrastinate, and you might discover that the difference between networking and not working really *is* a single letter.

As for the *places* to start networking, the opportunities are all around you, especially in these areas of your life:

- You can network where you work.
- You can network where you live.
- You can network where you exercise (or play a sport).
- You can network where you socialize (but I'm not suggesting you hang out in bars).
- You can network where you worship (if you belong to a faith community).

In this chapter, I'll take a closer look at how you can network from scratch with each of these areas of your life.

Where You Work

Since networking is the art of building alliances, it behooves you to develop relationships with your hallway neighbors. Since much of your interaction with other employees happens during the course of eight-to-five workdays—the task force projects, the long meetings that bring various departments together, and the face-to-face exchanges with your superiors—networking at work should be an easy call.

Throughout my twenty-five years in business, I've always made it a point to befriend everyone I come into contact with inside my place of work. That's just good, commonsense networking, especially for someone young in his or her career. Remember this: the guy or gal in the next cubicle over may become your boss some day.

I understand that there's a hierarchy in business settings, which means an entry-level employee fresh out of college can't expect to become a BFF with the corporate CEO. (But if you're a scratch golfer, you just might find yourself being asked by the Head Honcho if you're "available" to partner him at a corporate golfing event.)

That's why I recommend swimming in your pond and developing relationships with your peers, the managers a rung above you, and key people outside your department. One way to get to know others is by volunteering for your company's "birthday committee," if it has one. Raise your hand and volunteer to help out with a food drive or community-outreach event that needs bodies.

> *Remember this: the guy or gal in the next cubicle over may become your boss some day.*

But the biggest thing you can do on a day-to-day basis is to eat lunch with others. Being willing to break bread with your colleagues will strike up all sorts of interesting conversations that could prove fruitful down the road. You'll learn who they are, and they will get to know who you are. I'm not saying that you have to hopscotch from table to table inside the employee lunchroom, but eating lunch alone in your cubicle or outside on a park bench—or with the same clutch of people each day—is counterproductive to good networking. A noontime workout in the company fitness center is another way to connect.

There's another compelling reason why you should want to network and get to know others at your place of work—it might save your job. Let's face it: we're headlong into an era when companies are shedding employees like Autumn Blaze Maple trees that scatter a parade of red, yellow, and gold leaves every October. Corporate decision-makers often have some leeway in making the hard choices about who stays and who goes, and I would imagine that many of these nightmarish decisions are highly subjective. That said, the decision on who gets the pink slip could rest on how well you're liked or intangibles like your attitude, your effort, and your ability to get along with co-workers.

Human nature being what it is, I would hazard a guess that managers and department heads—when given a choice—will choose those whom they know and have a relationship with over employees who failed to engage them.

Where You Live

When I was a graduate student at Notre Dame, Tami and I talked a great deal about where we wanted to live once I earned my MBA. Since we were both born and raised in Madison and had grown up in large families (I had eight brothers and one sister and Tami had five younger sisters), all roads pointed to Wisconsin. We used to laugh that we had a thousand relatives waiting for us back home, but the fact of the matter was we viewed our extended families as solid anchors in our lives.

With "Wisconsin or Bust" as our objective, I started working on finding my first job a year before the Notre Dame Business School handed me my MBA degree. The motivation to have a good job lined up was certainly there: Tami had given birth to Kyle and conceived Conor during our two short years in South Bend—which only goes to show you what Notre Dame grad students did for amusement. I also had $50,000 in student loans to contend with, not to mention maternity bills since we didn't have health insurance.

To spur myself along, I gave myself the goal of becoming the owner of a privately held manufacturing company, preferably in Wisconsin or a bordering state. The biggest problem, however, was my profound lack of money. To get around that obstacle, I came up with an unconventional idea: find a business owner in his sixties who was phasing into retirement but wanted to bring in a young guy with a lot of energy to eventually take over the company.

But how would I locate such a person? That owner would be a needle in the haystack, to be sure, especially in those pre-personal computer and pre-Google days of 1983. As far as I knew, there was only one way to find a business owner matching my parameters, and that was to lock myself in the Notre Dame library and thumb through business directories, writing down each company address by hand on 3x5 index cards. I stayed on that mission like a bulldog on a bone until I compiled a massive list of thirteen hundred target companies between Chicago and Minneapolis.

I hired a consultant to mail out thirteen hundred letters of inquiry over the next year, whereby I offered to learn the business from the owner and then trade any sweat equity and money I could beg, borrow, or steal to purchase the company at some later date.

Here is an excerpt from a sample letter sent out by my consultant:

January 24, 1984

Ms. Kristine K. Krier
Alexander Grant & Co.
2 East Gilman Street
Madison, WI 53708

Dear Ms. Krier:

I represent Joe Sweeney, who is interested in structuring a unique opportunity in small business. Joe is a talented and ambitious young man. He comes from an entrepreneurial family background with his father and all eight of his brothers owning their business or professional practice. Needless to say, Joe is very familiar with the challenges, demands, and rewards of small business ownership.

As a May 1984 candidate for MBA from the University of Notre Dame, Joe is taking a non-traditional approach to his career. As his family background and training would indicate, he is primarily interested in owning a business. However, Joe recognizes the risks and demands that accompany owning any business. While he is by no means risk averse, he believes there is an approach to business ownership that would fully prepare him while providing benefits to current management.

On behalf of my client, I am contacting various business professionals who work with and advise business owners. You may currently be working with a business owner who has expressed an interest in eventually getting out of business in five to seven years. One option the owner might consider is an arrangement in which he is systematically bought out over a period of time by a successor that he personally selects and trains to assume his responsibilities. This approach allows the business owner to remain active in the business until his desired retirement age. At the same time, he is training his successor <u>and</u> being bought out based upon a fair, pre-determined schedule and value. When properly negotiated and practiced, this type of relationship creates a "win-win" situation for all parties. This is the type of relationship my client is interested in developing. For the right business owner, this relationship could prove to be the ideal way to receive full value for his business while eliminating the emotional/financial stress that frequently accompanies the outright sale of the business.

The consultant ended the letter by talking about me and my character in glowing terms that would have made my mother blush, but the correspondence certainly painted an interesting proposition. I received around eighty responses, and one of them led to my first opportunity at Pipkorn Steel, a steel fabrication firm in Waukesha, Wisconsin, and about fifteen miles west of Milwaukee.

In the late spring of 1984, our young family of three packed up our belongings in South Bend, settled into a two-bedroom apartment in Waukesha, and looked for the on-ramp to the Yellow Brick Road. While our episodes of "Married with Children" were rich and rewarding, I was finding Milwaukee a tough town to break into. Like most Midwest industrial cities, I encountered a lot of old wealth and blue blood, and I caught the vibe that those in respected positions didn't look favorably on hustling entrepreneurs. To these moneyed and long-standing aristocrats, I was an Irish-Catholic mongrel who didn't know his place yet. A street rat from the wrong side of the tracks.

Their unspoken questions floated in the air: *Where did you come from and where did you get your money?*

I did my best to ignore their withering looks and asked myself a more important question: *So how can I get connected with the community?* Of course, there are the usual avenues: the church, the country club, and community groups. Each had its pluses and minuses. As a Catholic, though, I wouldn't naturally run into Protestants or non-churchgoers on Sundays. I couldn't afford a country club, and community groups proved to be a hit-and-miss venture. Tami and I joined the Newcomer's Club, but it soon became evident that we were *trying* to make friends. As any fifth-grader can tell you, when you *try* to befriend someone, it isn't going to happen.

After six months of apartment living in Waukesha, we moved into our first house, which was located in the Milwaukee suburb of Fox Point north of downtown. Tami had just delivered our *third* baby in four years, and for all I know, we must have looked like Okie migrants from the Dust Bowl as our U-Haul rolled into the neighborhood.

Once again, we struggled to make friends. Fox Point was one of those village towns that didn't believe in sidewalks, which may be a selling point with some people, but the lack of sidewalks certainly made it more difficult to connect with your neighbors. People drove their cars into their garages, and down went the garage door. Six months after we moved to Fox Point, I still felt like I didn't know anybody.

Sure, I got along with the guys at work, but we were a small business with just forty or fifty employees. Unable to branch out, I felt like I was withering on the vine. I certainly didn't feel connected with Milwaukee at all.

In the summer of 1987, Kyle, our oldest, had just turned four years old, and Conor was just a year younger. On Saturday afternoons, I'd take them to a neighborhood park and try to teach them how to shoot a basketball. I *loved* basketball, and it was my sport in high school. I grew up playing pickup games in my parents' driveway until my hands—chapped from the cold—would split and bleed. I couldn't get enough of playing hoops, and I even went on to play college ball at St. Mary's University in Winona, Minnesota.

I continued playing basketball after college, and at Notre Dame, I loved the pickup games at The Rock—the Knute Rockne student athletic center where I'd burst into Coach Ara Parseghian's office almost twenty years earlier. After moving to Fox Point, I would go to the nearby park after work to pump jump shot after jump shot as a way to relieve the pressures of the workplace. You could call me a "shoot-aholic." I loved hearing the swish as the basketball passed cleanly through the rim.

Naturally, I wanted to give my boys the same thrill. When I took them to the park, though, I found that heaving a "bitty ball" toward a ten-foot high basket was simply beyond their capabilities. Then an idea began to form in my mind: what if Kyle and Conor could learn the proper way to shoot on a basket more their size?

By that time, I was part-owner of Arkay, the company that manufactured photographic-processing equipment. Some of the items we manufactured were four-, six-, eight-, and ten-foot-high camera stands for studio work—what we called monopods. What if I could mount a basketball rim and backboard on those industrial camera stands?

Late one afternoon, I grabbed one of the shop engineers at closing time and described my idea. He nodded, said my idea sounded feasible, and within a month, I drove home in a company van and unloaded four basketball standards in the driveway. Tami came out of the house with Kelly on her hip and said, "What has he done now?"

That's what the neighbors must have wondered when they drove past our house and gaped at four basketball standards—each with a different height—perched around the perimeter of our driveway. I went top drawer the whole way: each basketball standard came with a glass backboard. Their mouths must have really dropped when they saw me wheel out two basketball racks filled with twenty-four leather basketball balls. Tami thought I had gone bonkers.

After dinner, I'd take the boys outside and teach them the fundamentals of shooting, using the four-foot basketball standard. Then something interesting happened: three boys who lived across the street—Ben, Ari, and Danny, the sons of Rabbi Ron and Judy Shapiro—asked if they could shoot baskets with us. Since I had always fancied myself as a frustrated basketball coach, how could I refuse? I kept our shooting drills fun, and when we were done with making layups and practicing set shots, everyone got an ice-cold Coke.

In a way, I was reliving my childhood. Back in middle school and high school, there was always a mob at our house during basketball season—November to March—playing pickup games in our driveway. Without fail, Mom had popcorn and pop ready for us when we wanted a break from the action—or needed to warm up our freezing hands. Those carefree days of yesteryear inspired me to purchase a real Coke vending machine—one of those vintage models—and rig it up so the kids didn't have to put in a quarter to get a Coca-Cola. I figured Tami could handle the popcorn.

You can imagine how the Shapiro kids told everyone in the neighborhood about shooting baskets and getting free Cokes at the Sweeney house. Soon, I had twelve-year-old boys with squeaky voices knocking on my door, asking if I could come out and play. Before I knew what hit me, a couple of dozen kids in the neighborhood were dropping by on Wednesday nights. This wasn't a free-for-all, however. I organized various drills, let the older kids play half-court games, and kept things moving. When darkness hit, everyone rushed for the Coke machine for a free soft drink.

We had more than a few curious parents drop by, who naturally wanted to know what all the ruckus was about. Tami prepared light hors d'oeuvres and set out a couple of bottles of wine, and before you could say Stag's Leap, we were meeting doctors, dentists, lawyers, and business owners.

TAKE A ROOTING INTEREST

Looking for a sure-fire way to bond with someone you want to get to know better or show a customer you really care?

Go to his kid's ball game.

There's something about standing on the sidelines or sitting in the bleachers together that creates a shared moment between the two of you. I still haven't forgotten the time when a well-connected Milwaukee CEO, John Arlotta, and his wife, Bobbie, came to Conor's high school football game when the championship was on the line. That happened seven years ago, but every time I think of John, I remember how we cheered on the exploits of Conor together.

It was a great bonding experience.

In other words, we were finally networking in the community.

The numbers kept swelling until our last Wednesday night hoopalooza—just before Labor Day—when I counted sixty-five kids in my driveway. We went out with a bang that first summer when I networked with the Milwaukee Bucks' executive vice president, John Steinmiller, to have Randy Breuer, their towering seven-foot, three-inch center, drop by and visit my driveway that last Wednesday evening. My Lilliputian players thought Randy was a giant.

The following summer, my Wednesday night basketball clinic grew so large that I decided to organize a weeklong basketball camp, totally free of course. Sweeney's All-Star Basketball Camp was held every July at Cardinal Stritch College in Fox Point, and my old high school basketball coach, Joel Maturi (who at the time was the assistant athletic director at the University of Wisconsin–Madison)

EMPIRE PHOTOGRAPHY

When fifty, sixty, and seventy kids started showing up for my Wednesday night basketball clinics, I decided to organize a weeklong basketball camp at Cardinal Stritch College in Fox Point. The camp was free, but the young players had to ask people to sponsor them by seeking pledges to the Midwest Athletes Against Childhood Cancer.

agreed to use one of his valuable weeks of vacation to run the camp. The only thing I asked the kids to do was to knock on doors and appeal for pledges that would go toward one of Milwaukee's biggest charities—the Midwest Athletes Against Childhood Cancer, or the MACC Fund.

They were instructed to say something along these lines: "Ma'am, I'm going to this basketball camp to help kids with cancer. I'm going to shoot two hundred shots. How much will you sponsor me for each shot I make?" We raised $10,000 that first year, and by the time Sweeney's All-Star Basketball Camp ended in 1994, we were taking in nearly $20,000 a year for the MAAC Fund. In all, we raised $100,000 for a very worthy charity.

JOEL MATURI: THE ULTIMATE SELFLESS NETWORKER

If there is anyone who shaped my character more than my parents, it was my high school basketball coach, Joel Maturi.

What an amazing example of selfless humanity! For eight summers, Joel gave up one of his invaluable weeks of vacation to run Sweeney's All-Star Basketball Camp, and all he got in return were some pats on the back and my admiration for what he did. In my world of networking, Joel was a rock star, an example of the selfless giver that I took to heart. He was the associate athletic director at the University of Wisconsin during those summer basketball camp years, and he did so much behind the sports scene in Wisconsin that he was recognized as the Wisconsin Sports Person of the Year in 1993.

Joel has been the athletic director at the University of Minnesota since 2002, where it's said he engineered a complete transformation of Golden Gopher athletics. Nothing about my great friend Joel Maturi surprises me since he exemplifies that networking is a place you go to give, not to get.

The key networking point to consider here is that I took one of my passions—basketball—and used that to open up double-sided networking doors. Once my Wednesday night basketball clinics started rolling, I found out that I now had a network I could tap into if someone asked me for the name of a good attorney, or an accountant, or a dentist. I expanded my network by hundreds of people, felt connected to the community, and made important contacts for the future because I did something I really enjoyed—teaching kids how to play basketball.

What's your passion? What do you like to do when you're not working? You can turn that passion into a great way to network if you want. I don't care if you're a championship Scrabble player, log-rolling champ, pie-baking king or queen, workout nut, or scratch golfer. You can take that passion and meet people with it.

Even better is if you can marry your passion with showing an interest in someone else's kids. Show me a Little League coach, and I'll show you someone who has a golden networking opportunity in front of him. Show me a Boy Scout or Girl Scout leader, and I'll show you someone that other parents *want* to get to know.

I followed my passion—playing basketball—and stumbled into one of my greatest networking experiences. You can do the same by identifying what energizes you.

GOT A MOVE IN YOUR FUTURE?

If there's one constant in the American character, it's our penchant for mobility. Sixty percent of us will move to a new community at least once in our adult lives, according to a recent Pew Social & Demographic Trends survey. Asked why they live where they do, movers often cite the pull of financial opportunity.[8] "Generally speaking, people move based on the economy," said Jed Smith, Ph.D., a research director for the National Association of Realtors, noting that the economy has been mediocre to bad in the last two years.[9]

Even if we stay in the same city, we still move around a lot. Around 11 percent of Americans change their residences each year, according to the U.S. Census Bureau, a figure that, surprisingly, was as high as 20 percent in the mid-1960s. Even though the percentage of folks changing residences has fallen off, that's still a significant number of Americans who move each year, whether it's around the block or to another state. Whenever you make a move, even if across town, you're practically starting over in building up a network, especially if you've changed jobs recently or been laid off.

Instead of looking at moving as starting all over or a demoralizing chapter in your life, remind yourself that you have a chance to reinvent yourself. Nobody knows you, right? Then you can be exactly who you want to be—or always wanted to be.

There's something moving about that opportunity.

Where You Exercise, Socialize, and Worship

I've lumped these three bullet points together because when it comes right down to it, it really doesn't matter *where* you interact with people you don't know but share a common interest with. What matters is *how* you take the initiative to approach others, how you introduce yourself, how you listen carefully to discover shared interests or goals, and how you use your shared interests or shared values as the basis for sustaining a new relationship.

Where do you like to spend your free time? Answer that question, and you'll discover your passion. If fitness and keeping the pounds off are important to you, then you're probably among the 30 million Americans who belong to some sort of health club.

You don't have to belong to a fitness club or gym to exercise, of course. Other options are available, such as working out at your place of employment or around the home. Then again, working out at a corporate fitness center might be a two-for-one networking opportunity: you keep fit *and* meet your work colleagues.

Exercise and networking go together like asking a friend to go on a power walk with you. I've seen three or four women take their morning or lunch break walking around downtown Milwaukee. You can also play in a tennis league, join a bicycling club, participate in yoga classes—the list is endless.

As for the social side, I think I showed how I view social occasions as a grand opportunity to network, like at the Christopher Doerr party. No matter the setting—from a lavish party to a simple stand-up business mixer, I've taken the initiative to approach others, introduce myself, and seek a bit of information that could reveal a common thread that we share. Since I'm a people person, it doesn't take any effort for me to move toward people, and with practice and an attitude of discovering shared interests and goals, you should be looking forward to casually networking at a social event as much as I do.

Which brings us to that other pillar of society—the church. The built-in advantage is that you're networking with people who hold the same values as you, or members of the same body, as the Apostle Paul described it. Every church member has unique talents and insights, and sharing these gifts with each other as a unified body strengthens the feeling of community.

NETWORKING AND LOVE

I can't tell you the number of people who've said, "Joe, you're a great networker. Can you find me a nice girl?" Or, "Joe, you know everybody in town. Can you find me a nice guy?"

You may be smirking, but this is a serious topic. I can tell by the earnestness of each request. When you're alone in life, finding the right person and building a future together is *very* important. That's why online social networking sites are runaway hits with young people today—there's an incredible desire for connection with others.

I remember the time a young woman asked me for help. Michelle was into triathlons and keeping her body in peak physical shape. "So where are you looking for guys?" I asked.

"Oh, I don't know," she replied nonchalantly. "Mostly in bars, I guess."

"But during the day, you spend a lot of your free time training for mini-triathlons."

"That's right," Michelle said.

"Well, what are you doing looking for a guy in a bar? Guys who do triathlons don't hang out in bars at night."

Networking for love follows the same path as networking from scratch: you begin by asking yourself what your passions are, and once you do that, you can begin to search the right places for people you can connect with. If tailgating on Saturday or Sunday afternoon football games is your thing, then celebrate the big game by asking your friends to tell *their* friends to join you in the parking lot before the opening kickoff. If tennis is your passion, then hang out at tennis clubs and sign up for tennis leagues and tournaments. If wearing black leather and riding Harleys is your favorite weekend pursuit, then find a motorcycle club in your city. If your religious faith is the most important thing to you, then join the worship team or sign up for a Bible study targeted for your age group.

I think a big problem with love today is what Johnny Lee sang about in the 1980s—that people are looking for love in all the wrong places.

"Church work and church attendance mean the cultivation of the habit of feeling responsibility for others," said Theodore Roosevelt, the twenty-sixth president of the United States. Churches always have various ministries that you can join to help others since faith without works is dead, as the Good Book says in James 2:20. When you do things for others, "unto the least of these," you do them for a greater cause.

If you are a part of a faith community, I would get plugged in to your local church or place of worship. That's something that Tami and I, as lifelong Catholics, have always thought was important, and our lives have been immeasurably blessed by others who've reached out to us, and we've blessed others by reaching out to them. When it comes to networking with friends and folks you meet at church, this really is a place where you go to give, not get.

Time to Go for It

So what do you really like to do? Work out in a gym? Sing in the church choir? Belong to a book club?

When you're networking from scratch, you have to take the things you enjoy and look for ways you can plug yourself into those activities so that you can meet others and begin to build your network. This is the time to look out, not in.

This is also the time to think about big, wild, audacious goals—and how networking will get you there. I'll share my insights and describe how I networked to get Green Bay Packer quarterback Brett Favre some help when it looked like he was going to lose everything.

Networking from Scratch

- **What are you passionate about? What do you like to do when you're not working?** Networking from scratch is all about taking what you enjoy doing and turning that pleasure into an activity that puts you in circulation with others. When I found a creative solution to playing basketball in the driveway with my two sons, I unwittingly opened up a huge networking opportunity.

- **Identify your passion, and then think of a creative way to involve others.** Start today by looking around you. Who can you network with? Don't expect others to come to you—you have to go find them! Shortly after I moved my young family from Notre Dame to the Milwaukee area, I knew it was up to me to get connected with my new community and take active steps to putting myself into circulation.

- **Ask yourself good questions.** Here's one I was asking myself back in the mid-1980s: Why did I move my family to a city I didn't know to work for a small company? The answer was because that's where my job was. Once I worked that out mentally, my attitude blossomed. Milwaukee was my new hometown. It was up to me to get connected.

- **Make networking fun.** The kids in my neighborhood thought a vend- ing machine that spit out free Cokes was the coolest thing ever, and stressed-out moms were absolutely giddy after a couple of glasses of wine. Not only did young and old have fun in our driveway every Wednesday night, but we also met tons of nice neighbors and new business associates.

- **If you want to get close to a client or customer, show up at his kid's extracurricular event, like a game or performance.** He or she will know that you have gone the extra mile just by showing up.

- **Get plugged into worship and community groups, where you'll find like-minded individuals that you will want to get to know bet- ter and become friends with.**

- **Be a selfless networker like Joel Maturi, a humble guy who looks for ways to serve others.**

How to Network to Land a Superstar or Super Deal:

When Brett Favre Became My Big, Wild, Audacious Goal

CHANCES ARE you've heard of Brett Favre, the forty-one-year-old quarterback for the Minnesota Vikings. Three-time NFL Most Valuable Player. Super Bowl champion. Owns or shares most of the well-known NFL career records for quarterbacks, including consecutive starts, career passing yards, career passing touchdowns, and career pass completions.

His detractors point to another dubious record: most times "retired and unretired"—three. If it's one thing we've learned over the years with Brett Favre, it's that he's open to changing his mind.

Love him or hate him—and you can find plenty of Cheeseheads in Wisconsin who'll tell you that they don't know whether they should shake their fists or shake their heads in admiration for what he's done—Brett Lorenzo Favre leaves a trail of controversy behind him wherever he goes. His latest stop is in Minneapolis, where his cannon arm and leadership ability in sports' most difficult position—NFL quarterback—has won him a whole new legion of Minnesota Viking fans. Brett had an amazing season in 2009, surprising the pundits on NFL pre-game shows by leading a parade of Viking victories that landed Minnesota in the NFC Championship game.

At one time, I was Brett's sports marketing agent, and I helped take his off-the-field income from a paltry $65,000 a year to $4 million per annum, a sixty-fold increase. I got the chance to work with Brett Favre because I gave myself a breakthrough goal and saw it come to fruition.

When it comes to networking, it never hurts to have a BWAG in life—a Big, Wild, Audacious Goal. You know why big, wild, audacious goals are so great? Because they get you up in the morning, ready to tackle the day. They inspire you to make one more phone call, answer one more e-mail, and shake one more hand. They take you to places that you never thought you could get to on your own.

> *When it comes to networking, it never hurts to have a BWAG in life—a Big, Wild, Audacious Goal. You know why big, wild, audacious goals are so great? Because they get you up in the morning, ready to tackle the day.*

So let me begin with a series of questions:

What are you going to do for your big, wild, audacious goal? Do you have one? A couple? What would a quantum leap mean for you to get to the next level in your business? Does it mean going from $1 million in sales to $5 million? Networking with the top CEOs in your community? More face time with the decision-makers? Branching off on your own and starting your own business?

In this chapter, I'll discuss how having big, wild, audacious goals—and visualizing what you're going to do to make them happen—will take your career and your networking to the next level. I'll also share the secret of how you can land the superstar client, network with the top producers, or put yourself in the position to network at the highest levels.

Dropping Back to Pass

I've been asked a thousand times in my life a variation of this question: "How did you ever land a superstar like Brett Favre?"

I told you in an earlier chapter how I sold my 50 percent stake in Arkay—at a fortuitous time—to my partner. With a seven-figure check in my hand, I used the proceeds to purchase two manufacturing companies, Lotzwood and Stanwood, which expanded my business and networking horizons—but put me in a tight financial bind (see "Networking in the Darkest Times" on the next page).

My connections were responsible for my hat being tossed into the ring when Wisconsin business and political leaders were looking to start the Wisconsin Sports Authority, a nonprofit agency dedicated to promoting America's Dairyland through sporting events. After being hired as the president of the WSA in 1992, I worked behind the scenes with the planning and construction of a new ballpark for the Milwaukee Brewers. Then I was part of the Milwaukee networking team that brought the 2002 Major League All-Star Game to Miller Park as well as several high-profile collegiate events to Wisconsin, including the NCAA Basketball Midwest Regional and the NCAA "Frozen Four" hockey tournament. On the gridiron front, I used my budding networking skills to recruit four NFL football teams to bring their training camps to Wisconsin's milder summer climate. Along with the Green Bay Packers, the national media called the five NFL teams with Wisconsin training camps the "Cheese League," a play on major league baseball's spring training leagues: the Grapefruit League in Florida and the Cactus League in Arizona.

All of those are nice accomplishments to have on your résumé, but they pale in comparison to the best thing that happened to me at the Wisconsin Sports Authority during the early 1990s: building an enduring relationship with Craig Leipold, chairman of the WSA Board of Directors. When our friendship blossomed, I asked Craig to be one of my first wingmen, and he brought me into his confidence as well. Over the last twenty years, I've been Craig's "go-to" guy and was one of his top advisors regarding several hundred million dollars in sports transactions when Craig sold the Nashville Predators NHL hockey team in 2008 and subsequently purchased the Minnesota Wild NHL franchise.

Besides putting on Hall of Fame dinners every couple of years—remember Bob Costas?—the Wisconsin Sports Authority hosted an annual event to name the "Sports Person of the Year" in Wisconsin. Well, in 1995, there was this young quarterback wowing fans at Lambeau Field, leading the Packers to the NFL playoffs with an 11–5 record and advancing all the way to the NFC title game before losing to the Dallas Cowboys. His name was Brett Favre, and that season, the Green Bay Packers quarterback was named the NFL's Most Valuable Player.

NETWORKING IN THE DARKEST TIMES

When I sold my 50 percent stake in Arkay at a providential time, I'm sure you're thinking: *Shoot, Joe, I can't relate to that.*

I hear you, but now it's time for you to listen to the rest of my story, which I think you *will* be able to relate to.

I will concede that life was good after the Arkay check was deposited into my savings account. Our fourth child, Brendan, had just arrived, meaning Tami and I had four children under six, so now I had more time to help around the house. We also did some fun things, like take a few trips and visit some of my brothers and Tami's sisters around the country.

I also "treated" myself by training for the Boston Marathon, which I successfully ran in under four hours, and camped out at the driving range, where I grooved my swing.

The diversions were nice, but I was itching to get back into the game when the right opportunity presented itself; after all, I was in my early thirties. My accountant tipped me off to a couple of companies, Lotzwood and Stanwood, that were takeover prospects. Located in northwestern Wisconsin, both businesses were manufacturers of hundreds of different wood products and employed 125 workers.

I did my due diligence—or at least thought I did—and pulled the trigger with another partner. I plowed a good chunk of my cash into the two companies, but we leveraged ourselves to the hilt. You'd think I had learned something from my Arkay days about the wisdom of using debt to supplement an investment, but I did it anyway, even though Cousin Bobby *strongly* advised me to walk away from the deal. Too bad I didn't listen to my wingman.

After consummating the deal, I'll never forget the frantic phone call I received from my partner, who had moved to Eau Claire—215 miles northwest of Milwaukee—as part of a "meet and greet" with the management staff. (Lotzwood was located in Eau Claire, and Stanwood was located thirty miles east in Stanley, Wisconsin.) Upon further review, he said, both businesses were hit hard by the 1990 recession. "I need you to come up here, Joe, on the double. We've got to get these companies turned around." I could hear the panic rising in his throat.

Here's where I made Dumb Move #2: Instead of renting a home—since we never had any long-term plans to live in Eau Claire anyway—Tami and I went house-shopping and purchased a 150-year-old dilapidated mansion that could have doubled as the *Addams Family* mansion.

We moved into a torrent of broken pipes and broken dreams. Major clients of Lotzwood and Stanwood were going bankrupt left and right. Accounts receivables were nearly worthless, and our accounts payable stood in arrears. A sick-looking balance sheet revealed the financial reality: both companies were sinking faster than the *Titanic*.

I remember burying my face in my hands after surveying the gaping holes in the companies' financial records. *How in the hell am I going to get out of this mess?* I was personally guaranteed on the bank loan. My butt was on the line big-time.

My options were few, but over the next week, I slowly realized that I had the wrong mindset. Instead of figuring out a way to dump a pair of troubled companies, I turned the equation completely around. Who would *benefit* from picking up Lotzwood and Stanwood? Who could turn these two lemons into lemonade? Once I turned around my way of thinking, I put together a networking plan.

I came up with a list of a thousand companies, far and wide. Then I narrowed the list to five hundred, then my Top 100, Top 50, Top 10, and finally my Top 5. Long story short, we sold one, liquidated the other, took care of our bank debt, and got out of town.

Looking back to what transpired from 1990 to 1991, I can honestly say that this was probably the darkest time of my career. I plunged into a business that I knew little about. I uprooted a young family and moved them four hours away from friends and family support. For one of the few times in my life, I felt adrift, without moorings or any sense of direction. My gut churned day and night with guilt: one, for thinking I knew the wood manufacturing business; and two, for making a snap decision to purchase a weird home that would always be difficult to resell. The guilt nearly consumed me.

Networking got me out of a deep, dark hole. Not only did working our contacts get our businesses sold, but our social network—our friends and relatives back in Milwaukee and Madison—offered love and support at a time when Tami and I needed it most. In times of trouble, whom else can you count on? That's why I keep hammering the idea that investing in people *today* could help you during the tough times tomorrow.

If you're facing a similar situation, with your back up against the wall, this is not the time to go Lone Ranger. Even the Masked Man had a faithful companion, Tonto, whom he could call upon. "Two people are better off than one, for they can help each succeed," wrote King Solomon, the wisest man who ever lived. "If one person falls, the other can reach out and help. But someone who falls alone is in real trouble."[10]

There wasn't any doubt who the Wisconsin Sports Person of the Year for 1995 would be. As we made plans for the February 1996 dinner, it was my job to get Brett to Milwaukee in the off-season—a Costas-like order. Like a San Juan Capistrano swallow, Brett migrated back to Hattiesburg, Mississippi, where he loved to hunt and fish once the football season was over.

I didn't have to send Brett a box of Brewer brats to get his approval, though. He graciously said he'd be honored to receive the Sports Person of the Year award, and that was the start of our relationship and our friendship.

We connected on several fronts, even though he was twenty-six years old and I was thirty-seven. I had three boys and a girl; he came from a family of three boys and a girl. We shared similar passions like working out, playing golf, and interacting with people. We just hit it off.

A couple of months later, I asked Brett and his attorney, Bus Cook, who handled his Packer contracts, if they wanted to play golf with Craig and me at the North Shore Country Club south of Green Bay.

Early on in the round—I think it was the second hole—we were talking about the Sports Person of the Year dinner and what a good time everyone had. Then Brett looked at me. "Hey, Joe," he said. "When I was in Milwaukee for the award dinner, you seemed to know everybody, and you have a good business mind. Do you think you could get me a few deals?"

My pulse quickened. The thought of marketing Brett for beaucoup bucks sounded exciting. "That's interesting to hear you say that. But haven't you been getting any calls?" I figured that winning the NFL's Most Valuable Player trophy would have raised Brett's national profile considerably and that major companies would be beating a path to his door with endorsement deals.

"Barely anything," Brett said. "And nothing like Michael Jordan. He has to be making a boatload of money with that Nike Air deal and all the other things he has going on."

Bus, who was in our foursome, said Brett needed someone to aggressively pursue sports marketing opportunities.

"So do you think you can get me some business deals?" Brett repeated as we stepped on tee box at the third hole.

Could I? That was like asking me if I could go dribble-drive to my right on the basketball court.

I smiled. "Sure, Brett. But instead of getting a few deals, why don't we set up a business for you and invite other athletes to join us? Bus can continue doing the contracts, and we'll handle the business planning, marketing, appearances, and off-the-field revenues for you and other players."

Brett was all over that idea.

Before I go much further, you may be wondering, *But what about your job at the Wisconsin Sports Authority, Joe?*

To be honest, I was looking for a new challenge. I had been at the Wisconsin Sports Authority for four years, made my mark, but in my heart of hearts, I was a private-sector guy, meaning that I saw myself plying my skills in the business world and not quasi-governmental entities like the Wisconsin Sports Authority.

Suddenly, I had a big, wild, audacious goal to chase after—becoming a sports marketing agent. When this opportunity fell into my lap, leaving the Wisconsin Sports Authority was a no-brainer.

Brett, Bus, Craig, and I kept talking, and by the time we reached the 18th hole, we had hatched a plan: I would leave the WSA to become president of a new company called Sports Management Group, or SMG, and Brett Favre would become our first client—and one of the shareholders. Brett, Craig, Bus Cook, and I would each own a 25 percent stake in the company.

Talk about a big, wild, audacious opportunity. Having Brett on board—and someone with skin in the game—prompted other Packers and NFL players to sign up for representation by SMG. It wasn't long before we were representing five or six Packers, a half-dozen NFL players, a handful of coaches, and a couple of PGA golfers. We also started producing *The Pack Attack*, a weekly football show syndicated throughout Wisconsin and Minnesota. But our bread-and-butter was, by far, the one wearing the dark forest green No. 4 jersey belonging to the Green Bay Packers, and he was about to have his breakout season in 1996.

The Packers kept winning, and I kept things clicking for Brett in the endorsement world. The 1996 Packers were a powerhouse club that steamrolled opponents on the way to posting a league-best

RICK WOOD

While Brett Favre came into his own, winning two of three Most Valuable Player trophies, Packers teammate Reggie White was barreling into the opposition for six seasons, including 1996 and 1997, when the Green and Gold reached two Super Bowls and won one. In the mid-'90s, I brokered an advertising deal with Edge shaving gel featuring the two players.

13–3 record in the regular season. Defensive end Reggie White, the "Minister of Defense," anchored a tenacious defensive unit. Brett riddled NFL secondaries with pinpoint passes that looked like they were thrown on a zip line.

Following two relatively easy wins in the playoffs, including a 30–13 victory against the Carolina Panthers in the NFC championship game at Lambeau Field, the Packer faithful screamed "The Pack is back!" I was there that day and shared the excitement as well. The last time Green Bay had reached pro football's ultimate stage— the Super Bowl—was back in 1967 during the Vince Lombardi glory days…just two weeks after I dropped by Coach Ara Parseghian's office as an eight-year-old.

My phone rang off the hook during the two-week break between the NFC championship win and the Super Bowl on January 26, 1997. I must have fielded a hundred phone calls a day, mostly for Brett, although SMG represented around a half-dozen Packer players. One of the calls was from a high-up marketing VP with the Walt Disney Company. He wanted to know if Brett would shout "I'm going to Disney World!" to the cameras—if the Packers won—while he ran off the field through the confetti and stringers back to the safety of the locker room. Then when the commercial aired the following week, an unseen narrator would say, "So, Brett Favre, what are you going to do next?" It was a great payday for five seconds of his time.

I briefed Brett the morning of the game, told him about the Disney deal, and said I would be looking for him on the Superdome floor (Super Bowl XXXI was played in New Orleans) after the game.

After the final seconds ticked away, a Disney film crew followed me as I chased after Brett in the chaos. I managed to corral him as dozens of pushy TV camera guys, photographers, and reporters jostled for position. A Fox camera crew was there, too, so for nearly seven seconds, we were live on national TV before one hundred million people, including a thousand relatives back in Wisconsin who were all saying the same thing: "That's Joe on the field with Brett!"

I paved some free space and then got the Disney film crew into position. A sweat-soaked Brett, with helmet aloft, looked toward the cameras and let out a joyous, "I'm going to Disney World!" And then he disappeared into the scrum again.

The commercial never aired, however, because kickoff/punt return specialist Desmond Howard won the Super Bowl MVP for scoring the game-clinching touchdown on a Super Bowl record 99-yard kickoff return. The prerequisite to participation in the Disney "What's Next" campaign was winning the Super Bowl MVP, so Brett lost out, even though Disney still paid him handsomely for his time. Too bad his enthusiastic rendition of "I'm going to Disney World!" never aired.

Everything changed for Brett after Super Bowl XXXI. We found out in short order that executives and companies were willing to throw hundreds of thousands of dollars at Brett if he'd only stop by their sales conference or company golf outing or employee appreciation event. Two hours of his time for $200,000. Within a year, I marketed Brett Favre to the hilt with Corporate America, and he was soon raking in $4 million a year in off-the-field income (which included a sweetheart deal with Nike)—an amount about equal to his Packers salary but more than sixty times what he earned before SMG came into this life.

TICKET TO RIDE

Hitching up with the Brett Favre bandwagon before he exploded into American households was an awesome experience and something I'll be telling stories about the rest of my days.

The persona you know him by—the good-ol' boy, the hayseed from Mississippi—wasn't an act. That's plainly who Brett was and wanted to be. Even his well-publicized forays into self-destruction had a silver lining: he gave us a public connection to common struggles.

During the Packers' two-year Super Bowl run in 1996 and 1997, everyone wanted a piece of Brett. As his marketing agent, our arrangement called for me to be compensated 20 percent off the top of what he earned off the field—endorsements, appearance fees, and the like. It was also my job to handle the zillion requests that came his way—big and small.

To help him focus on what was best for him, as well as reflect the soft parts of his heart, we helped set up, with Bus Cook's assistance, the Brett Favre Fourward Foundation, which funneled aid to disadvantaged or disabled children in Wisconsin and Mississippi. Locally, he was behind the Boys and Girls Club of Milwaukee, and I can't tell you the number of Friday afternoons that Brett dropped by Children's Hospital, wearing his Packers jersey, to visit the sick youngsters in the cancer ward.

One day, I was feeling a bit frustrated from dealing with the requests flooding the office. Could Brett speak before an elementary school assembly? Participate in a 5K walk for Huntington's Disease? Send a note of encouragement to a young boy paralyzed in an automobile accident? Fly to New York and appear on *David Letterman*? All were worthwhile requests, but they were what we in the office called "non-rev" appeals: no money involved. I also handled other zero-income tasks, like answering thousands of letters from fans—mostly for photos and autographs—and managing Brett's travel schedule during the off-season, which had him zigzagging across the country like a quarterback scrambling out of the pocket. When Brett was out on the road, there were dozens of flights, hotels, and rental cars to book.

That day, I was on the phone for probably the seventh time with Brett, going over the recent requests as well as his travel schedule, when my frustration got the better of me. "Brett, have you noticed something? Ninety percent of the things I'm doing for you right now, I don't make any money."

Brett paused for a moment. "Hmm," he began. "That might be right, but that 10 percent is pretty good, isn't it?"

I never envisioned becoming a sports marketing agent, but when a young, up-and-coming Green Bay quarterback named Brett Favre became my first client in the mid-1990s, I suddenly had a big, wild, audacious situation on my hands. Later, when addictions to alcohol and painkillers threatened Brett's marriage and on-the-field performance, I networked with a counselor who specialized in addictions to write Brett a letter urging him to seek outside help.

What Brett and I didn't know at the time, however, was that all the fame, money, and adulation would set him down a road of dangerous addictions. I wasn't the one to turn him around—his wife, Deanna, gets credit for that—but I did my part by networking to get the help he needed.

Overcoming Addictions

After being a sports marketing agent for a number of years, I discovered that the entire sports industry is an industry of addiction.

This wasn't a major revelation. To me, it was logical and simple. The sports world is primarily classical conditioning that starts at a young age, usually after puberty, as budding sports stars start to make their mark. When you can run faster, leap higher, shoot better, and flat-out beat your competition, you have coaches kissing your behind and adults telling you that you'll be a rich and famous professional athlete some day, scooping up millions for playing—what is at the end of the day—a game.

Star athletes are coddled from high school, right through college, and into the pros. Everything is taken care of for them; all they have to worry about is performing on the field or in the arena. Hearing thousands of fans scream your name or cheer for your team is *physically* addicting. The feel-good neurotransmitters serotonin and dopamine release from the brain, and the result is a sensation that feels quite good. You'll frequently hear famous athletes say that they're "on a high" after winning a big game or championship.

When the cheering stops, though, it's difficult to let go of that high. Some athletes look to other avenues to make them feel good again: drugs, alcohol, and women come to mind. And the addiction cycle keeps feeding on itself.

In May 1996, just weeks after the launch of SMG, Brett shocked the sports world—and his new marketing agent—when he voluntarily entered the NFL's substance-abuse program because of a dependence on painkillers that he had developed over the previous two seasons. At a press conference, he said, "It's very serious. It's something I have to take care of."

Like a blindside blitz, Vicodin was something that Brett couldn't escape. The painkillers wrapped their arms around him and wouldn't let go—but there was no referee to blow the whistle and stop the play. His addiction to Vicodin eventually consumed Brett to the point where he lied to doctors, stole painkillers from teammates, and even re-swallowed Vicodin tablets swimming in his own vomit. He gulped downed painkillers by the handful. Six pills a day soon became eight, then ten, then fifteen.[11]

I knew nothing about this at the time, but as Brett's newly minted sports marketing agent, I was pleased to see him taking steps to seek treatment. But a few years later, he looked like he was falling off the wagon again. I'll never forget one Friday afternoon and evening when I watched Brett drink *way* too much alcohol, pop pills like dime-store candy, and get obliterated. Yet thirty-six hours later in ninety-degree heat at Lambeau Field, I stood on the sidelines and witnessed Brett take an unbelievable blindside shot from Tampa Bay defensive end Warren Sapp, all of 300 pounds. The vicious hit tore off Sapp's helmet and silenced the Lambeau Field

I was on the Lambeau Field sidelines that hot afternoon in September when Tampa Bay Buccaneer Warren Sapp blindsided Brett Favre with a hit so violent that it tore off Sapp's helmet. Brett shook off the hit and threw for four TDs that Sunday afternoon.

fans. But Brett shook the cobwebs away, regained his composure, and threw for four touchdowns like he was playing pass-and-catch in one of those Wrangler jeans commercials. *No problem, dude.*

Yet those of us who knew Brett off the field had a sinking feeling that his addictions to alcohol and painkillers would eventually sack him—or land him in an early grave. As our association lengthened, the question in my mind was no longer, *How can I help Brett get another endorsement deal?* but, *How can I help Brett?*

The reality was there was only so much I could do. I couldn't babysit him, and what he did in his private life was his private life. But as I saw him slipping deeper into the abyss, I marshaled my forces and sought out people who help *me* help Brett. In other words, I networked.

One of the people I called was Mike McGowan, a drug-and-alcohol counselor who became an invaluable, behind-the-scenes advisor to me. Mike specialized in addiction counseling and gave me clarity on how to proceed with this, even though I had been through interventions with other people. He suggested that I write a letter saying it was time to get some outside help. He dictated much of the letter, saying that I needed to speak the language of drug addicts and alcoholics.

Here's a copy of the letter:

SPORTS MARKETING & MANAGEMENT GROUP, LLC

December 16, 1998

Brett Favre
3071 Gothic Court
Green Bay, WI 54304

Dear Brett,

I am writing to you because I care about you as a person and as a friend. Because I have a high degree of respect and admiration for you as a person, I wanted to share my thoughts with you in light of my conversation with Deanna earlier this week.

Since my discussion with Deanna Monday, I've been thinking about a lot of things. All of them focus on how I can help you, and be your friend and not just your marketing agent. I've been your friend and partner now for several years and I care a great deal for you, Deanna, Brittany, and the entire Favre family. Because I love you like a brother, it hurts to see you and Deanna going through such tough times in your relationship, and I stand ready to help in any way that I can.

Frankly, I am scared to death for you. You and I know that a big part of the problem is the drinking and drugs and it is starting to get really scary with serious life threatening and career implications. I know you are embarrassed by some of the recent things that have happened. Because you are human, I know that you, too, must be scared about what is happening and when it will ultimately and inevitably break out into the open. I believe it is time we develop a game plan together to get your marriage, your life, and your health back to where you would like them to be. In the short term we need to establish a plan so that we can sort through the difficult questions that you face.

The options and consequences at this point are fairly clear. One option would be to do nothing, but I don't think anyone, including you favors that approach. Another option would be to take a big step and seek serious, professional assistance. I believe an outside professional can show you the proper direction to get things back on track.

I am telling you how I feel because I am worried about you and care about you as a friend more than I can express in this letter. Give me a call and let me know your thoughts.

Sincerely,

Joe Sweeney

111 East Kilbourn Avenue • Suite 2800 • Milwaukee, WI 53202 • 414-277-6780 • Fax: 414-277-6790

The letter was mailed in late 1998, right around the same time that his wife, Deanna, had reached her limit. In her autobiography, *Don't Bet Against Me*, she had this to say about his behavior in 1999:

I had all his belongings packed and waiting in the courtyard of the house. I'd become so desperate that I'd called a divorce attorney...He [Brett] came into the house and begged me to let him stay, but I was firm. "If you're not going to quit drinking, you can leave," I told him. "I'm not going down that road again; I'm done. I've already spoken to an attorney..."

The attorney called while Brett was begging me to reconsider, and Brett heard me tell her I was ready to file; that I was done and there was no changing my mind...[Later] I told Brett that if he didn't get out of my house, I would call 911. I called his agent [Bus Cook] and Bus came to pick him up. Brett told Bus to take him to the airport because he was going to check himself into rehab again.

Brett realized that if he wanted a life with me and the children, he couldn't drink again. He gave it up completely, and it's been eight years since he had a drink.[12]

Listen, we all have demons in life. Some of us have bigger demons than others. How we deal with these demons will determine how our lives turn out. Don't believe me? Look at Elvis Presley, John Belushi, Chris Farley, and yes, even Michael Jackson. Brett Favre was going down the same road as those people, and they all died before their time. Whether you like Brett Favre or not, I respect him. By examining his dark side and turning things around, Brett not only got the help he needed, he saved his marriage, extended his career, and most importantly, saved his life. I'm certain that had he not changed his habits, he would not have played as long as he has—or even be alive today. The way he handled himself is a prime example of a successful turn-around story.

It wasn't an overnight process, though. His wife, Deanna, informed me they were opting out of doing any more major marketing or endorsement deals in order to remain focused on what was really important in their lives. Things eventually wound down a couple of years later, and we officially parted company when Brett left SMG.

I'll always be grateful, though, for the big, wild, audacious partnership with one of the premier quarterbacks in the NFL. My experiences with Brett created unique and memorable moments in time in my professional career.

Networking for the Future

Remember how I said I would share my secret on how you can land the superstar client, network with the top producers, or put yourself in the position to network at the highest levels?

Well, here it is: you want to start networking with people *before* they get big, become a superstar, or get promoted to the executive suite. Bottom line: the people you network with today could become the superstars of tomorrow.

That's why I urge you to network with co-workers, friends, classmates, colleagues, fellow parishioners—people just like you—before they start movin' on up. You want to reach out to others *before* they get that big promotion or leave to start their own company.

I call this my "rising tide lifts all boats" theory. If your friends and networking contacts do well and rise within their careers, you'll rise as well, especially if your boat is hitched to theirs—either because of your strong bond of friendship or a work-centric relationship built on trust and performance.

When you stop and think about it, it's very difficult to "network" or even socialize with a senior vice president or company CEO who's twenty or twenty-five years your senior anyway. You're in different orbits, different stages of life. But if you create bonds with the people around you—your peers—they are the ones who can hire you or bring you aboard their ship when they go on to bigger and better things someday in the future.

The idea is to catch people on their way up. Develop relationships today because you never know what tomorrow will bring. If I stop and think about it, I know I caught Brett Favre on the way up. He was just another darn-good young quarterback with a small-market team when we joined forces in the spring of 1996, but then he had a breakout season a few months later and exploded. I was there at his side, thanks to networking efforts that put me in a position to become his sports marketing agent. The same idea works in the everyday work world: you want to catch people on the way up.

But Joe, what if I don't know who's going to make it my office or my world?

You don't know who will make the big jump, and that's why you should continue to look at networking as a place to give, not to get. Sure, you don't know who'll rise to the corner office, but that shouldn't matter in the way you treat people. You treat all people the same, and your goal should be to reach out to *everyone* you can.

You can't *try* to be in the right place at the right time because that's not the way life works. You just are. But I

> *The idea is to catch people on their way up. Develop relationships today because you never know what tomorrow will bring. If I stop and think about it, I know I caught Brett Favre on the way up.*

think you put yourself in the right place tomorrow by networking *today* with your colleagues and friends.

Having a Big, Wild, Audacious Goal

1. Set a big, wild, audacious goal—one that is obtainable. Believe it to be obtainable and be prepared to have this goal stretch you and take you out of your comfort zone.

2. Figure out how to play in areas that others consider work. For instance, Brett Favre and Bus Cook thought that "running" a sports marketing business with budgets and forecasts was work, but I loved playing in that sandbox. I made myself more valuable as a networking partner by being willing to take an area that didn't interest my colleagues.

3. You can always try to be at the right place at the right time, but life usually doesn't work that way. Still, it never hurts your cause to think about what the right place would be.

4. Set a big, wild, audacious goal to begin a relationship with someone who is a superstar to you. It'll never happen if you don't try.

5. Follow your passions—what you really like to do—and you might find yourself excited about a big, wild, audacious goal that you never thought possible but looks plausible.

6. Remember that a big, wild, audacious goal can and will come to fruition if you believe it's possible, close your eyes and imagine it happening, and act like you believe it's already going to happen.

7. Start networking now for a better future tomorrow. The people you befriend today will undoubtedly move on to other opportunities, and they could bring you along. Hitching your wagon to theirs won't happen tomorrow if you don't reach out today.

Networking Is Not All Black and White

ONE OF THE FIRST Green Bay Packers to sign up with SMG was LeRoy Butler, an All-Pro strong safety and all-around good guy. LeRoy—pronounced L'Roy—holds a special place in Packer hearts because he is credited with inventing the "Lambeau Leap."

I loved working with him, and this isn't his former sports agent talking. I found the affable, easygoing LeRoy easy to market: I got him his own radio show on WKLH in Milwaukee; a Nike contract; a Cellular One endorsement deal; and a ton of appearances. I also helped him start his very own LeRoy Butler Celebrity Golf Tournament, a charity outing that benefited the LeRoy Butler Foundation for Breast Cancer.

My favorite LeRoy Butler story happened in 2001, his final season, when he called the Monday morning after a Packer game to inform me that his father had died of a heart attack the previous day.

"I'm sorry, LeRoy. How can I help?"

"I was wondering if you could come to the funeral. That would mean a lot to me."

I was touched. "Sure," I replied. "Just tell me when and where, and I'll be there."

"It's next week, back home in Jacksonville. I'm going down right after the Bears game Sunday."

"You're on, but isn't that a little long to wait to have a funeral service? That's more than a week from today."

LEROY BUTLER: THE STORY BEHIND THE LAMBEAU LEAP

In a late-December home game during the 1993 season, the Green Bay Packers were playing the Los Angeles Raiders. Silver and Black running back Randy Jordan took a swing pass at the Raiders' 35-yard line, but he got popped by strong safety LeRoy Butler, forcing a fumble. Reggie White picked up the loose football and lumbered down the field ten yards before instinctively lateralling to the speedier LeRoy, who sprinted the remaining twenty-five yards into the end zone.

The "Lambeau Leap" was invented during the 1993 season by All-Pro strong safety LeRoy Butler, wearing Packers jersey No. 36, when he picked up a fumble, sprinted into the end zone, and spontaneously leaped into the arms of cheering Packer fans.

Instead of spiking the ball or high-fiving his teammates, LeRoy made a spontaneous leap into the outstretched arms of joyous Packer fans packed in the south bleachers, setting off another frenzy of raucous cheers. LeRoy had so much fun that following that historic touchdown, the Packer players tried to outdo each other by seeing who could leap *farther* into the stands, even though they first had to scale a six-foot wall. Today, the Lambeau Leap is one of the more unique and exciting touchdown celebrations that bonds players and fans, and jumping into the stands is widely imitated throughout the NFL. At the Packers Hall of Fame in Green Bay, you can even try your own "Lambeau Leap" at one of the exhibits.

For a guy with a story like LeRoy's, it's amazing he ever made it to the highest level of the game—professional football in the NFL. He was born in Jacksonville, Florida, on the wrong side of the tracks: the crime-infested Blodgett Homes housing project on the West Side. His parents separated when he was a toddler, but his mother, Eunice, supported LeRoy and his four siblings by working, first as a secretary and later as a nurse.

The streets he grew up on "had more chalk lines marking dead bodies than hopscotch lines," LeRoy was fond of saying. He was born so pigeon-toed that doctors had to break bones in both of his feet at the age of eight months to correct the deformity. Learning to walk was a struggle, and young LeRoy spent much of his early youth in a wheelchair. At age six, he was forced to wear the same kind of leg braces that Forrest Gump had to wear.

What happened next sounds like something from a Hollywood drama. LeRoy was sitting at the window, watching other neighborhood kids play kickball, when an older sister, Vicki, raced out of the apartment and accidentally knocked LeRoy out of the wheelchair. The leg braces flew off as well. LeRoy picked himself up, and lo and behold, discovered that he could walk normally. Not only that, he could move pretty well. He immediately ran outside and joined the kickball game in progress. Overnight, he was the fastest kid in the projects—a speed demon.

There was no holding LeRoy Butler back. He was a high school blue-chipper and first-team All-American at Florida State. After the Packers drafted him in 1990, he quickly emerged as a star in the NFL and undisputed leader of the Packers' defensive secondary, but today, his greatest legacy was coming up with an infectious way to celebrate a Green Bay Packer touchdown.

"We know you white folks," he chuckled. "You die and you bury 'em right away. We black people, we just chillin'."

I laughed. The following Monday, I flew down from Milwaukee to Jacksonville. One of his old friends, Arthur Johnson, picked me up at the airport and drove me straight to the funeral home that reeked of formaldehyde.

I stepped inside the dark foyer and was introduced to other family members, which allowed me to express my condolences to James Butler's family. Eunice, his first wife and LeRoy's mom, was there, and so was his girlfriend.

We made small talk, paid our respects, and then formed a procession over to LeRoy's home. A stream of old friends from his neighborhood passed through, and most were content to play card games, shoot pool, or hit LeRoy up for some "walking-around" money. They certainly had the street slang going. Every five minutes, I would nudge LeRoy and ask, "What did he say?"

After everyone had left, I was shown their guest room and slept like a baby—until I heard the door open the following morning and four little eyes locked with mine. The door slammed shut, and I heard one of the girls running down the hall, shouting, "Mommy, Mommy, there's a white man sleeping in the guest bedroom!"

I showered, dressed, and walked into the kitchen, where I found LeRoy setting out cereal boxes for LoReal, his nine-year-old daughter, and Gabrielle, her seven-year-old sister. His wife, Rhodesia, was cradling their energetic nine-month-old daughter, Danielle, while she sucked on a bottle of formula. I helped myself to some cereal, and then LeRoy motioned that it was time to go.

I rode to the church with Leroy and the Butler family. As we walked into the simple clapboard church, though, I made a quick move and ducked into the back row. LeRoy, from his strong-safety position, intercepted me. "No, no, you's coming with us," he directed. Next thing I knew, I was standing respectfully in the first row with the immediate Butler family. Behind us, the small Baptist church filled to the brim.

I had never been to a black church. I looked at the church program and noticed that beneath the "Order of Service" an advisory read, "Subject to change as the Lord leads us." I wasn't sure what that meant.

We started with some old Negro spirituals, which were quite moving. Then the piano player switched to some up-tempo songs, and the red-robed, all-black choir started swaying—just like in the movies. Things were starting to hop, and the faster music lasted another ten, fifteen minutes before the preacher got up to say a "few words" on behalf of the dearly departed. Well, it turned out to be a torrent of speech, but I'm getting ahead of myself. What happened is that the preacher took his time building to an emotional climax to his sermon, which he punctuated with raspingly rhythmic exhortations about how "death's *str-aaahng* grip" would be "ree-laxed at the gates of heaven." Every few sentences, the energetic preacher—who was

ED ERKMANIS

I represented LeRoy Butler as his sports marketing agent, and when he called and asked me to attend his father's funeral in Jacksonville, Florida, in the middle of the Packer season, I was touched. Here I'm pictured with LeRoy (left) and an old friend from Jacksonville, Arthur Johnson.

working up a good sweat—would remind his flock to "shout glory to His name!"

They shouted all right. A chorus of "Amens" and "Preach it, brother" popped up from the pews in response to the preacher's uncontrollable enthusiasm.

I mumbled a self-conscious "Amen" or two, just to be polite. This wasn't like any Catholic funeral I had attended. By the fifth or sixth exhortation, though, my "Amen"s were becoming more robust. I was loosening up. The next time the preacher called for a response, I nearly shouted, "Amen, brother!" and pumped my fist, prompting a sideways glance from a wide-eyed LeRoy.

The service ran long—I guess that's what they meant by "Subject to where the Lord leads us"—and Arthur Johnson rushed me back to the airport so I could make my flight on time. As the Delta Airlines

737 lifted into the sky, a surreal feeling fell over me, as if I had just been part of something that was a dream. I asked myself: *What happened back there?*

I knew what happened: I was a white man in a black man's world. A minority. Part of a different culture. Several hours later, after changing planes in Atlanta, my flight began its final descent into Milwaukee. I had a window seat that late afternoon, and as I looked down upon a familiar city that had been my home for more than seventeen years, I remembered the shocking news that had been all over the newspapers in recent weeks. One of the headlines in the *Milwaukee Journal Sentinel* stood out in my memory:

Milwaukee Is Most Segregated City in America

The shocking news stemmed from the latest U.S. Census report. According to the 2000 Census, an analysis of where blacks and whites lived in Milwaukee and how isolated each race was from each other confirmed what many of us had known for decades: the Cream City was the No. 1 racially divided city in the country.

In Milwaukee, everyone knew that African-Americans lived north of the Menomonee River, in the "Negro district," as it was known in the pre–Civil Rights days, while whites congregated in their own neighborhoods south of the river and in the suburbs ringing Milwaukee's inner city.

In demographic terms, 37 percent of Milwaukee's six hundred thousand residents were African-Americans, but I knew that several thousand feet below me the disparities between the races were glaring in nearly every social index: income, child poverty, education, and housing. The result was a cauldron of crime, high unemployment, and fatherless African-American homes. They'd also taken the biggest hit from the decline of the manufacturing economy over the last twenty years when most of the breweries and auto parts factories were shuttered. They used to say that all you needed was a strong back and an alarm clock to support a family in Milwaukee, but those days were gone.[13]

Those were the sorts of conflicting feelings I wrestled with while my flight feathered in for a landing at Mitchell Field in Milwaukee.

I haven't forgotten that experience in Jacksonville, and I'm drawing upon it as I write this chapter on how African-Americans, as well as other minorities in this country, can benefit from networking in what is, unfortunately, a mostly white corporate world in America. While companies are fully integrated today, in many areas of the country, however, including old Midwest industrial cities like Milwaukee, the sea of faces in the conference rooms and executive suites are uniformly white.

That's the reality, but things are changing, and more rapidly than you might think. The nation is becoming more racially and ethnically diverse, according to the U.S. Census Bureau. Minorities, roughly one-third of the population, are expected to become the majority in 2042. Non-Hispanic, single-race white people are projected to lose population in the 2030s and 2040s and comprise 46 percent of the total population in 2050, down from 66 percent in 2008.[14]

To whites reading this chapter, I challenge you to intentionally look for ways to network with minorities now not only because it's the right thing to do, but because it makes sense to network with people of color today since the racial makeup of corporate business *will* change in the near future, as the U.S. Census Bureau is predicting. Like I said in the last chapter, the people you network with today could be the ones who can bring you along when they go on to bigger and better things in the future.

I'm glad to hear that, Joe, but how does that help me? I'm a young person of color, working in a business where I can count the number of other minorities on staff on one hand. How can I network in a white corporate world?

My quick answer: just like you network with your friends and colleagues of the same race. In other words, you still do the 5/10/15 plan, you still look at networking as a place to give, not

> **You must make sure you network outside your race.**

get, you still add wingmen to your life, and you still make connections with peers today who could go on to bigger and better things tomorrow—and take you with them. You must make sure you network outside your race, the same advice I just directed toward the white people reading this chapter.

But I will be the first to admit that since I'm a white Irishman, I don't have the life experiences to address minorities on how they can best network in today's work environment. That's why I've dipped into my networking pool and asked Ulice Payne, a close friend of mine and one of the best networkers in the country, to tell us his up-by-the-bootstraps story and share his advice to minority readers of *Networking Is a Contact Sport.*

Up Close and Personal: Ulice Payne

Ulice Payne—his first name is pronounced *You-lis*—was born on November 23, 1955, to humble and simple beginnings in Donora, Pennsylvania, a borough twenty miles south of Pittsburgh on the Monongahela River. Donora was your typical Rust Belt town of fifteen thousand in the 1950s, a place where coal mining and steel manufacturing were the Twin Towers of the local economy. The town is forever memorialized by the infamous Donora Smog of 1946, where an inversion layer trapped dirty pollutants emitted from the American Steel and Wire plant and the Donora Zinc Works. By the time the three-day inversion lifted, seventy had died and hundreds more would finish their lives with damaged lungs and hearts.

Ulice grew up in the same house his mother had been born and raised in—a modest home that was seventy yards from the steel mill gate where his father, Ulice Sr., punched a time clock five, six days a week. For a black male with an eighth-grade education, that's all he could aspire to in those days.

He could, however, prepare Ulice and his older brother, Bernie, for a better future, and Ulice Sr. accomplished that through instilling a strong work ethic and tough-love discipline. "I was afraid to screw up because if my mother told my father after he got home from work that I was in trouble, he spanked my ass," Ulice said. "It was 'Yes, sir' and 'No, ma'am' around our house. My parents wanted my brother and me to get more out of life, and they were constantly encouraging us to do well in school."

A college education was seen as a way out of Donora's steel mills and coal mines—or athletics. "Stan the Man" Musial, the famed St. Louis Cardinals first baseman who compiled a .331 lifetime batting

RICK WOOD

Ulice Payne, a member of the Marquette University basketball team that captured the NCAA crown in 1977 under Coach Al McGuire, enrolled in the Marquette University Law School after his playing days were over, which led to a meteoric rise to the top of the Wisconsin business world. He became the first African-American to run a major league club when the Milwaukee Brewers named him president and CEO. Ulice says that no matter what your color, you have to understand the common language in business, which is money and serving clients. Here, we are pictured after a Bradley Center Sports and Entertainment board meeting.

average, hailed from Donora. So did Ken Griffey Sr., and Ken Griffey, Jr., for that matter. Dozens of Donora's favorite sons went on to star in collegiate sports.

Junior, as he was called by his parents and relatives, continued to grow like a weed throughout childhood until he reached six foot six inches tall at Ringgold High School. His height, quickness, and superb jump shot were the reason he was named a high school All-

American. (A jock quarterback named Joe Montana also played on the Ringgold High basketball team.) Because of his basketball prowess, Ulice was heavily recruited. A college coach named Al McGuire coaxed him to join his up-and-coming program at a small Catholic university in Milwaukee known as Marquette.

On the first day of practice, the acerbic McGuire pulled Ulice over to the side and informed him, "You're going to play defense."

Ulice's eyes blinked. He fully understood the importance of Coach's directive. Chasing and harassing the other team's best scorer all over the court meant very little energy would be left over to play offense. If he didn't score points or lead the team in scoring, then there was no way he would ever be voted All-American.

"Why do you want to do that, Coach?" Ulice asked.

"Because you're my best athlete, and that's where we need you."

I guess Al McGuire, crazy like a fox, knew what he was doing. He coached his brains out in 1977 when his Marquette basketball team ruled March Madness, capturing the NCAA championship against North Carolina in the finals. I still haven't forgotten how excited I was that a Wisconsin team captured the national basketball crown—a first in the Badger State since the 1941 University of Wisconsin team won it all in college basketball.

Even though playing on the national stage was quite an experience, it was in the college classroom where Ulice had his horizons broadened. "At Marquette, I began to see how many smart people there were out there," he said. "You think you're hot until you get to college, sit in the classroom, and hear other kids say things that you never thought about before. That became part of my networking style, to listen to people who knew things that I didn't and get to know them."

Ulice stayed on at Marquette after his basketball days were over, enrolling in the Marquette University Law School. After he was admitted to the Wisconsin bar, he became a law clerk for the U.S. District Court in Wisconsin before joining several law firms, where he reached managing partner and started a meteoric rise to the top of the Wisconsin business and sports worlds.

In 2002, Ulice made history when he became the first African-American to head up a major league baseball franchise when the

Milwaukee Brewers appointed him as CEO and president. That landed Ulice at No. 14 on *Sports Illustrated's* list of "101 Most Influential Minorities in Sports."

The high-visibility role with the Brewers paved the way into the boardrooms of a number of major companies such as Manpower, Inc., Northwestern Mutual, Wisconsin Energy Corporation, and Badger Meter, Inc. Until his resignation in 2009, Ulice served seven years as chairman of the Bradley Center Sports and Entertainment Corporation, which is where I got to know him since I was a member of the Bradley board. (The Bradley Center, an 18,600-seat arena, hosts the Milwaukee Bucks, Marquette University basketball team, and numerous concerts and corporate events.)

When I asked him if he could be my go-to guy in my "Networking Is Not All Black and White" chapter, Ulice stepped onto the court. Here's what he had to say during our question-and-answer time:

JOE: How would you describe your networking style, given the racial makeup of Corporate America today?

ULICE: I'm with you that networking is a place to give, not to get, but I'm not sure if I have a unique networking style, and what I mean by that is that I just try to be myself. In the end, most people are the same, we truly are. Most people in life want to have a few laughs, have a few friends, have a healthy family, be comfortable in their homes, and go on vacation every now and then. For me, being real is where networking begins.

If you're not comfortable with yourself, then it'll be hard for you to relax with others or for others to be comfortable with you. So to me, being comfortable with myself goes back to my humble beginnings. My parents never let me get a big head. No matter how

> "In the end, most people are the same, we truly are. Most people in life want to have a few laughs, have a few friends, have a healthy family, be comfortable in their homes, and go on vacation every now and then. For me, being real is where networking begins."
> —Ulice Payne

well I did in school—and I did well—or how well I played basketball, I was still "Junior" to them.

Nobody wants to be around know-it-all guys, or women for that matter. That's why my networking style is driven by who I am, who I want to associate with, who I give my phone number to, and who I give my e-mail address to.

JOE: You've had a lot of success in the legal world, the business world, and in the sports world. If you look at everything that you have done in your life, you are an African-American who has networked and worked hard in a predominantly white business culture. What are some things that you would tell someone of color who wants to get connected?

ULICE: The first thing I would say is remember the environment you are in, and in the business world, it's all about money. Keep in mind that in the capitalist system, businesses exist to meet the needs of people. Whether you're a funeral director, a nurse, an engineer, or running a small business, all businesses are designed to meet the needs of people, so you have to understand that. And it is always about the money because if you don't make money in business, then you can't be in business.

You have to understand that the common language we all speak in business is money. It's the common denominator that goes through black and white or Asian and brown. If you understand that, then we all have something in common. Then we're really not so different. Then we are thinking alike, regardless of our background, regardless of our race, and regardless of our religion.

The second thing about this black-and-white piece is knowing who you are. When I walk into a room, I know that I look different than everybody else most of the time. I just keep on going so we can get past that.

If I sense any tension in the room, I'll try to knock that out. How? By talking about the things we have in common, and for most businessmen and businesswomen, it's how we can do good business so that we can all make some money. If you talk about money, the white guy is going to say to himself, *Hey, he's okay*. That's why I've said that in a business environment, green slices through black and white.

JOE: But you have a style and an aura about you the instant you walk into a room that transforms any black or white issue. I'm talking about the way you present yourself, the way that you speak. Are you aware of that?

ULICE: I'm not consciously aware of it, but again, it goes back to who I am. I feel confident about myself; therefore, I don't try to be someone that I'm not. That is usually a disarming quality, is it not? I'm sure you've met people, who, by their actions, seem uptight. To me, that's a problem.

If you're not comfortable in your own skin, I don't care what education you have, people will feel that. When I walk into a room, I'm not looking over my shoulder. I'm not afraid to look you in the eye. Not afraid to say "I didn't know that," because I realize that I'm not the smartest man in the room many times, nor do I have the most money in the room.

I think that attitude disarms a lot of people who don't know me. They may see that I'm six foot, six inches tall, have dark skin, and stand out in a crowd, but I don't let that bother me. If it bothers you, then you should talk to your psychologist about it.

JOE: If I would ask you to take a young inner-city black man under your wing, how would you mentor him? As you know right here in Milwaukee, we live in the most segregated city in the country, where 50 percent of the black males are unemployed. What advice would you give to them?

ULICE: You can no longer say it's the white man's fault. For many years, especially back in the sixties, there was always sort of the rationale that we were poor and uneducated because they wouldn't let us get into schools. And that was true to a large degree a generation ago. But that's changed, right?

Sure, there was a time we had to live in bad housing because we can't live in white neighborhoods, and banks were all redlining at one time, but that's gone away to a large degree if you can do business. The fact that you are black isn't going to change.

You're going to die as who you are, so you'd better get over that, or you'll take that bitterness to the grave with you.

I'm talking about taking 100 percent responsibility. We can't use our racial history as an excuse. Things have changed. For God's sake, we have a black president in Barack Obama. We have black CEOs on Wall Street.

I'm thankful that growing up, I was taught never to use racism as an excuse. My mother said, "You're supposed to go to school every day. You're supposed to get good grades." That was just the expectations that we had within our family.

I think what has happened is that over time people have lowered their expectations about what they want to get out of life, saying it's the white man's fault.

JOE: But what about the unemployment situation, especially during this recession?

ULICE: The unemployment picture, Joe, is a social piece that goes back to family, in my view. In the inner city, where guys are 50 percent unemployed, it's often because of their family structure. The questions I would ask them would be these: Did you ever have a job? Did you ever have to work a part-time job? Did you have a job at home when you were growing up?

I had chores growing up in Donora: washing the car, putting out the garbage, and cutting the eight-by-twelve-yard area of grass in our backyard. My brother and I had two jobs every night. One guy washed the dishes, and the other guy dried and swept the kitchen floor. We had to wash our own clothes. Nothing was given to us. I had a paper route, delivering the *Pittsburgh Post-Gazette* every morning at five o'clock. On cold days, my mother—before she had to go to her job—drove me around in her car. Whether she drove me or not, the fact of the matter is that I had a job at eleven years old.

Society has certain issues and challenges, but fundamentally you can get a job if you're used to doing a job. Many times, African-American men haven't had to work at home, so they don't know what it's like to have to go to work every day. Or they work for two weeks, pick up a paycheck, and don't go back.

There are no excuses. You can always find something to do. It may be McDonald's, it may be working for the county picking up garbage in the parks, but it's a job.

JOE: I heard Chris Gardner, whose life was the basis for the movie *The Pursuit of Happyness*, speak to an audience. He was almost as smooth as you, Ulice, but he said the most striking moment in his life was when he went on *Oprah* with his son, Christopher. Oprah asked the boy what it was like to be homeless, and he said: "You know what? I never felt I was homeless because every morning I woke up, my father was there." The No. 1 problem, and you hit on it, is when the father is not present in black *and* white families.

ULICE: The welfare system is set up today to discourage the father from being part of the family since support stops or is severely curtailed if he marries the mother of his child. The child is better off with the father in the house because he can be there to say things like, "Pick your clothes up," "Wash that car," or "Clean those windows."

I have been so blessed that all four of my grandparents had a sense of family. The man was home. The woman ran the household. He went out to get the money, and when he got home, I got the belt when I needed it. You know what I mean?

I grew up that way. My cousins all grew up that way, and we are that way with our children. But it is societal. If you don't have that family base, I think it is very hard for society to solve the problem.

Teachers in the public schools today will tell you that they can't teach a kid if he goes home and is not required to do his homework. So how can you blame the school system for their children's absence or lack of performance in the classroom? It goes back to the family.

The most important photo in my possession was taken when my son was born. My wife, Carmella—she's Mexican-American—and I named him Ulice III, and the photo shows him at four weeks of age, being held by my father in his one good arm after he suffered a stroke.

I see that photo every morning on the way to taking a shower. That photo grounds me. Reminds me who I am and what's most important. That's the man who gave me a whupping when I deserved one and gave me the discipline I've needed to succeed in the business world.

I carry that photo of the three Ulices—Ulice, Sr., Ulice, Jr., and Ulice III—in my head all the time.

Turning a Corner

Now I'd like to give the floor to another African-American, Donnie Walls, who's a young family man in his late thirties. I first met Donnie...well, let's hear directly from him:

I first met Joe back in 1992 when I was a college senior playing basketball at Assumption College in Worcester, Massachusetts. I didn't know Joe at the time, even though I had grown up in Milwaukee, where I was a high school standout on the basketball court. It seems that Joe knew another player on the Assumption team from Milwaukee, a teammate named Demetri Beekman, and Joe flew out to Massachusetts one weekend to watch Demetri in action. After the game, Demetri introduced me to Joe, and Joe immediately invited me to join them for dinner.

Demetri, an African-American like myself, had actually spoken to me about Joe being a good family friend at a previous occasion. I figured that their relationship must be really solid since he came all the way out to Massachusetts to see him play a basketball game.

Joe took us to one of those nice white tablecloth restaurants after the game, where we talked about life and basketball. I remember him asking a lot of questions about me, like my background and my family. I told him that I didn't know my father or have a relationship with him; it was just Mom and my brother and me, and we talked through what that was like. I think I had become a good judge of character being on my own a lot, and Joe seemed to be a straight shooter. After the dinner, he handed me his card and asked if he could stay in contact with me.

I heard from Joe shortly after he got back from Milwaukee, and he gave me a standing invitation to drop by the house at any time. I took him up on that, so whenever I went home, I made a beeline for the Sweeney home, where Tami cooked the best meals—everything from baked chicken to pot roast. I loved coming over and hanging out, shooting baskets in Joe's driveway, and playing two-on-two games with his boys.

Our relationship progressed to the point where I became an extension of the family. At Thanksgiving and Christmas times, I would obviously spend time with my immediate family, but then I'd race over to the Sweeneys', where there was always a setting waiting for me at the dining room table.

After college, I played on an exhibition basketball team out of Columbus, Ohio, called Veritech Rep and then flew to the Czech Republic, where I played in a professional league for three months. That was fun seeing the world, but Joe reminded me that sooner or later I had to get serious about what I was going to do next in life, so I enrolled at U.S. Sports Academy in Mobile, Alabama, for graduate school.

One of the things I had to do to earn my graduate degree, besides writing a thesis, was a mentorship. I knew just the person to ask: Joe Sweeney. During my last semester, I moved back to Milwaukee so that Joe could be my "official" mentor, even though we both knew he had taken me under his wing long before.

I can assure you that it was an unbelievable learning experience working with Joe as my mentor. In terms of professionalism, he showed me how to dress a certain way, present myself a certain way, always be prompt and on time, and how to write a good business letter. In a nutshell, he showed me everything that it takes to succeed as a professional.

He invited me to attend business luncheons with him, where I watched him interact with others. He could definitely work a room because he knew so many people, and many of them spoke highly of him. You couldn't help but learn from him. His contacts seemed endless, and he always had the ability to get things done. There was no person that he would not call. He never hesitated to pick up the phone. He would always say, "You never know what the guy on the other end of the phone might say."

Joe tried to get me to go to the Notre Dame Mendoza College of Business, but I opted to attend law school in Houston, Texas. I had a change of heart, though, so I decided to get my teaching credential with the idea of becoming a high school teacher and coaching basketball. I had been married a few years to LaShonda, so I needed a career that could support a family, and Joe supported that decision.

We're still in Houston, where I teach P.E. at Lee High School and coach the boys' basketball team at Bellaire High. My goal is to someday coach at the college level, but one step at a time. We'll see where the connections I've made in basketball circles take me.

On the family front, since Joe had four kids, I had to have four kids. LaShonda and I accelerated things a bit, though: we have two boys and two girls ranging in age from one to four. No twins. "You move fast," Joe kidded me. Then again, I was always quick on the basketball court.

So what can African-Americans learn from my story about networking? I think it's this point: doors will be either open or shut depending on your mindset. You have to do your homework and be prepared to deliver results. In the coaching world, the bottom line is wins and losses. In the business world, the bottom line is what you can bring to the table financially.

> *"Doors will be either open or shut depending on your mindset. You have to do your homework and be prepared to deliver results."*
>
> *—Donnie Walls*

Joe taught me to be relentless. To never give up. If you really want something that bad, don't be afraid to write a hundred letters to get a meeting with a guy. Call all your contacts and be persistent. A lot of times, I don't think we African-Americans are persistent enough. If something doesn't go our way, some of us play the race card.

One thing my mother taught me was a strong work ethic. She certainly had an unbelievable one. There was not a day I can recall where she did not get up and go to work because she had to provide for her two boys. Joe's the same way. You could call Joe at seven in the morning, and he's up working out or already starting his day. It's all about how much you're willing to work. That's true in business, and that's true in my world—athletics.

I know that Joe is going to go out and speak to businesses and their employees about *Networking Is a Contact Sport*. I've thought about what I would say if I was asked to say a few words at one of his seminars.

Let's say Joe is addressing one hundred agents from a major insurance firm. Let's say the group consists of eighty-five Caucasians, five Asians, and ten African-Americans. If I looked out and saw that everyone was sitting next to someone the same race, I would understand. There's something innate about migrating toward others with the same racial characteristics as you, but I would urge the audience to stand up, move around, and mix things up a bit. Meet someone new. Don't limit yourself mentally.

Then I would remind the audience of an old saying: never judge a book by its cover. You can't tell what someone is like on the inside from what you see on the outside. Then, since I would only have a few minutes—Joe likes to keep things moving—I would finish by saying that networking isn't all black and white, and that I'm living proof of that. Black, white, brown, and Asian, we can all network together, and the sooner we start doing so, the better for us and the better for our nation.

Wrapping Up

Thanks, Donnie. You make me proud.

Let me close with this thought: in April 2008, I celebrated my fiftieth birthday in a big way when Tami and I invited fifty of our closest friends and family members to our home for a big bash. "Fifty for My Fiftieth" was the theme of that special Saturday evening.

Only two people—besides my immediate family—flew in from out of town to be there. One came from Jacksonville, Florida, and the other took a flight from Houston, Texas.

I think you've figured out who they were: LeRoy Butler and Donnie Walls.

When it comes to relationships and networking, that says it all, doesn't it?

Networking Is Not All Black and White

While segregation still exists in this country, the races can—and should—work together, and networking is a great way to break down age-old barriers.

If present demographic trends continue, whites will cease to be in the majority in less than thirty years. The United States has always been a melting pot, a multiracial country, and this will continue happening in coming decades.

1. If you're white, you need to be intentional about your efforts to network with African-Americans, Hispanics, and Asians. Treat others as you would want to be treated.
2. If you're a member of a minority group, learn the language of business, which is making money. Let your common goal of growing your business transcend any racial differences.
3. Whatever industry you're in, *learn* the language. In government, it's governing; in education, it's educating; and in business, it's money.
4. Ulice Payne reminds you to be comfortable in your skin and put others around you at ease. Don't act hesitantly when being introduced to others. Offer a firm handshake and look people in the eyes.
5. Be on a one-man or one-woman mission to break down barriers, one contact at a time. Seek out common ground—your favorite teams, your favorite foods, or your favorite hobbies, sports, and pastimes—and build upon those shared interests.
6. No matter what your situation, avoid the victim mindset and take 100 percent responsibility for what happens in life.

Women and Networking:
A Different Approach

I HAVEN'T TOLD an Irish joke yet, so I'm due. In light of my family background, this one seemed appropriate:

> Mrs. Donovan was walking down O'Connell Street in Dublin when she met Father Flaherty.
>
> The Father said, "Top o' the mornin' to ye! Aren't ye Mrs. Donovan, and didn't I marry ye and yer hoosband two years ago?"
>
> "Aye, that ye did, Fadder," she replied.
>
> "And be there any wee little ones yet?"
>
> "No, not yet, Fadder."
>
> The Father said, "Well, now, I'm goin' to Rome next week, and I'll light a candle for ye and yer hoosband."
>
> "Oh, thank ye, Fadder," she replied, and then they parted ways.
>
> Some years later they met again. The Father asked, "Well now, Mrs. Donovan, how are ye these days?"
>
> "Oh, very well, Fadder!" she replied.
>
> "And tell me, have ye any been blessed wit wee ones yet?"
>
> "Oh yes, Fadder! T'ree sets o' twins and four singles, ten in all!"
>
> "That's wonderful!" the Father exclaimed. "How is yer loving hoosband doing?"
>
> "E's gone to Rome to blow out yer stinking candle."

My parents didn't have t'ree sets of twins and four singles, but they did welcome ten children into the world—nine boys in succession until our caboose—Mary Beth—arrived on the scene. With nine older brothers and a home environment that resembled a locker room more than what you'd find in the pages of *Better Homes & Gardens*, Mary Beth was a tomboy on the order of aviator Amelia Earhart.

Given a family background of mostly brothers, for me, Joe Sweeney, to write about women and networking seems a bit of a stretch, right up there with having my own cooking show on the Food Network. But I'm still going to suit up for this critical chapter because it's important that readers understand how men and women approach networking differently. We have much we can learn from each other.

For those of you of the male persuasion, I don't want you to skip ahead, because women have made incredible gains in the last twenty-five years, especially in leadership positions. I'm sure you have female colleagues at your place of work, so there's some good information ahead that will not only help you network with women but will give you a greater appreciation for how men and women think and act differently, especially in a business setting. You'll also learn about what women do well, like establishing a good rapport before getting down to business, as well as advice on how *you* should comport yourself in a work environment populated with members of the opposite sex.

THE SIDETRACKED HOME EXECUTIVE

I'm aware that plenty of career-minded women marry, have children, and decide to hop on the "mommy track" for a decade or two. That's what Tami and tens of millions of moms like her have done, and I salute that choice.

If you become a mother, leave your job, and decide later on to return to the workforce, networking can help you get back in the game. One thing that may help is staying in contact with colleagues back at your old place of work—something you're probably already doing. People change positions frequently today, though, so while it's good to maintain those ties, there's a good chance you'll have to start all over in terms of networking.

Then again, just because a friend moved over to a different firm or business doesn't mean he or she couldn't hire you for *that* company.

Stop the Presses

Ladies and gentlemen, before we go any further, I must acknowledge a stunning discovery. Please pay close attention to this profound statement of fact:

Women are different than men.

Or, put another way, men are different than women.

Deep, I know.

Many social scientists in recent years have dispelled the idea that men and women are essentially the same underneath the obvious physical differences. My parents would call that commonsense thinking and a recognition that God created the sexes to complement and complete each other. While men typically act more aggressively and have the single-minded drive to accomplish tasks, women tend to be more supportive. Whereas women tend to value love, communication, beauty, and relationships, a man's sense of self is often defined by his ability to achieve results.

> *While men typically act more aggressively and have the single-minded drive to accomplish tasks, women tend to be more supportive.*

Men and women think and speak differently. *Men Are from Mars, Women Are from Venus* author John Gray writes: "...a multitude of scientific studies have clearly indicated many differences between men's and women's brains as well as in the way they use them." There are two sides of the brain, the left brain and the right brain, and the left brain houses more of the logical, analytical, factual, and aggressive centers of thought, while the right side of the brain harbors feelings and imagination as well as relational, language, and communication skills. "In general, women tend to use both sides of their brains simultaneously, while men use one side or the other," Gray said.[15]

These differing characteristics are why women relieve stress by talking with others about their feelings while guys prefer *not* to talk about their feelings and "retreat into their cave," as Gray described it. Women complain about problems because they want their problems to be acknowledged, he wrote, while men complain about problems because they're seeking solutions.

Deborah Tannen, Ph.D., an Oxford-trained specialist in linguistics who's studied the differing conversational styles of men and women, confirmed these dissimilarities. Men grow up in a world in which conversation is often a contest, she said, either to achieve the upper hand or prevent other people from pushing them over. Men are socialized to win, while women are socialized for acceptance. For women, a conversation is seen as a way to exchange confirmation and support, not an opportunity to speak authoritatively and command respect.

Dr. Tannen used an example from her own life to demonstrate her point. At one time, she and her husband—also a professor—held academic positions in different cities, which necessitated being apart most of the week. Friends made comments like, "That must be rough," or "How do you stand it?" She naturally accepted her friends' sympathy and even reinforced it, saying, "The worst part is having to pack and unpack all the time."

When her husband heard those comments, though, his back stiffened because he viewed them as being mildly critical of their unconventional working arrangement—and henceforth their marriage. He sought to win over their friends by reminding them that their teaching and research schedules meant four-day weekends, four months off in the summer, and long vacations. (Note to self: for your next career, consider becoming a college professor.)

At first, Deborah Tannen was put off by her husband's defiance and didn't understand why he chose to say those things, but she came around to his point of view. "I now see that my husband was simply approaching the world as many men do: as a place where people try to achieve and maintain status," said Dr. Tannen. "I, on the other hand, was approaching the world as many women do: as a network of connections seeking support and consensus."[16]

As this simple story illustrates, men and women have fundamentally different networking styles. Women engage in "rapport talk" and men use "report talk," said Dr. Tannen, which means that men talk to exchange information whereas women converse in order to strengthen their relationships. "Men should accept that many women regard exchanging details about their personal lives as a basic ingredient of intimacy, and women should accept that many men do not share this view," she wrote in *You Just Don't Understand.*[17]

Susan Wehrley, a growth and leadership consultant from Milwaukee, told me that men can learn from women how to begin conversations and show interest in learning more about the other person, while women can learn from men how to close a conversation by "asking for the sale," as they say on the street.

What many guys do after the conversational preliminaries have run their course is reach into their breast pocket and whip out a business card. The next sentence comes out by rote: "Here's my contact information. I sell 401(k) retirement plans. When can we have lunch?"

It would be far better, said Susan, if men could think of a way to establish a rapport as women do. You do that by looking for openings—any opening—that can move you beyond the "Nice to meet you" phase. A sample idea: *Pleased to meet you, Magnus. Is that a Swedish name? Have you ever visited Scandinavia?*

"You have to establish a friendly connection and engage that person—especially if she's a female—before you can offer a business card," Susan said. "And never accompany a card with a hard-sell invitation. Instead, say something like, 'It's been great meeting you and getting to know you better. Here's my card if I can ever help.'"

> *"You have to establish a friendly connection and engage that person—especially if she's a female—before you can offer a business card."*
> —Susan Wehrley

Women, on the other hand, are more engaging and ask open-ended questions to establish a connection. They will inquire about your family, if you have kids and what ages they are, and how they're doing in school and sports. Women share feelings and gather people close to them much better than men do, but many never get to the "here's my card" part because of their reluctance to "trade in" on their relationship.

"As a result, women 'networkers' are all too often not taken as seriously as males," Susan said. "To succeed in networking, women have to become a little more results oriented—asking for the order, as they say. So many women fail to do this. I've heard some women say, 'I've gone to every Chamber of Commerce mixer in the state of Wisconsin, I've been networking a lot, and everyone likes me, but I don't have anything to show for it.'"

Chances are, according to Susan, the lack of results was because these women failed to follow through as though it were a business transaction.

Sheila Stewart, an author and coach for woman entrepreneurs, says that there will be times that women have to "man up" in the corporate marketplace.

Empowering Women

It's time to meet Sheila Stewart, who says that working women can be feminine, successful, and happy, but there will be times when they'll have to "man up" in the corporate world.

When I heard Sheila speak at a business networking event in Los Angeles, I was in the midst of writing this book. I was so impressed with Sheila's presentation that I intercepted her to ask if she would be willing to share her insights with women reading *Networking Is a Contact Sport*.

With a networking spirit that was out to give, not get, Sheila said yes.

Calling herself a "serial entrepreneur," Sheila started out in hotel management after graduating from the University of Denver in the early 1990s. She has steadily climbed the corporate ladder, creating a national reputation as a marketing expert and building an award-winning advertising agency. These days, Sheila, who is the author of *Backwards in High Heels: A Woman's Guide to Succeeding in Business*, spends much of her time coaching other women entrepreneurs.

I began by asking Sheila what women should know about networking. She had this to say:

Every single day, women hear thousands of thoughts swirling through their brains—a "little voice" offering a running commentary or making the most self-deprecating statements. I would say that 85 percent of the circulating comments inside women's heads are negative. Here are a few of my favorite examples:

- *Who do you think you are? Aren't you too young for this? Too old?*
- *What makes you think you can succeed in business? You'll never be successful.*
- *What makes you think you can go into that conference room and succeed when you're the only woman? You aren't prepared well enough.*
- *The guys are looking at you, and they know you're not as pretty as those new hires.*

When I started my career working for the largest hotel-management company in the world, I was the only woman on the fourteenth floor who wasn't a secretary—and the only woman in that department traveling with men. It took me a while to gain my footing because I heard the same negative thoughts as well: *What makes you think you can manage the industry's largest trade show? You're fresh out of college. You can't supervise multimillion-dollar budgets. You're in way over your head.*

I had to periodically dump my "head trash" so that it wouldn't hold me back. You will have to make the same trip to the county landfill as well. The thing about head trash is that you absolutely cannot ignore it, push it aside, or stifle it. You have to completely acknowledge that your thoughts and feelings are real and then deal with them.

A great way to acknowledge your feelings is to write them down in a journal, something I do almost every single night. Record all your thoughts and feelings—the good, the bad, and the ugly. Once you write them down, you can visually make a connection and start dealing with them. Tell yourself, *I don't really believe that. That's not the way I think. That's not who I am.*

Do women have more of these negative thoughts than men? I don't know the answer to that, but I do know that women are wired differently than men. Men typically need a goal or a deadline to focus on, and they can concentrate on only one overarching task at a time. Women, on the other hand, are multitaskers, capable of juggling several assignments. I've had women tell me they have washable chalk in their bathroom shower so they can write themselves notes as they lather up and get ready to attack the day. We're used to doing several things at once because that's how our brains work.

I see the differences between men and women whenever I'm in a networking environment, like at a reception or mixer. When men introduce themselves, it's all about egos: *I'm John Smith. I'm in real estate and I flipped four thousand mansions last year. I charge $4 million per mansion, so I generated a little over $239 million, which makes sense since I have five degrees and own ten companies. And who are you and what do you do?*

> "*I see the difference between men and women whenever I'm in a networking environment, like at a reception or mixer. When men introduce themselves, it's all about egos.*"
> —Sheila Stewart

A woman would never do that with another woman or a man. She would be more likely to start asking questions to elicit information from the *other* person. If it's a man that she's talking to, she never wants to come across as arrogant or braggadocio. That's because we operate from the right side of the brain, which is the heart.

I counsel women, when they are meeting men, to "man up" and get in touch with their right brain, if they can. If you don't believe in what you're doing, guys can smell fear or doubt a mile away. You have to have the power and confidence within, and that comes from here—the gut. You have to play big or go home. If you don't, you'll get left in the dust.

I like Sheila's insights, especially the refrain to "man up" when you find yourself in a predominantly male environment. That doesn't mean barking orders or bossing people around. Rather, it's about adopting a communication style that stays on point, one that is bottom-line oriented. It's also about using the language of the workplace—the abbreviations, the shorthand ways of describing procedures and work flow, and trendy buzzwords like "value justification," "business objective," "lean initiatives," and my favorite—"benchmarking."

A balance must be sought, however. Talking in jargon—"We're seeing incremental improvement in user engagement, but until our brand identity has been measured for success metrics…"—doesn't do anyone any good. You still have to sound believable, be relaxed, and act comfortably in your skin.

But guys, we can "woman up," too. We need to manifest the characteristics of establishing trust and rapport at the front end of our networking interactions, taking our time to listen before speaking, and to empathize before pursuing our agenda. The idea of creating some sort of intimacy—or bonding, to use a more masculine term—with our networking contacts is a practice that can help us in our business careers as well as our interpersonal lives.

Sexual Tension in Networking

During our conversation, Sheila addressed the sexual tension that can arise between men and women. In a workplace where people of the opposite sex interact with each other for eight, nine, and ten hours a day, where they are physically close, where they are thrown together on projects, where there is bantering and flirting going on, there's a fine line between innocent cooperation and a sexually charged atmosphere. In an age where sexual harassment lawsuits ruin careers, break up relationships and marriages, and cost companies huge settlements, this topic must be discussed.

I observed to Sheila that it must be very difficult for attractive women to either network or get their work done because some men—especially in a social setting after consuming an adult beverage or two—have a tough time corralling their minds or their tongues. So they make inappropriate comments, often with double meanings, to see if there is a reciprocal response.

"What should women do in those situations?" I asked Sheila.

"It's all about the energy you put out," she replied. "If you're confident as a woman with all aspects of your life, confident with your knowledge, confident with your looks, there is no sexual tension. There might be sexual energy from him, the man you are talking to or interacting with, but it is not fueled by your energy because you are putting out a different energy than he is."

"But what should an attractive woman do if a guy is hitting on her but he holds the keys to a $32 million account?" I wondered. "How should she deal with that?"

"I've done a lot of work in certain industries where their language can often stray from proper discourse," she replied. "Your first response should be not to add fuel to the fire. You can acknowledge the comment in passing, but do not reciprocate in any manner, if that makes any sense. Sometimes I have been in situations where the guy was doing that to test me, to see how I would handle his borderline remark. I decided not to overreact, ignore the pass, and stay focused on business. Other times in those situations, I've made a snicker and said sarcastically, 'Oh, aren't you funny,' and then got right back to business. The important point is to keep the conversation moving *away* from the sexual stuff."

If you're a guy reading this, listen up, because any unwelcome comments of a sexual nature can be considered to be sexual harassment, which is legally viewed as a form of sex discrimination. As someone who has sat on the board of directors of nearly two dozen companies, I can assure you that sexual harassment charges are big deals, expensive to defend, and a huge black mark in your personnel file—if you're not fired.

So watch what you say.

It's Good to Have Girlfriends

I had one more important question for Sheila: "Do you have an inner circle of women that you confide in or bring into your confidence?" What I really wanted to know was whether Sheila had wingmen in her life.

She did, but she used another term. "Yes, I do," she replied. "Every woman needs to have six girlfriends on speed dial. When you've had a rough day at the office, or a tough business trip, or whatever it is, you need to call your six girlfriends, talk it all out. If you call your husband or boyfriend, he'll want to figure out how to 'fix' the situation when all you're really interested in doing is venting about your dilemma, the fix you're in, or the boss who doesn't quite get it."

Having these six Girlfriends—with a capital G—hasn't always been the case for Sheila. "I didn't have Girlfriends until four years ago when I was going through what I call my COD—Crap-Out Day. I needed an inner circle of women I could draw upon; women who would listen to me vent about things that were going on in my world because I don't typically do girl talk. I'm not the type who goes to bunco parties on Thursday nights. That's not who I am, and I don't get any enjoyment out of that. Instead, I have a network of six powerful, strong Girlfriends, and I cherish those relationships. I know that somebody has my back."

While I was pleased to hear about the Girlfriends that Sheila had taken into her confidence, she also told me that development happened only four years ago. I asked her why.

"Because I started my career in a predominantly good ol' boys network, so everything in my early career was based on men," she replied. "I always believed that if I rolled up my sleeves and did business like a man, I would be fine; but I found out that I needed more. It was lonely being the only woman in the boardroom. Where could I go? I couldn't go to clients because I didn't want them to think that I was in any sort of trouble or inexperienced. If I did, they could have pulled their business. So I had to hold it in, which is when I went through my crap-out phase with all the physical ramifications. That's when I realized that I needed to start talking about my issues with other successful women."

I stopped Sheila right there. "Let's say I'm Betty Smith. I live in Bettendorf, Iowa, I run an insurance company, and I feel all alone. How do I position or frame up my six Girlfriends? Do you say, 'Do you want to be my Girlfriend?' How do you ask that question?"

"What you need to do is you look at who's in your network now and where you want to be. So when you go looking for Girlfriends in your network, it's almost like you need a combination of three levels of women: those who just started their careers or business ventures; those who've found their niche in their business or corporate life; and those who are well-established in their careers, be it in their business or in a corporate setting. They will help you stretch your mind and push you to play big in your environment."

And support you like a big sister.

Gail Lione: Revved Up to Serve Others

Milwaukee is the twenty-third largest city in the United States, but in many ways, it still feels like a small Midwest burg where everyone knows your name.

If you shoehorned a couple of hundred Milwaukee business types into a crowded bar and asked them to name the most respected leaders in the local business community, Gail Lione's name would be on the lips of many. As the Executive Vice President, General Counsel, and Secretary for one of the most testosterone-charged companies in the United States—Harley-Davidson, the iconic maker of motorcycles with a distinctive design and engine exhaust note— Gail Lione is a trailblazer for the way she's integrated herself into the Harley-Davidson culture as well as the Milwaukee community.

HARLEY DAVIDSON

Don't get the idea that Gail Lione, the Executive Vice President, General Counsel, and Secretary of Harley-Davidson, doesn't like to let her hair down. This corporate lawyer loves to gun her Harley chopper during summer rides.

The reason why Gail is well-respected in local business circles is because she throws herself into community involvements—the ultimate networking experience. I know Gail from serving on the Bradley Center Board of Directors with her (the board chaired by Ulice Payne), but that's just a warm-up for her civic duty. She currently serves on the boards of the Milwaukee Art Museum, the YMCA of Milwaukee, and the Greater Milwaukee Committee. Until the end of 2007, she served on the United Way board and co-chaired the 2004 United Way campaign, which raised $37 million for Milwaukee charities.

You could say that Gail brings a truckload of corporate world experience to any boardroom. From having sat beside her in day-long meetings, I can attest to her sharp legal mind and attention to detail.

So when I asked Gail if I could interview her for *Networking Is a Contact Sport* to get her perspective for some do's and don'ts for women and networking, she initially demurred. "I might not be the best person for you to talk about that," she said. "I actually have huge issues with the word 'networking' because of the perception that networking is all about handing out business cards and getting in front of as many people as you can. To me, there's a superficiality about that. I have always approached my life not from the standpoint of collecting friends but from the standpoint of building communities of people who share the same passion for things in life."

> *"I've always approached my life not from the standpoint of collecting friends but from the standpoint of building communities of people who share the same passion for things in life."*
> —Gail Lione

Wait a second, Gail. We can ride alongside each other on this networking highway. "Just so you know," I said, "the whole idea of *Networking Is a Contact Sport* is that networking is a place you go to give, not to get."

"If that's your operating premise," she replied, "then I support that because I really do believe that networking is about building communities that share your passion—like opera, ballet, social outreaches, or legal services to those who are underrepresented."

Gail said that as a woman, she feels the best way she can "network" is to mentor young attorneys—women *and* men. "The value to me is that you see things through their eyes," she said. "Developing relationships with younger attorneys makes *my* work more meaningful. I feel like I'm contributing something important to my community when I connect with others."

Gail Lione is in one of the top legal positions in one of the top-branded companies in the United States. Even though she doesn't consciously think about networking every moment of the day, she certainly *gets* what networking is all about.

Thanks, Gail, for the reminder to discover what your passion is, get involved in the community, and nurture others through mentoring.

Saints Preserve Us

As I bring this chapter on networking and women to a close, let me tell you why the joke about Mrs. Donovan and her ten children was so funny to me. You see, I ended up marrying a woman whose grandparents got married late, in their thirties, but ended up still having ten kids, just like Mrs. Donovan. Instead of t'ree sets of twins and four singles, though, Dorsey and Betty Botham started with *two* sets of twins, back to back, before delivering six singles. Two years into their marriage, they had four kids to care for.

Remember, this double-double happened in the 1930s, long before fertility drugs and in vitro fertilization came around. The first set of Botham twins were Jane and Dorsey James, Jr., but their parents—for whatever reason—nicknamed them "Nip" and "Tuck."

Tuck married a woman named Ginny, and they had six daughters, one right after another, with my future wife, Tami, being the oldest. Unlike my parents, though, Tuck and Ginny decided not to test fate in their quest for a boy and stopped at six daughters.

Meanwhile, I grew up in a crowded home with nine rambunctious males, where if one of my brothers was off base or out of line, he got called out on it. In fact, I learned that it was a sign of weakness if you didn't demand that your brother back up what he said or make him aware that you were on to him about a certain issue. (*"Hey, Mike, we all know that you've been lying about dating Jennifer."*) We were always calling each other out in front of others—even at the dinner table.

Meanwhile, Tami grew up in a sorority house with five sisters. We're talking a well-run ship: clothes neatly folded and no cut-down humor. The household *modus operandi* was "Peace at all costs."

So think about it: someone who's trained to call people out—that would be me—marries a young woman who was raised to keep the peace at all costs. Given these differences, it took a lot of work on both our parts to understand one another and communicate effectively. And just as couples learn to relate better through studying each other, women in the workplace need to learn the language of men if they're interacting with them for their job (and men need to learn the language of women).

But watch how you communicate that language. One of the things that vividly illustrates the differences in communication styles between men and women is tone. I'm going to step into the Stereotypical Zone for a moment, but a lot of times, men are flat-out direct in their speech and decision making. Tami thinks I can be rude at times, but I'm not. I'm just direct in my tone and language. In my world, those are attributes, and if a male manager or executive is perceived as tough and hard-nosed, he's said to be a *good* businessman.

Not so on the female side. If a woman is tough and hard-nosed, she'll get a reputation for being a shrew, or worse. But if she's nice and sweet to everybody, then the rank-and-file think they can walk all over her. It's a real catch-22 for women—and very unfair.

What I've learned from great female networkers is that you should combine your heart and your head. Don't be given to emotional mood swings. Don't take yourself too seriously. Focus on getting the job done. Be pleasant to be around, even self-deprecating, and others—men and women—will be drawn to you and want to network with you.

Women and Networking—A Different Approach

1. Bring levity to the situation. Great networkers (male or female) have a great sense of humor and are funny and upbeat. I'll take a person with humor much more seriously than someone without one.

2. Use self-deprecation to defuse situations. Having a biting spirit won't endear you to others.

3. As Sheila Stewart says, gather up any negative thoughts—"head trash"—and banish them. What's past is past, and any questions about your abilities are irrelevant.

4. Look for several women that you can put on speed dial. Women need wingmen (or Girlfriends) in their lives.

5. Become involved in your community—from volunteering in your children's classroom to helping out with breast cancer awareness walks. It's a great way to network.

Networking
in a Facebook
and Twitter World

I'VE ALWAYS BEEN an early adopter of technology.

Back in 1996 and 1997 during the height of my Brett Favre sports marketing days, I juggled three cell phones even though they were about as portable as paving bricks. I also signed up with AOL back in the mid-1990s so that I could use this new innovation called "electronic mail."

Nearly fifteen years later, I still have my original AOL e-mail address—it's like a teddy bear that I can't give up—that goes straight to my smartphone and iMac at my downtown office. If I had a buck for every time Elwood Edwards informed me "You've got mail," I could afford one of the newly remodeled Club Suites at Miller Park.

When I'm on the road or out of the office, I rely on my BlackBerry, where I can make phone calls, receive voicemails, and keep abreast of a blizzard of e-mails. For all the high-tech gizmos in my life, however, I must confess that I'm not an authority regarding social networking sites such as Facebook, MySpace, and Twitter, or online professional networking websites such as LinkedIn, Plaxo, Spoke, XING, and Yahoo! Kickstart, which are virtual communities focused on business-related interactions and relationships instead of purely social ones.

There have been hundreds of books written on social networking, but if you're looking for a great book on this topic, I recommend *The Zen of Social Media Marketing* by Shama Hyder Kabani, a social media wizard and president of the Web-marketing firm Marketing Zen.

I certainly understand how social networking can help advance our careers and help us meet like-minded individuals online. But I'm also finding that a great deal of time spent on social networking sites is not really productive, and that online interactions are often superficial and unimportant. This creates an opportunity for you, as I'll explain in a bit.

Let me give you a few examples of what I think really works in the world of social networking.

First of all, social media provide a superb research tool. Let's say that you meet some people at your child's school play or at your house of worship and you'd like to find out more about them. If they have Facebook pages, you can learn where they went to high school and/or college, or you can view pictures of the entire family or the most recent soccer game. In other words, you can use this information to break the ice the next time you see each other.

Social media can also be a great way to promote a business. For example, ever since *Sex and the City* ignited a cupcake craze by featuring Magnolia Bakery in New York's Greenwich Village, cupcake bakeries have sprouted around the country.

On the West Coast, Sprinkles Cupcakes opened up the first cupcake bakery in Beverly Hills. So how could they create a Hollywood-like buzz where their freshly baked treats would inspire long lines of devoted movie stars and serious epicureans alike? By launching a "fan page" on Facebook and offering a free cupcake each day to the first fifty people who showed up at each of its locations across the country, including the original Beverly Hills shop as well as bakeries in Chicago, Dallas, Phoenix, and Palo Alto, California.

What a promotion! More than 135,000 people have signed up as fans of Sprinkles's Facebook page, and each morning they receive a Facebook announcement giving them the "secret word" for the day. A typical message: "Another manic Monday? The first fifty people to whisper 'sugar rush' at each Sprinkles receive a free cupcake of their choice!"

Talk about having customers beat a path to your front door—patrons who probably purchase a few extra ginger lemon, chocolate coconut, and red velvet cupcakes to satisfy their sweet cravings later that day.

That's an excellent way to promote your business on Facebook, which has become the great white shark in the social networking ocean. More than 300 million people have signed up for Facebook, and half of them visit the site every day. My oldest son, Kyle, jumped on Facebook in 2004, and he was soon joined by Conor, Kelly, and Brendan, as well as millions of others. The principal reason why Facebook has become a phenomenon is the simplicity of uploading photos to your personal page and creating posts on your wall for your Facebook friends to comment on.

> *More than 300 million people have signed up for Facebook, and half of them visit the site every day.*

That's the good side to social networking online. But I would like to offer a contrarian view to the conventional wisdom regarding the Facebook/Twitter social networking world, and it's this: Are we really more connected today with all these technological gadgets and applications? In my mind, being virtually connected and personally connected are two entirely different things. Sure, we need both in today's world, but I would caution that the *quality* of your network is more important than your *quantity*. I'd rather see you connected with 300 "live" people than 300 "friends" on Facebook. When I hear a nineteen-year-old boast that he has 1,325 "friends" on Facebook, I really wonder what that means.

Besides, have you thought about what a "friend" is lately? Here's my definition: a friend is someone you know well enough to have a genial give-and-take discussion or friendly argument with. A friend is someone you can grasp in a hug or tap on the shoulder. A friend is someone you chat up at a backyard barbecue or church picnic. In other words, I think a friend is someone you share an experience with.

The personal touch always trumps being electronically connected. Sure, the world has changed and there are important connections made online, but if you're looking about where *best* to invest your time at work and after work, I'd seek out people that you can look in the eye, not some pixelized image viewed on an LCD screen.

One of the things that bothers me about today's wired world is that some people never leave their homes or apartments and still say they feel "connected." I would argue that unless you reach out and touch someone, you really don't know him or her.

Perhaps I say that because I've always been a hands-on type of guy, one who likes to hug and tease people. A personal phone call, a written letter, or a handwritten note mean a hundred times more than being on the recipient list of an impersonal e-mail blast or text message. I believe in the virtue of getting on the phone, sending out a book, or mailing a note of encouragement or recognition. That's how you stand out from the pack, and standing out is what my style of networking is all about.

Figuring Out Who Your Friends Are

Let's say you become a fan of mine on Facebook after reading *Networking Is a Contact Sport*. You've become a fan for the right reasons—you want to learn more about how to become a better networker by reading the insights I share as well as tidbits from others who've joined my online community.

You and I could have one hundred fruitful exchanges on Facebook, an engaging online dialogue, but we would not be as well-connected as we'd be if we sat across a table and broke bread together just one time.

That's why this would be a good time to figure out who your real friends are, and I have a way to help you. It's a ranking system that you can use to figure out who's important in your life. I call it the Friend Assessment Quotient, or FAQ.

Everyone you come into contact with, including your Facebook friends, can be categorized on a scale of 1 to 5. Here's an outline of the FAQ scale:

- **1s are people you don't know.** Here in America, there are about 300 million you don't know, but they are still potential clients and customers.
- **2s are the people you *barely* know or know by name and not much else.** They can also be people you'd like to get to know or sound like they would be interesting to meet. I would put Paul McCartney, Nelson Mandela, and LeBron James in this latter category.
- **3s are your acquaintances, people you've met before and know well enough to wave hello to at parents-teacher night or kids' soccer games.** Maybe they work for the same company but in a different department. You know them by sight but haven't socialized with them yet.
- **4s are your friends, and this is actually a wide-open category since there are different levels of friends.** There are friends that you enjoy chatting with after a high school football game, but you don't see yourself inviting them over for a Super Bowl party. At the other end of the spectrum, there are genuine friends that you would invite to your Super Sunday bash or one of your special birthdays that end in a zero. Some of these 4s could be your Facebook friends.
- **5s are your lifelines, your inner circle, and your wingmen.** They are your close friends that you'd call if you had a flat tire or needed someone to watch your kids when a family member

---

TWITTERING AWAY

Twitter is hot right now—kind of like the "wildcat" offense in the NFL. Is it a fad? Fox football analyst Troy Aikman, a former Dallas Cowboy quarterback, said something rather profound: "Everyone is doing it because they feel like it's what they're supposed to do, yet nobody really knows why they're doing it."

Nonetheless, I plan to Twitter when *Networking Is a Contact Sport* is released, although I'm not sure the world cares whether I went on my morning jog. I'll do my best to come up with something interesting to say before my 140 characters are used up. (You can follow me at @networkingjoe.)

had to be rushed to the emergency room. They have your back, and you have theirs.

Study this list. Even though the whole idea is to not put people in boxes and "categorize" them, do you see the point? We all have friends who are 2s and 3s. Maybe you met them one time at a mixer and you exchanged business cards. Maybe they're old high school classmates, members of the same church, or people who belong to your swim club. Sure, you're friendly to each other, but at the end of the day, you have a superficial relationship.

If you were a 2 or a 3 with me and you sent me an e-mail about your life insurance business, I wouldn't make a major purchase like that without having you step inside my living room, shake my hand, and let me get the measure of you. I have to see the whites of your eyes before I'll do business with you.

I prefer to invest my limited hours on this earth spending time with people I'd like to get to know (my 2s), spending more time with my 3s so that they can become 4s, and checking in with my wing-men—my 5s—who *are* my best friends. I'd do anything for them, and I know they feel the same way about me.

In conclusion, to be the most effective networker in today's high-tech world, you need to combine the new technology with the old-school way of connecting, which is to reach out and touch someone. In my next chapter, I'll introduce you to two Master Networkers who've reached and touched someone throughout their professional lives.

Networking in a Facebook and Twitter World

1. There is no substitute for the personal touch.

2. Use the Internet to stay connected, but stay connected to yourself. Ask yourself if your social networking relationships are moving the ball down the field or just a mechanism to spin your wheels.

3. Remember that the words you type in and the pictures you post on social networking sites like Facebook are there for the world to view. These days, many human resources directors, as part of their background checks, routinely perform a Facebook search of every job applicant, looking for incriminating photos that could disqualify them from hiring. Some companies can access photos that you've deleted from your Facebook page—like the one where you were plastered and holding a red plastic cup of booze.

4. Step back and look at the commitments in your life. If you find yourself too distracted by e-mail, Facebook, Twitter, etc., you need to decide how much time to devote to social networking.

5. Ninety-nine percent of the time, the particulars shared on Facebook and Twitter is TMI—too much information. I don't want to know that the traffic was horrible during your morning commute. I don't need to know that you have a "touch of stomach flu." I'm sorry your daughter needs braces, but I don't need to read about it.

6. View Twitter like a giant cocktail party. Just as you'd never start promoting your products or services the minute you meet someone at an event, take things slow and natural on Twitter. Promote in moderation and in no more than 10 percent of tweets.

7. Steer clear of topics like politics and religion, which can be divisive. You can cause all sorts of grief with 140 characters.

8. If you've been going back and forth with someone via e-mail and haven't resolved things by the third exchange, pick up the phone and connect with that person.

9. If you're over fifty like me, try to make at least one new friend a year with someone under twenty-five, which will help you understand the Net Generation.

10. It's important to be conversant and comfortable with technology, which can provide incredible new opportunities that weren't possible before.
11. With the speed of changing technology, it's crucial to educate yourself on what works for you to stay in contact with others. Remember, though, that the personal touch can be lost.
12. Don't confuse sending out tons of e-mails or two dozen tweets a day as qualifying you for Master Networking status.

The Master Networkers:
Bud Selig and Craig Leipold

WHAT IS A MASTER NETWORKER? Is it someone who always follows up on referrals, maintains a positive attitude, and never eats alone? Perhaps, but I think there's more to becoming a top networker.

I measure whether someone is a master networker not by the *quality* or *quantity* of their network but by what they've accomplished *with* and *for* others. Master networkers remain upbeat in a bad situation, keep their word, and don't think too highly of themselves or their position. But what master networkers have that others don't is *passion*—a passion to connect with others and a passion to be part of things greater than themselves. Master networkers know that these twin goals are not mutually exclusive. They understand that without great connections with other like-minded individuals, great accomplishments can never happen.

I could easily scroll through my BlackBerry and come up with a couple of dozen examples of "master networkers," but I'm going to limit myself to two: Bud Selig, a Milwaukee native who's the commissioner of Major League Baseball, and Craig Leipold, owner of the Minnesota Wild NHL hockey franchise. Their interesting stories and their passion for networking should prove instructive on how you can adopt a networking mindset.

Bud Selig: The Master Networker from Milwaukee

He's known around the country as the "Commish"—the chief executive of Major League Baseball who negotiates labor and television contracts, oversees the sport's umpiring crews, and maintains the integrity of the game.

Although Bud Selig is not universally loved around the country, he's certainly Milwaukee's favorite son for what he has accomplished in baseball over nearly five decades. He was instrumental in bringing Major League Baseball back to Milwaukee in 1970 following the departure of the Milwaukee Braves for the greener pastures of Atlanta in 1965.

As owner of the Milwaukee Brewers (formerly the bankrupt Seattle Pilots), he spearheaded the efforts to build a new ballpark, known today as Miller Park. He stepped into the role of Acting Commissioner in 1992 at a time when Major League Baseball was fractured between the owners and the players union, and he helped put baseball back on its feet after a crippling 232-day baseball strike canceled the last six weeks of the 1994 season and World Series. Bud Selig was named Commissioner in 1998, a position that he plans to hold until 2012 when he retires at the age of seventy-eight.

I know Bud Selig, but not because we run in the same circles; believe me, Bud networks with the highest circle of influencers of anyone I've ever known. We first met back on a cool, drizzly night in June 1984 when I attended a talk given by Bud in the bowels of Milwaukee County Stadium to local up-and-coming business executives. He delivered an interesting presentation about the economics of baseball, and I came away suitably impressed.

Our paths started crossing more frequently in the early 1990s when I was president of the Wisconsin Sports Authority. I was part of several committees that worked with the Brewers and the Wisconsin State Legislature to finance a new baseball stadium as well as bringing the 2002 All-Star game to Miller Park. Before the Bob Costas Hall of Fame dinner, I called Bud and made a personal plea for his attendance. "Bud, you gotta come," I said. "Your old shortstop, Robin Yount, is being inducted for his twenty seasons with the Brewers."

"Really?" Bud said.

"And by the way, Uke [referring to Brewer broadcaster and comic Bob Uecker] is inducting Robin. You know that Uke will have us in tears laughing." The acting commissioner bought a table and was in the audience that magical night.

Bud lived north of Milwaukee in Bayside, which abuts my hometown of Fox Point. There were Sunday afternoons during the off-season when I would spot him going for a walk—all alone. On more than one occasion, I stopped Bud and asked him, "Hey, Bud, you want to walk with someone?"

"Sure, Joe," he'd say, and we would have the most fascinating conversations as we exercised our legs and our minds.

As I thought about whom I wanted to name as my "Master Networkers," there was no doubt that Bud Selig would top my list. I called the commissioner's office with a request to drop in and interview him, and bingo, within a week, I found myself on the thirtieth floor of Milwaukee's U.S. Bank Center, Wisconsin's tallest skyscraper at forty-two stories. The view of Lake Michigan from the commissioner's office is awesome. (Isn't it something that Bud moved the commissioner's office from New York City to Milwaukee, Wisconsin?)

I was particularly interested in asking Bud how he networked back in the 1960s to convince wealthy patrons to back him in a quest to return Major League Baseball to Milwaukee after the Braves left for Atlanta.

Before I share his answers, let me give you a little background about Bud so that you can understand the context. Allen H. "Bud" Selig was the son of parents who owned a car dealership in West Allis, a Milwaukee suburb. When I read disparaging stories about Bud, sometimes the writer will make a snide remark that Bud was a "used-car salesman" so untalented that "he couldn't sell GM cars in West Allis, Wisconsin," which is another way of saying that Selig couldn't sell snow cones in Las Vegas during a summer heat wave.

Bud was never a car salesman. Following graduation at the University of Wisconsin—his roommate, Herb Kohl, would one day be a U.S. Senator from Wisconsin and owner of the Milwaukee Bucks—Bud began his career in the "family business" by working in the front office of his father's dealership.

Bud was a huge baseball fan growing up, and the commissioner-to-be was watching from the upper deck at Milwaukee County Stadium on September 23, 1957, when Hank Aaron clinched the National League pennant for the Milwaukee Braves with a monstrous two-run, walk-off home run in the bottom of the eleventh inning. "One of the greatest moments of my baseball career. So dramatic. So emotional," Bud said.

He got the baseball bug and purchased some public stock in the Milwaukee Braves while he was still in his late twenties. Then some ominous dark clouds began appearing on the horizon in 1964: Bud was hearing reports that the Braves' majority owners, based in Chicago, were looking to move the club to the Deep South—Atlanta.

What? And leave Milwaukee baseball fans in the lurch, including one of the Braves' biggest boosters, Bud Selig?

"I was twenty-nine-years old and a baseball fan, and the possibility of the Braves moving was heartbreaking," he said.

He needed backers—financial angels—to get a major league team back in Milwaukee. A plan formed in his mind to form a consortium. So he started networking.

Bud often ate lunch at the Milwaukee Athletic Club. (Remember in Chapter 1, "The Art of Networking," how I described the venerable Athletic Club as a place where the movers and shakers of Milwaukee would meet over lunch and after work?)

One day, Bud was having lunch with Bill Anderson, the Milwaukee County Stadium manager. They were talking baseball when Bud spotted Bob Uihlein, the chairman of the Joseph Schlitz Brewing Company, at another table. (Back in the 1960s, Schlitz Beer was something to which you could raise a foamy glass. The brewery was the Anheuser-Busch of its day. Schlitz was known as the "beer that made Milwaukee famous," and everyone could repeat its advertising slogan: "When you're out of Schlitz, you're out of beer.")

Bud leaned over to Bill, who obviously knew Bob Uihlein well since plastic cups of Schlitz were sold by the thousands at each Braves game. "Do you think you can introduce me?" he asked.

No problem, Bill Anderson replied.

"So I went over to Bobby and poured out my heart about baseball and what I wanted to do [to keep baseball in Milwaukee]," Bud remembered. "I said we needed to form a group. After an hour, a big hand went out, and he said to count him in."

Bud then approached Ben Barkin, a prominent public relations director at Schlitz who knew everybody in Milwaukee, and they would spend evenings brainstorming about Bud's secret ambition. Barkin set the wheels in motion for Bud to meet Edmund Fitzgerald, a patron of Milwaukee arts and civic projects and the son of a family that owned Great Lakes shipyards. In 1975, the freighter *SS Edmund Fitzgerald*, named for Edmund's father, sunk on Lake Superior and claimed the lives of twenty-nine crew members. (And now you know the rest of the story behind Gordon Lightfoot's 1976 song, "The Wreck of the *Edmund Fitzgerald*.")

After hearing the earnestness in Bud's voice, Edmund said he wanted in, too. "So now I have Bob and Ed going into this group with me," Bud told me. "My only contribution to the group was Herb Kohl, who was my college roommate. Ed gave me two more names of people that could help us: Dwayne Bowman, who owned Bowman Dairy in Madison, and Oscar Mayer. I remember saying to Ed Fitzgerald, '*The* Oscar Mayer?'"

Yes, that would be the one—the famous name behind Oscar Mayer wieners.

"So I first went to see Dawyne Bowman in the morning. Talk about networking," Bud said. "He was an older gentleman, a very nice man. Mr. Bowman was the former president of the Wisconsin League, and he wanted in, even though I asked him for a lot of money. Next I visited Oscar Mayer. When I walked into his office, I introduced myself to his secretary. 'I'm Bud Selig. I'm here to see Oscar Mayer,' I said. My heart was pounding at this point.

"'Oh yes, we're expecting you,' the secretary said.

"The secretary took me to his office, and there was Oscar Mayer waiting for me," Bud said. "We talked for a half hour, and he said to me, 'Buddy, I've been a Cubs fan since the 1920s, and I love baseball. I love what you're doing.' He came around his desk and gave me a big hug and said, 'I'm in.' Oscar Mayer turned out to be one of the most wonderful human beings I ever met, and he would always call me on my birthday, July 30. He was the kindest person. I only put my father and Lee McPhail [former general manager of New York Yankees and president of the American League] in that class."

Bud took the elevator to the lobby, and the first thing he did was find a pay phone to call Edmund Fitzgerald with the good news about Oscar Mayer. "I kidded Ed about my meeting," Bud said. "I said, 'When are you going to give me a tough job? That was easy.' Then Ed Fitzgerald got off a great line. He said, 'You're either the greatest salesman who ever lived or the luckiest son of a bitch I ever met.'

"To make a long story short, we got everyone we wanted. My father was stunned and amazed at whom I was seeing."

I asked Bud what we could learn from his experiences in putting together a group to bring baseball back to Milwaukee in the 1960s.

"Networking takes so many different forms, but you have to have the people skills and the patience so that people understand you, have confidence in you, and faith in you that you not only know what you're doing, but you'll do it. This group was a diverse bunch of people, but it was held together by me. It took five and a half years to get a team here, and it tried a lot of people's patience, except mine."

> "Networking takes so many different forms, but you have to have the people skills and the patience so that people understand you, have confidence in you, and faith in you that you not only know what you're doing, but you'll do it."
>
> —Bud Selig

Bud had mentioned the word *patience* several times in our interview. I asked him about that.

"Before I go into anything, Joe, I expect to know everything I can about it. I'm patient. I'm very, very patient. Some say too patient, but it's worked well for me and my career. Many of the things written about me say that I talk to every owner every day, but I do because if you really want to be successful, internally as well as externally, you have to have the ability to understand what people want. It's impossible to be successful at any level without having the ability to communicate—which you call networking—on a very consistent basis. To network, you really have to have the ability to listen and comprehend exactly what it is that you're trying to do and what needs to get done."

THE COMMISSIONER AND SISTER GEN

A few years ago, my son Conor traveled to Kenya to spend his summer on a mission trip helping the Sisters of St. Joseph, who minister to the impoverished, hungry, and ill facing dire circumstances in Sub-Saharan Africa. You can only imagine how proud I was about my son's service to the less fortunate.

Sister Genovefa Maasho, who I think is the Mother Teresa of Africa, led the Sisters of St. Joseph. She and her network of nurses and community health workers brought lifelines and rays of hope to those facing the scourge of AIDS, malaria, drought, hunger, and disease.

Conor traveled to Africa with Milwaukee nurse practitioner Karen Ivantic-Doucette, who had been appointed to the Presidential Advisory Council on HIV/AIDS. During their stay in Kenya, they learned that the Sisters of St. Joseph had a huge need for a truck that could bring life-saving medicine, food, and nutritional supplements to families in rural and hard-to-reach parts of central Kenya.

Upon their return to Milwaukee, Conor and Karen discussed who they could approach and ask for money to buy the Sisters of St. Joseph a much-needed truck. Conor suggested Bud Selig, who was practically a neighbor to us. A phone call was made, and within a week, Conor, Karen, and Dr. Ian Gilson visited Bud at his home one evening after dinner. They presented the need, and Bud wrote a check to cover the purchase of a truck right on the spot.

Fast-forward a couple of years, and Sister Gen happened to visit Milwaukee while I was writing this book. It was a pleasure to invite this Kenyan nun to our home. During dinner, she mentioned that someone named Bud Selig had sent a sizable check so that the Sisters of St. Joseph could purchase their truck. "Do you know this Bud Selig?" she asked in her clipped Kenyan accent. "I must meet him. I must talk to him and thank him."

I don't think Sister Gen—an African native—knew the difference between a baseball bat and a catcher's mitt, but she did know that Bud Selig lived in Milwaukee, which is why she asked about him. She had no idea that Bud and I knew each other or had networked in the past.

When I asked Sister Gen if she would like to thank the commissioner in person, her eyes lit up. "Yes, I would be very happy if that could happen," she replied.

The next day, I sent an e-mail letter to Bud outlining the connection between him and Sister Gen and her desire to thank him in person for the donation of a truck. "If you are able to spare ten minutes of time before

When Sister Genovefa Maasho, a Sister of St. Joseph nun from Kenya, told me that she wanted to thank "this Bud Selig" for donating a truck to her ministry, I helped make that meeting happen. Sister Gen had no idea who Bud Selig was or what the Commissioner of Major League Baseball did, but she wanted to say thank you in person, and Bud was generous with his time.

she returns to Kenya, it would mean a great deal to Sister Gen," I wrote. "These are challenging times for our community, our country, and our world. Thank for making a difference in the lives of so many people."

I received an almost immediate response: "Bring Sister Gen over any time it's convenient."

Three days later, I escorted Sister Gen into the commissioner's office— this was in August during the pennant race—and listened as Bud asked her question after question about her ministry in Kenya. What struck me as being quite remarkable was witnessing a passionate networker with a large heart—and a Jewish faith—bonding with a Catholic nun over the shared goal of helping others in need.

We were in Bud's expansive office for a good hour, and when we stood up to leave, Bud said, "Sister Gen, your visit has made my week."

Besides communicating with many of the thirty major league baseball owners on a daily basis, he and the owners meet four times a year. "I've developed a personal relationship with all of them. I know them pretty well now," Bud said. "They know me pretty well. I'm proud of the fact that most of our votes are 30–0, but it only comes after a lot of talking, a lot of conversation, and a lot of work. That's where patience comes in again."

I asked Bud, "What has your greatest networking challenge been?" I would imagine that being commissioner of thirty different major league teams, each with a different agenda, would be like asking a herd of cats to round up a pack of dogs. Not only does he have to be a master networker, but he must also be a master consensus builder.

"When I took over in 1992 as acting commissioner, baseball was in really tough shape," he replied. "One of the problems was that the owners had been split. We had a horrible relationship with the players union. The past commissioner [Fay Vincent] was caught in the middle. The owners were fighting each other. Then we had the strike and lost a World Series.

"I had to get the owners to work together. Today, even though we have heartaches from time to time because of different agendas, there's no more ripping each other in the press, no more ripping the commissioner. That's what you need to do. That's what networking is all about. You have to create a constructive, positive situation that enables you to get what you have to get done," Bud said.

"But how did you get the owners to stop ripping each other?" I wondered.

Bud said he told the owners about a book written by Michael Shapiro called *Bottom of the Ninth: Branch Rickey, Casey Stengel, and the Daring Scheme to Save Baseball from Itself*, which described how, in the late 1950s, attendance was declining and professional football was about to sweep the country. Up-and-coming cities that wanted teams of their own were being rebuffed by the owners, and in response, Congress was threatening the revoke the sport's antitrust exemption. Baseball had to figure out what to do with television and create new fans. Fans were bored with the New York Yankees winning all the time: between 1949 and 1957, the Yankees won eight pennants and six World Series.

"The interesting part to me was how fractured the owners were fifty years ago," Bud said. "They fought each other. They fought with the commissioner of baseball at that time, Ford Frick. As a result, baseball had a great problem. That can't happen today. One thing you learn in life is that you have to learn to disagree, but do it in a very reasonable way. A lot of people never learn that lesson, but that's how you turn people around. You turn issues around by continuing to understand the other person's position, and then you see what you can do about it."

"So you never made it personal," I ventured.

"You bet. There were times I wanted to, and there were times I felt aggrieved, but you don't do that because you have to keep your eyes on the goal. My father used to say, 'Good, you're mad. Now what?' Anger doesn't do you any good. You just have to figure out what to do and how to do it. Joe, you'll remember that a fair amount of people were critical of the tax [to build Miller Park], the one-tenth of a cent sales tax. We don't have to get into all that, but today, there are no critics left. It's remarkable how that works. That's why if your goal is one that's worthwhile and you commit to getting the job done, it will happen thanks to strong networking and good communication."

Commissioner, you nailed it.

Craig Leipold: A Wingman and Close Friend

He's been one of my closest wingmen, best buddy, trusted confidant, and perennial prankster. If I didn't have eight older brothers, I would say he's the brother I never had.

Our paths crossed when I became president of the Wisconsin Sports Authority in 1992 and Craig was an interested sponsor for the nonprofit entity charged with promoting sports in Wisconsin. I was thirty-four years old at the time; Craig was four years my senior. Our frenetic energy and shared sense of humor—sarcasm and put-downs galore—meshed like a six-gear Screamin' Eagle transmission set on a Harley-Davidson. His interest led to a board position with the WSA and eventually the chairmanship of the board.

Craig is a fellow Wisconsin native who grew up as the younger of two sons of Betty Jo and Werner "Lefty" Leipold, who worked his way up to vice president of Kimberly-Clark, a manufacturer of paper-based consumer products in Neenah, Wisconsin.

Craig is forever reminding me that he was a fourteen-year-old kid shivering in the stands at Lambeau Field on December 31, 1967, when the Packers won the unforgettable "Ice Bowl" against the Dallas Cowboys in the coldest recorded game in pro football history. The frigid NFL championship game was played in thirteen-below-zero degree temperatures and a forty-six-below wind-chill factor at kickoff. With sixteen seconds remaining and the temperature dipping further to eighteen below zero, the Packers found themselves two feet from victory. The field was a sheet of ice. With no timeouts, down 17–14, Packers quarterback Bart Starr followed guard Jerry Kramer into the end zone. The Packers' gamble won, and the phrase "frozen tundra of Lambeau Field" entered the American sports lexicon.

Craig loved sports growing up. He started playing golf at age eight at the Ridgeway Country Club in Neenah, and then he picked up basketball and baseball. His entrepreneurial spirit manifested itself early when the nine-year-old boy "networked" with some construction workers in the neighborhood. Craig discovered there was a thirsty market for cold beer on hot summer days, and the youngster made a killing peddling brewskis at a nearby job site until his father discovered the missing beer from the basement refrigerator.

Craig stuck with the usual teen jobs after that. Just before his senior year of high school, however, Lefty was transferred to a Kimberly-Clark division in Conway, Arkansas, and that's where Craig finished high school. He stayed in Conway and attended Hendrix College, where he earned a degree in political science.

He followed his father's footsteps by joining Kimberly-Clark as a paper products salesman and was given the state of Arkansas as his sales territory. This was the late 1970s, and being assigned a territory that included Bentonville, Arkansas, where a small regional discount chain called Walmart was located, was a lucky development. Selling paper towels, toilet paper, and Kleenex to the fastest-growing retailer in the world was easy work. The new "super salesman" was quickly promoted to Kimberly-Clark's headquarters in Wisconsin.

In the early 1980s, Craig saw the potential in assembling a sales team that would sell consumer packaged goods to small retailers by phone instead of by more costly "sales calls" by on-the-road company reps.

"I asked around if Kimberly-Clark would ever do this for other companies, and the answer was no," Craig said. I admire what happened next: even though he had a bright future with Kimberly-Clark, he decided to go for it anyway. Craig left the company at age twenty-nine to start Ameritel Corporation, one of the nation's first telemarketing firms.

"Networking helped me get Ameritel off the ground," Craig said. "As it turned out, the Senior Vice President of Sales at Kimberly-Clark and all the sales department assisted my start-up by becoming one of the very first customers of my new company. They also introduced me to sales executives from other consumer products companies who later became clients of Ameritel."

The new company blossomed, and at a sales meeting in Miami with executives from Johnson Wax in 1985, there was a golf outing at Doral's Blue Monster course. Craig was assigned—I tease my buddy that he rigged the pairings—to a foursome with an athletic blonde named Helen Johnson. "The second I saw her legs, I said, 'That's it,'" Craig remembered.

See, I told you golf is a great networking game.

Craig and Helen fell in love, and he married an heir to the S.C. Johnson fortune. The Racine, Wisconsin–based company is the manufacturer of home cleaning products like Pledge, Windex, and Shout, and pest-control products like Raid, Baygon, and OFF!

Craig sold his half of Ameritel to his 50 percent partner for a princely sum not long after the marriage and purchased Rainfair, a 125-year-old rainwear manufacturer and importer. Our paths crossed a few years later at the Wisconsin Sports Authority, and as our friendship deepened to wingman status, Craig told me about his dream to one day own a professional sports franchise.

One day—this would have been in 1996, right around when Craig and I formed the Sports Marketing Group with Brett Favre—I got a phone call from my golfing chum. He had a networking request.

"Can you call Jeff Sauer and get me a copy of *The Rules of Hockey*?" he asked.

Jeff Sauer was the hockey coach the University of Wisconsin. "What do you need a hockey rulebook for?" I asked.

"Because I'm about to spend $80 million to buy a pro hockey franchise."

I nearly dropped the phone. "Listen, Craigger. You don't know the difference between offside and icing, and you're telling me that you're buying a professional hockey team?"

"Sounds crazy, but the National Hockey League is looking at expanding its league, and I'm going to try and get a team and put it in Nashville."

Craig was awarded the Nashville franchise in 1997. Talk about starting from scratch in a small city dominated by the country music industry and Southeastern Conference college football. "You have to picture this guy from Wisconsin going to Nashville with the idea of introducing hockey into a very traditional Southern city that only knows music and football," Craig said. "People didn't know hockey. They certainly didn't know me. We didn't even have a name yet."

After conducting a citywide contest, Craig named the team the Nashville Predators and set about selling hockey in a locale where sports fans thought ice was for soft drinks, not something you skate on. The NHL gave Craig nine months to sell 12,000 season tickets in a market where naysayers joked that the fans had fewer teeth than the players.

"We needed credibility in a hurry, and to get credibility, we turned to the music industry because Nashville is all about music," Craig said.

Networking Going Country

Craig's idea was to have Music Row stars such as Garth Brooks, Amy Grant, Vince Gill, Martina McBride, and Brooks & Dunn pitch the Predators on billboards, print ads, and TV spots. How could he get to them?

Through networking.

"I didn't want to go through their agents because things would get complicated with all sorts of demands for money," Craig said.

"Agents put up walls, like Joe did with Brett Favre, where you could never get through to the player.

"We had hired a Nashville advertising agency to handle the Predators' account, and they had a pretty good Rolodex. If they didn't have a phone number for Amy Grant, then they knew somebody who could reach her and inquire if I could call her. I remember phoning Amy and asking if we could meet so that I could explain what I was doing with the Predators and why I needed her help. A new professional sport was coming to Nashville, and a successful NHL franchise would be good for the city. The Nashville city fathers had recently built a $144 million, 17,000-seat arena with the idea of luring an NBA or NHL franchise to Music City, so there was a lot on the line."

What resulted from Craig's networking efforts with the top music names in Nashville was a series of billboards and print ads, including one in which Garth Brooks had his front tooth blacked out to promote the Predators. Amy Grant, Brooks & Dunn, and Lorrie Morgan also did similar billboards and TV spots.

The marriage between country music and hockey did more than put fannies in the seats—it also put Grammys into Nashville Arena. Vince Gill and Reba McEntire supported the team by their presence, turning Nashville from a honky-tonk attraction to a hockey-tonk town.

The expansion team was the model of stability and continuity in the Nashville community. During the team's first decade, the Predators won their share of games—around half—with the same general manager and head coach. Craig was welcomed into the NHL owner fraternity as a strong advocate for a more "fan-friendly" professional game, which included rule changes to increase offense and establish "shootouts" to settle ties in regular season games. NHL commissioner Gary Bettman also appointed Craig to serve on the League's Executive and Audit committees.

After ten years of helping to make the Predators a success, Craig sold the franchise in 2007 for $193 million and a month later purchased the Minnesota Wild for $260 million, the NHL franchise based in Minneapolis-St. Paul. Once again, he's thrown himself into the community by signing a ten-year lease for a twenty-four-hundred-square-foot, fourteenth-floor penthouse suite at the St. Paul Hotel, steps from Xcel Energy Center, the home arena. "I like the fact that I can walk from where I'm living to work, and I don't even have to go outside in the winter," he said.

Craig wouldn't say this but I can: when you're an NHL owner—or occupy any sort of top gun position in life—you don't *have* to network. Most of the time, it's people coming to you asking for this or that, but still inside Craig is the hustling kid from Neenah, Wisconsin, carrying a cooler of ice-cold Blatz beers to the construction workers.

For opening day of the 2009–2010 season, I flew from Milwaukee to watch the first game with Craig. I booked a room at the St. Paul Hotel, and two things impressed me. One was how he interacted with the St. Paul Hotel doormen, who wear distinctive long black coats with black top hats. It's almost like they're a throwback to the Gilded Age of the late nineteenth century, a genteel time when the upper crust were catered to by the working class. The St. Paul Hotel doormen play off that image and are unfailingly polite. "Good morning, Mr. Leipold," they would chorus as he entered or exited the elegant and historic hotel.

> *When you're an NHL owner—or occupy any sort of top gun position in life—you don't* have *to network. Most of the time, it's people coming to you asking for this or that, but still inside Craig is the hustling kid from Neenah, Wisconsin, carrying a cooler of ice-cold Blatz beers to the construction workers.*

Craig would have none of the formality. "Just call me Craig," he would instruct the doormen before engaging in several moments of friendly banter. If you witnessed the interaction like I did—which I've done numerous times over the years—it was a reminder that my friend had not lost the common touch.

Later that morning, I left the hotel in my jogging outfit to go for a little run. I stepped outside and jogged down West Fifth Street toward the Xcel Energy Center, the nineteen-thousand-seat multi-purpose arena where the Wild play their home games. I heard a loud band playing, and a celebratory mood was in there. I picked up my cadence to get a closer look.

Even though it was mid-morning and opening night was still ten hours away, a steady stream of cars was snaking its way to the arena. A closer inspection revealed the reason behind the traffic jam: Minnesota Wild employees, dressed in forest green or red team jerseys, were handing out cups of coffee and doughnuts to drivers and passengers.

And then I saw him—Craig Leipold passing out coffees and shaking hands of Wild fans. Here was the team owner, in the trenches with his front-office staff, pressing the flesh and thanking the fans with a wave, a wink, and a hot cup of java. I was so impressed that I never went on my morning jog. I just wanted to watch Craig in action.

What's the moral of the story? Extreme wealth and a heady and public position as a professional hockey team owner hadn't changed the man from a middle-class family in Neenah, Wisconsin. Sure, his circumstances had changed significantly, but when you stripped away the veneer, Craig Leipold hadn't forgotten where he came from.

I said as much when *The Minneapolis Star Tribune* interviewed me for a profile piece on the "No. 1 fan" of the Minnesota Wild. I characterized Craig in this fashion: "Craig is a big business guy who runs in big political circles, but he walks with kings with the touch of a common man. He is as down-to-earth as anybody I've ever met. The greatest thing I can say about him is that he has a hundred best friends who all think that Craig is *their* best friend."

To me, that's the sign of a great networker—a person where a lot of people feel they are best friends with him or her. That means he's connected with a lot of people who feel like they can go to him because his enthusiasm and energy are contagious. I've seen him help people he barely knows when they hit tough points in life. Through my connections in the sports world, I've heard that whenever some of his hockey players get traded or let go, many will call Craig and say, "Mr. Leipold, I'm grateful for who you are and the opportunity you provided me."

And that's what networking is all about.

Craig Leipold (left) and Mark Leopold—can you believe how close the spellings of their last names are?—are my closest friends and confidants. These two helped me formulate a plan to bring Bob Costas to Milwaukee for the Wisconsin Sports Hall of Fame dinner.

The Master Networkers: Bud Selig and Craig Leipold

Joe's Recap

1. If you find your passion and follow it, you'll never work another day in your life. Bud Selig and Craig Leipold are textbook cases about this.
2. Reach out and don't be afraid to ask. Bud asked investors to pitch in so that Milwaukee fans could still enjoy major league baseball, and Craig asked country music stars to help him promote hockey in a Southern city.
3. Become a consensus builder.
4. Find people who play in the areas that you find work.
5. Be a great listener . . . and then listen some more.

6. Hire the best advisors, and then listen to them, too.
7. Become an incredible giver, and people will notice and be attracted to you.
8. Master networkers never lose the common touch, no matter where they are or what their position in life may be.
9. Master networkers approach networking as a place to give and serve—even if it's coffee and doughnuts to hockey fans and season ticket holders.

13

Networking Will Enrich Your Life

WE ALL HAVE OUR little routines in life, and I'm no exception. Many mornings I stop by Sendik's Food Market to pick up a coffee during my morning commute to downtown Milwaukee. I know most of the clerks behind the cash registers, which is what you can expect in Wisconsin when you're a regular customer and gregarious like me. After Kenny finishes ringing me up, he'll look me in the eye and say, "The usual, Joe?"

"You got it, Special K. The same deal as always."

I pay cash every time, and what happens in the next few minutes is an experience you can't buy. Usually, just before I reach my car in the parking lot, a young mother, a middle-aged businessman, or a senior citizen who's out of breath will call out, "Wait! I want to thank you!"

I'll look up, and the grateful individual will thank me profusely and pump my hand. "That's such a nice thing you did! I can't believe what just happened!"

What transpired is that I left some extra cash behind when I purchased my morning coffee. When the next customer moved through the checkout line, the clerk calmly said, "The man ahead of you thought you'd be blessed by this, so he left enough to cover your purchase."

I'm hesitant to tell this story because the Good Book says not to let the right hand know what the left hand is doing when performing an act of kindness, but handing over a few extra bucks at Sendik's is my way of participating in something I call PFE, or Pay Forward Enterprises. I got the idea for PFE after seeing the movie *Pay It Forward* a decade ago, which starred Haley Joel Osment as a boy who launches a goodwill movement that can only be described as a charitable pyramid scheme. "Paying it forward" meant the recipient of a favor does a favor for a third party rather than paying the favor back.

That concept appealed to me, so I decided to set up my own Pay Forward Enterprises, which I fund monthly. The looks of shock and disbelief on people's faces have been reward enough, although one time my altruistic deed benefited me. It seems that a woman who received some free groceries drove home and told her husband about our interchange in the Sendik's parking lot. Her husband was trying to sell his business and needed the services of an investment banker. One thing led to another, and we eventually got the engagement at Corporate Financial Advisors. What occurred was an unexpected bonus, but that's just a footnote to the bigger picture of how doing things for others—which is what networking is all about—can enrich your life.

When I say that networking can enhance your existence, what I mean is that being a source of comfort and strength for others— through your networking efforts—reaps long-lasting benefits on both sides of the equation. When you offer a shoulder to lean on, extend good advice, make a phone call, send an e-mail, or share good times and laughter, you're showing that you're *more* than just a networking contact. Those acts of random kindness, as some call it, nurture friendships and convey to others what it means to be a good friend.

Networking can also be good for *your* health and mental outlook. Reaching out and touching others boosts your self-esteem—my Sendik's story is a prime example—and lifts your endorphin level, which are the "feel-good" hormones. Doesn't it make sense that we feel good when we *do* good for others?

There are added benefits as well. The connections forged from networking can:

- increase your sense of belonging
- give you purpose in life
- reduce stress
- improve your self-worth
- help you weather traumas and give you a sense that everything is going to work out in the end
- propel you to make even deeper bonds with your friends, which would make them wingmen in your life

Networking Is Like the Growing Roots of a Tree

I understand that you may prefer a smaller circle of friends and acquaintances, but extending your reach can benefit you *and* your more diverse network of friends. Just as you plant a tree in the backyard and want it to grow, so should you feel the same way about networking.

In fact, we can look at a tree and see parallels to networking. The roots of a relationship must sink into the fertile, moist soil and grow in its own time. As the root system begins to branch out, a sapling and then a small trunk appear out of the ground. The trunk grows into a sturdy base that sets a firm foundation for further growth. Next come the branches, which represent the maturity you have to reach out and touch others, much like I did at Sendik's. Sure, sometimes relationships can grow dormant just like trees, which shed their leaves every fall in preparation for the cold winter months. But come springtime, trees grow back and become stronger and higher than before, and that's what can happen in networking when you have a strong foundation. Your sunny disposition will draw others into your networking circle.

Finally, let me finish the tree metaphor by reminding you that just as trees rings are measured in years, not months, so are relationships. People need time before they can trust you or discover that you're not being their friend just so you can get something or "call in" a favor sometime in the future.

While we all agree that networking helps your businesses and advances your career, what gets overlooked far too often is that networking supplies you with a rich set of experiences, expands your contacts, and provides the framework for living a life of significance. That's what I mean when I say that networking can enrich your life.

THE BAMBOO ANALOGY: WATER . . . AND THEN WAIT!

Unlike normal crops that you can harvest annually, bamboo takes a lot longer to grow. According to the stories I've heard, you take a little bamboo seed, plant it, water it, and fertilize it for a whole year, but nothing happens. The second year you water and fertilize the bamboo plant, but again nothing happens. The third year you water and fertilize it, and again nothing happens. Talk about discouraging . . .

But when you continue watering and fertilizing the seed the fourth year, suddenly the Chinese bamboo tree sprouts and grows *ninety feet in six weeks*!

All those years, the bamboo was growing roots that became the foundation to support massive growth. That's why the way bamboo grows is much like networking—you need patience as well as persistence without losing track of the long-term perspective.

The Search for Significance

I mentioned in the Introduction that I've probably purchased more than three hundred copies of Bob Buford's book, *Halftime: Changing Your Game Plan from Success to Significance.*

Bob's book resonated with me because I was fast approaching the "halftime" of life—middle age. Bob argued that it doesn't matter who you are or what you do, you should take a "half-time intermission"— a quiet time of deliberate decision making, restructuring, and passionate contemplation of your heart's desires.

The message of *Halftime* hit me like a ton of bricks. As I reflected during my morning and evening commutes about what I wanted to accomplish during my second half of life, I pondered several questions posed by Bob, including this one: Where do you want to go from today to the end of your life?

That's a complex question that can lead one down many different roads, but "upon further review," as NFL referees say, everything crystallized for me: at the end of our lives, it doesn't come down to power, money, or fame. Everything comes down to the people we meet, the connections we make, and the value of the relationships we build. *That's* what gives life meaning and makes all the difference in the world.

I was reflecting on some of those thoughts when I was getting dressed to celebrate my fiftieth birthday a couple of years ago. It was around five o'clock on a Saturday afternoon, and in less than ninety minutes, Tami and I would greet fifty special friends and family members knocking on our front door on April 23, 2008.

Being surrounded that evening by people who meant the world to me was something I'll treasure the rest of my days. I really appreciated sharing that moment with Mom and two of my brothers, Mike and Mark, who both flew in to be there. But what really hit home was spending some time with Eddie Erkmanis, Mike Hayes, and Donnie Walls—three young men I had mentored over the years.

I met Eddie when he was a senior on the Marquette University golf team and hired him as an intern at SMG, our sports agency. I showed him the ropes, and a few years later he ended up running our golf division. He showed such great executive skill that he was promoted to president of SMG following my departure.

Mike, the son of close family friends, was a Marquette law student unsure about what he wanted to do in life when he took me into his confidence. He allowed me to mentor him, and like Eddie, Mike interned for me at SMG. He later negotiated the contract with General Mills to put three-time NFL MVP Brett Favre on the front of orange Wheaties boxes.

I introduced you to Donnie Walls and his compelling story in the "Networking Is Not All Black and White" chapter. Seeing Donnie and his wife, LaShonda, that night reminded me how proud I was to see that this responsible father of four had broken the inner city's cycle of poverty and despair.

Suddenly, the time that I took to mentor these three young men all came rushing back to me: the early morning pickup games on the basketball court; the unexpected times when we discussed significant issues or dilemmas in my office; the special evenings around the Sweeney dinner table; and countless conversations over the phone. Sure, I had poured out hours and energy to help them succeed, but what I received back was worth far more than rubies and gold. Witnessing the fruit of my efforts left me feeling humbled and unworthy of their gratitude.

SERVING OTHERS

"Many people measure their success by wealth, recognition, power, and status. There's nothing wrong with those, but if that's all you're focused on, you're missing the boat. Using your time and talents to serve others— that's when truly meaningful success comes your way."
        —Ken Blanchard, co-author of *The One-Minute Manager*

And that's the thought I want to leave with you as *Networking Is a Contact Sport* comes to a close. At the end of your life, will you be filled with regrets because your focus was on yourself? Or will your life be one that touched others because of your service to them?

There's an incredible scene at the end of *Saving Private Ryan*, one of my favorite World War II movies. James Francis Ryan, now in his seventies, stands with his family in the cemetery above Omaha Beach, where Allied Forces launched the greatest invasion ever on D-Day, June 6, 1944. The aged Private Ryan, trembling and filled with anxiety, turns to his wife. "Tell me I have led a good life," he pleads, a quasi-question that underscores his realization that six decades of his existence was purchased through the death of Captain John Miller (played by Tom Hanks) and six other U.S. soldiers.

It's a profound statement that speaks to the issue of meaning in life. We ultimately all want the same three things in our lives. We all want the feeling that we belong to something greater than ourselves. We all want to love and be loved, and we all want to know that our lives had substance and significance. That's why I believe that at the end of our lives, we will all have one final exam, and it's not a take-home exam and you can't have a do-over. The exam consists of just one question. Our Creator will ask us: *Were you a giver, or were you a taker in life?*

If you were a giver, then you leave this world a little bit better than when you arrived into this world. If you were a taker, then you leave this world having missed out on what was really important. We came into this world with nothing, and we will leave with nothing. How much money you accumulate or the number of toys you buy does not determine success in life, but how you gave of yourself to others with your talents, your imagination, your personality, and your physical energy. That's the very essence of what networking is all about—a place you go to give, not to get, because you'll receive much more than you'll ever give.

If you approach life and networking with this mindset, I guarantee you that you will pass your final exam.

Joe's Final Recap

Thank for joining me! If you adopt the following key summary points into your life, you'll become a Master Networker.

Remember:

1. Relationships make the world go round.
2. No matter where you are, keep an eye out for networking opportunities.
3. When you're attending a mixer or social event, be intentional about meeting the right people, but don't hand out business cards unless asked to do so.
4. Networking 101 is working the 5/10/15 program, which means five meetings or encounters, ten letters or pieces of correspondence, and fifteen phone calls could result in five "engagements" or business-making opportunities.
5. If you're unemployed, remember that *who* you know is often more important than *what* you know. This is the time to let everyone you know that you need a job.
6. Knowing what personality type you are can help you understand how you network best and how best to network with others.
7. Don't fly solo through life. Ask someone—or several close friends—to be your wingman. Everyone needs a confidant.

8. If you're new to a community, look for ways to get connected with others by coaching youth sports, volunteering with civic groups, signing up for the PTA, or joining a church. Identify what your passions are and do something that you're passionate about.

9. Everyone needs a BWAG—a Big, Wild, Audacious Goal. What's yours?

10. If you're a member of a minority group, learn the language of business. Networking can break down racial barriers.

11. Understand the differences in how men and women network.

12. Social networking on the Internet through platforms like Facebook and Twitter extend your outreach, but keep in mind that e-mail messages and voicemails will never replace face-to-face contact and looking someone in the eye.

13. Find a mentor early in your career and become a mentor later in your career. One of the e-mails that gets forwarded around the Internet is the "Charles Schultz Philosophy," even though the late creator of the *Peanuts* cartoon strip never said those words. Still, the point was a good one. If you were asked to name the most recent Best Actor Oscar winner, or the last Super Bowl or World Series victor, or the last *Dancing with the Stars* champions, you probably couldn't do it. No one remembers the headlines of yesterday very long.

    But if you were asked to name the teacher who impacted your life the most, or the friend who helped you through a difficult time, or five people you'd enjoy spending time with, those are the people who've made a substantial difference in your life. They aren't lauded by Hollywood or given a ticker-tape parade down Broadway, but those were the people and mentors who cared about you and enriched your life.

Endnotes

1. Katie Byrd, "Conversation Starters and Techniques," published at ezarticles.com at <http://ezinearticles.com/?Conversation-Starters-and-Techniques&id=98106>.
2. Dean Calbreath, "6 Workers for Every Job, Feds Say," *San Diego Union-Tribune*, November 11, 2009, page C1.
3. "What is the average number of occupations one will have in their lifetime?" A question-and-answer on Askville by Amazon at <http://askville.amazon.com/average-number-occupations-lifetime/AnswerViewer.do?requestId=16930824>.
4. "Job & Career Networking," an article on the Career Playbook Web site at <http://www.careerplaybook.com/guide/networking.asp>.
5. "Best Jobs in America," an article on the CNNMoney.com Web site at <http://money.cnn.com/magazines/moneymag/bestjobs/2009/jobgrowth/index.html>.
6. Rick Hampson, "For some, hard times are a gateway to new careers," *USA Today*, October 11, 2009.
7. Robert "Waldo" Waldman, *Never Fly Solo: Lead with Courage, Build Trusting Partnerships, and Reach New Heights in Business* (New York: McGraw-Hill, 2009).
8. D'Vera Cohn and Rich Morin, "American Mobility: Movers, Stayers, Places and Reasons," Pew Research Center, December 17, 2008. <http://pewresearch.org/pubs/1058/american-mobility-moversstayers-places-and-reasons>
9. Sam Roberts, "Slump Creates Lack of Mobility for Americans," *New York Times*, April 22, 2009. <http://www.nytimes.com/2009/04/23/us/23census.html>
10. Ecclesiastes 4:9–10, New Living Translation
11. Gary D'Amato, "Dependence on painkillers brings Favre to new low," *Milwaukee Journal Sentinel* newspaper, October 22, 2005. <http://www.jsonline.com/sports/packers/45266162.html>

12. Lance Allan, "A Shocking New Brett Favre Revelation," on the TMJ-TV Web site, May 20, 2009. <http://www.todaystmj4.com/bloggers/lanceallan/45578767.html>

13. Stephanie Simon, "The Old South, Up North," *Los Angeles Times*, December 30, 2002. <http://articles.latimes.com/2002/dec/30/nation/na-segregate30>

14. "An Older and More Diverse Nation by Midcentury," a press release from the U.S Census Bureau News, August 14, 2008. <http://www.census.gov/Press-Release/www/releases/archives/population/012496.html>

15. John Gray, *Mars and Venus Together Forever: Relationship Skills for Lasting Love* (New York: Harper Paperbacks, 2005), page 71.

16. Deborah Tannen, "Can't We Talk?" an article condensed from her book *You Just Don't Understand* at <http://raysweb.net/poems/articles/tannen.html>.

17. Deborah Tannen, Ph.D., *You Just Don't Understand* (New York: Ballantine Books, 1990), page 122.

Contact Information

Joe Sweeney is available to speak about how networking can grow your business, expand your influence, and make life richer and more meaningful when you connect with friends, acquaintances, business colleagues, and even strangers. If you or your company would like to book Joe Sweeney for a speaking engagement, contact him at:

Joe Sweeney
Corporate Financial Advisors
111 E. Kilbourn Avenue, Suite 2800
Milwaukee, WI 53202
414-259-8900
joe@NetworkingContactSport.com

For bulk purchases of *Networking Is a Contact Sport,* please contact Joe Sweeney directly.

For more information, visit www.NetworkingContactSport.com.